MIRANDA HART

THE UNAUTHORISED BIOGRAPHY

MIRANDA HART

SOPHIE JOHNSON

JOHN BLAKE

Huge thanks to Paddy.

Published by John Blake Publishing Ltd,
3 Bramber Court, 2 Bramber Road,
London W14 9PB, England

www.johnblakepublishing.co.uk

www.facebook.com/Johnblakepub   facebook

twitter.com/johnblakepub   twitter

First published in hardback in 2011
This edition published in paperback 2012

ISBN: 978 1 85782 796 5

British Library Cataloguing-in-Publication Data:

A catalogue record for this book is available from the British Library.

Design by www.envydesign.co.uk

Printed and bound in Great Britain by CPI Group (UK) Ltd

3 5 7 9 10 8 6 4 2

Papers used by John Blake Publishing are natural, recyclable products made
from wood grown in sustainable forests. The manufacturing processes conform
to the environmental regulations of the country of origin.

Every attempt has been made to contact the relevant copyright-holders,
but some were unobtainable. We would be grateful if the appropriate
people could contact us.

CONTENTS

1 THE QUEEN OF COMEDY   1

2 THE EARLY YEARS   13

3 GROWING PAINS   25

4 HERE COME THE GIRLS   36

5 FRINGE BENEFITS   49

6 RADIO DAYS   62

7 OPPORTUNITY KNOCKS   75

8 GOING INTO HYPERDRIVE   89

9 NOT GOING OUT   103

10 THE WRITER'S JOURNEY   114

11 MIRANDA ARRIVES AT THE BEEB   129

12 ADVENTURES IN A JOKE SHOP   142

13 REALITY BLURS   157

14 THE BOY NEXT DOOR   169

15 YOU HAVE BEEN WATCHING   180

16 CLASS DISMISSED   196
17 THE ART OF THE PRATFALL   208
18 THE DIFFICULT SECOND ALBUM   223
19 THE RISE OF THE OFFICE TEMP   238
20 DOING SOMETHING FUNNY FOR MONEY   251
21 WHAT'S NEXT?   266

THE QUEEN OF COMEDY

'Hart, 37, has arrived as the statuesque darling of BBC light entertainment, arguably even its saviour.'
– Dominic Cavendish, *The Times*

All hail Queen Miranda! A sudden hit in British comedy, she is our sweetheart of light entertainment. At first glance, it seems her success happened overnight. At the 2010 British Comedy Awards, she won a hat-trick (or 'Hart-trick', thanks *Daily Mail*). The following year she topped it up with another win for Best TV Comedy Actress and secured her place in the comedy spotlight. Before this barrage of awards, most would not have known who Miranda Hart was, let alone recognise her by her first name alone. Now, she is one of our best-loved comedians, slowly nudging herself towards national treasure-dom. Her self-titled sitcom propelled Miranda to fame and into the nation's hearts and has itself achieved cult TV status. The show is based on a persona she developed in her stand-up, an immature singleton who giggles at the word 'bottom'. Her cosy comedy receives ratings of over 4.4 million thanks to furious word-of-mouth and glowing reviews – and her appeal may yet broaden still further.

On why she thinks she has become such a sensation, Miranda has suggested it might have something to do with a British love of failure: 'My aim was to tap into that universal truth that we all feel awkward in life, but hide it to varying degrees. Everyone feels like a dick at some point in their life – probably every day.' But she seems almost oblivious to how successful she has become. Talking to *Stylist* magazine, she said that she doesn't feel like a role model, or that she has become 'one of the most popular female figures in comedy'. When asked how she felt about suggestions that people are inspired by her comedy, she responded humbly, 'I find it hard to believe really. If it is true, it's amazing.'

Miranda's self-titled sitcom arrived in 2009 during an era when comedy was becoming popular again, taking over the TV listings. A sea change of sorts had begun with *Live at the Apollo*, which has spun off into *Michael McIntyre's Comedy Roadshow*: a stand-up comedy vehicle that introduces the nation to acts working the gig circuit around the UK. Panel shows are abundant: if *Have I Got News For You* and *Never Mind The Buzzcocks* were once the big boys in town, they've now been joined by *Mock The Week*, *Would I Lie To You?*, *QI*, *8 Out of 10 Cats*, *Shooting Stars*, *Celebrity Juice*, *Ask Rhod Gilbert* and many more, all jostling for our attention. Ricky Gervais is in America, spreading the good word of British comedy, and Matt Lucas and David Walliams have become international stars. *Miranda* is waving the flag for sitcoms, harking back to our tradition of *Are You Being Served?*, *Dad's Army* and *Keeping Up Appearances*.

Her journey to becoming a multi-award-winning comic started with three nominations at the Royal Television Society (RTS) awards in March 2010. She won Best Comedy Performance but in her other categories others took the trophies home – Best Comedy Writer, where her co-writers James Cary and Richard Hurst were co-nominated, was awarded to Iain Morris and Damon Beesley for *The Inbetweeners*, and Best Scripted Comedy went to single-camera show *The Thick of It*. Speaking to Davina McCall on Twitter, who she made friends with on the Sport Relief cycle from Land's End to John O'Groats, she shrugged, 'Genuinely not bothered about winning. Just lovely to be there. In fact, don't want to win – terrified of speeches!' Speaking in a later interview, she said that she found it a surreal and nerve-racking experience. 'I don't really remember it but I got up and said, "I haven't won a prize since junior high jump in 1980" and I ran off. Everyone kind of went "Oh".'

Soon after the RTS bash, in May 2010, came two BAFTA nominations – Female Performance in a Comedy Role and Situation Comedy. In the end, the accolades went to Rebecca Front and *The Thick of It*, respectively, but Miranda was just excited to be there. She told one red-carpet interviewer that she had only recently learned of the nominations and couldn't believe her luck, 'I literally can't quite believe it. It's like I'm looking down on myself. It's very, very exciting... 12-year-old me would be going mental right now... It's just amazing to be in the company of people I admire.' In the category of best female comedy performance, she was nominated alongside Rebecca Front (from *The Thick of It*), Jo Brand and Joanna Scanlan (both from *Getting On*). Miranda imagined an all-girls-together revolution. 'I think it would be rather marvellous if all four nominees could get up together and make some screamy, girlie-based speech. You never know. The joint winners are…'

Alas, such a spectacle did not arise, and Rebecca Front took the award for her portrayal of Nicola Murray. Front claimed she was staggered, assuming she hadn't won because she was sat in the middle of a row. For the Situation Comedy category, Miranda was contending with *Peep Show*, *The Inbetweeners* and *The Thick of It*. As well as winning this category, *The Thick of It* team owned the night, with Peter Capaldi taking the prize for Male Performance in a Comedy Role.

After the BAFTAs, Miranda had time for a quick dress change before heading off with her 'telly mum', Patricia Hodge, to the Monte Carlo TV Festival in Monaco a few days later, where they were both nominated for Best Comedy Actress. But Miranda's big night was to come early next year. The British Comedy Awards 2010 were on their way and Miranda was up for four gongs – Best Comedy Actress, the People's Choice Award (for the King or Queen of Comedy), Best New British TV Comedy and Best Sitcom. The ceremony was held at the Indigo2 at The O2 Arena and was broadcast for the first time on Channel 4, formerly shown on ITV. Prior to the event, talk was all around regular host Jonathan Ross, who returned in 2009.

After the row over prank calls he made with Russell Brand, now commonly known as Sachsgate, Wossy announced that he would not be presenting the 2008 show and Angus Deayton took his place as host. Apart from this and the inaugural ceremony (presented by Michael Parkinson), Ross has hosted every ceremony. Every year, there is anticipation about the show, the host and the controversy he has brought with him. In 2006, he made a joke about Heather Mills and her prosthetic leg and was heavily criticised by the press. A year later, he wound up news journalists by suggesting he was worth 'a thousand BBC journalists', just as many redundancies were being made. This year, Jonathan and the show had a new home, a channel with a reputation for being more lenient towards 'challenging' comedy. After all, this was the channel that stood up for Frankie Boyle when he made a sexual joke about Katie Price's disabled son Harvey. The show has become legendary for creating memorable moments, including Julian Clary's famous comment about Norman Lamont in 1993. The format was being revamped for Channel 4, with the new award, the People's Choice, returning after an incident in 2005, where Ant and Dec were given the award, when it should have gone to Catherine Tate. This led to an Ofcom fine of £80,000 and, after further investigation around the British television phone-in scandal in 2007, led to a record fine of £5.675 million. Channel 4 was happy to pick up the show and brought back the phone vote, which was carefully overseen by the Electoral Reform Services.

The night was a big success for the organisers and, of course, the winners. The British Comedy Guide website, who were live blogging the occasion, confirmed that Jonathan Ross was on form, 'The customary Jonathan Ross speech is proving as popular in the room as always. Digs at Horne and Corden, Gervais and Carr have already been ticked off.' He also described Simon Amstell's acting as 'so wooden Ray Mears tried to make a canoe out of him'. But it's all part of the spirit of the night, as Dara O'Briain, who presented Michael McIntyre with the gong for Best Male TV Comic, says, 'These are the most openly bitchy awards ceremony because, frankly, we just don't mind! This is Jonathan's front room.' And he can take it as well. Russell Brand's recorded video message for winning Outstanding Contribution to Comedy teased him about the Sachsgate scandal: 'Jonathan, you're a father figure, what were you thinking?'

Other winners of the night included Jo Brand, *Peep Show* writers Sam Bain and Jesse Armstrong, Charlie Brooker for *Newswipe*, Kayvan Novak, *Horrible Histories*, John Bishop, Samantha Spiro, Harry Hill, *Would I Lie To You?* and Peter Capaldi. The lifetime achievement award went to Roy Clarke OBE, creator of *Last of the Summer Wine*, *Open All Hours* and *Keeping Up Appearances*, a fine moment for lovers of the traditional sitcom. *The Inbetweeners* won Best Sitcom, which *Miranda* was also nominated for. But the highlight of the evening, the woman of the match, was Miranda Hart.

Even as Jonathan Ross was telling viewers about the nominations for the People's Choice Award, and explaining how to vote, she had the support of the room. The British Comedy Guide website wrote at the time: 'Sounds like Miranda will be a very popular winner for the People's Choice Award; the only cheer we noticed from the auditorium.'

Even before the event, a critic for the *Telegraph* wrote up who they thought should win in each category: 'This will go to a public vote, so it should be a straight fight between McIntyre and Hart. Whichever of them wins, it'll be a victory for gentle, friendly, uncynical comedy. I'd take McIntyre, although it would be nice to see empress of slapstick Hart lift the award, not least because she'd almost certainly drop it on her foot, mug to camera then fall over.'

As the evening built up, all signs pointed to victory for Miranda. First she won Best New TV Comedy for *Miranda*, as, although series two had just finished airing, the first series broadcast in November 2009 was eligible. Later, she picked up Best Female Comedy Actress, presented to her by Simon Le Bon from Duran Duran. As she accepted the award from the 1980s icon, real-life Miranda blurred with her sitcom alter ego as she flirted with him, 'Yes, I will go back to your hotel! Thank you very much, wow! Actually, not really, you're OK.'

Now, Miranda relaxed. Being up against Michael McIntyre, Ant and Dec, Harry Hill and David Mitchell, she didn't much fancy her chances. But when David Tennant opened the envelope, he gleefully announced, 'The winner of the People's Choice Award is... it's Miranda Hart!'

Her face showed her genuine astonishment as she staggered to the stage to make another dreaded speech: 'From Louie Spence to Simon Le Bon to David Tennant! Erm, this is a joke, right? Because Michael McIntyre and Ant and Dec are like proper famous and stuff, come on! I genuinely don't know what to say. I mean, terrified of the thought of getting up – I just spat! I just actually spat! ... I'm really so overwhelmed, as you can see, I'm making a total tit of myself. Thank you so much to everyone who voted. That's all I can say, really. Thank you.'

She was still in shock the morning after, saying on Twitter, 'Very amusing dream last night that I met Simon Le Bon and spat on stage at the comedy awards'.

In the aftermath of the British Comedy Awards, there was

only one person taking the headlines. Miranda Hart, the lady who walked away with three trophies, appeared on almost every chat show available – they all wanted her. Speaking to Alan Carr on his TV chat show, *Chatty Man*, she said she was still buzzing and couldn't quite believe it. He suggested that Simon Le Bon had been flirting with her too and she joked, 'Well, you know, he's only human.' She went on to confess an embarrassing moment she had on stage: 'I kind of held on to him for a bit too long... I gave him a hug and I could feel him slightly trying to withdraw, but I wouldn't let him go. And I was like, I'm doing this for too long, and it's on telly. Even then I couldn't quite let go.' Alan asked how she celebrated her victorious evening, imagining – as we might too – a night of champagne and revelry. In fact, she admitted that she and the cast went back to her house for a cup of tea and to enjoy the contacts of their goodie bags, 'within which was, literally, three packets of crisps and a pint glass that you might get at an Esso garage in the 80s. And then, a Creme Egg'. A cup of tea and a Creme Egg at home with her sitcom family – how quaint.

Adrian Chiles and Christine Bleakley spoke to Miranda on ITV's *Daybreak*, and congratulated her on her hat trick. Chiles said of the Comedy Awards, 'I mean that's a tough gig actually, isn't it? Because you've got to be funny. I mean, if you won a comedy award, you've got to stand there and be funny, otherwise they might confiscate it.'

Miranda wasn't sure she managed that as, in her words, she just 'spat and dribbled and embraced Simon Le Bon for a bit too long'. After time to regroup and find the right words, Miranda left a message for her fans on her website: 'Thank you to everyone who voted for me at the Comedy Awards. If you saw the show you will have seen how embarrassingly speechless I was to get the People's Choice Awards. I am such a fan of Harry Hill, David Mitchell, Michael McIntyre and Ant and Dec – they are all amazing entertainers. So to be considered amongst them, let alone win, was a genuine shock. A big fat thank you for your support. You have made someone whose dream it was to get into comedy very happy. I am apparently now officially called the Queen of Comedy, so no eye contact please, only speak when you are spoken to and back out of the room. Thank you subjects.'

So why was Miranda so surprised at winning? People were talking about her at water coolers around the country, she was getting big viewing figures, and journalists were singing her praises. But Miranda was so worried about reading something negative that she avoided reviews and wasn't aware of the glowing write-ups she was given. Despite the fact the Christmas special attracted 4.4 million viewers, she couldn't quite get her head around it: 'I thought they'd got that wrong. I suppose because you sort of hear these figures, but it's very hard to get a tangible sense of it being popular because it's just sort of numbers. And I haven't done a tour recently, I haven't been out and about so I haven't really got a true sense of it. I think that's why I was particularly shocked by the People's Choice Award.'

But this wasn't the end of the acclaim for Miranda and her series. March 2011 saw the RTS Awards, where she received two nominations to the previous year's three. On this occasion, she won both categories: Best Scripted Comedy and Best Comedy Performance. Miranda was very excited to have won but, as it says on her website: 'The highlight of the night was winning a dare to ask Ant and Dec for a bottle of champagne because the BBC aren't allowed to buy champagne for their tables. Ant and Dec were kind enough to oblige!'

In June 2011, the lady of light entertainment was awarded extra cool points when she was given Best Comedy Actress of the Year by *Glamour Magazine*. 'I thought I had won Most Glamorous Woman of the Year, so I am a little disappointed, but I'll take it', she commented.

Surely by now, this darling of light entertainment must be bombarded on the street, hounded by fans and unable to go about her daily life? Not quite. Approaching the broadcast of the second series, Miranda had been busy writing, rewriting, rehearsing and recording the show, so didn't notice much difference. On his BBC chat show, Graham Norton suggested, 'You were a working comic and you've guested on other people's shows, but now this show... presumably it's taken you to a whole different level of fame.'

She replied that she does occasionally get recognised on the street, but then proceeded to tell how, recently in the waiting room at her doctor's, the nurse called out her name, 'Miranda Hart', and she heard someone say, 'Ooh! Do you think it's her off the telly?' After looking up to check, the lady concluded, 'Oh, no it's not.'

Online, however, is a different story – Miranda has a legion of fans. There are numerous blogs dedicated to the comedian, where admirers post screenshots of their favourite moments in the show, funny clips, and fan videos of her character and Gary set to love songs.

Some are asking the question whether it has been too much too soon. Andrew Pettie, writing for the *Telegraph*, says she is 'at the moment at which a steady groundswell of approval becomes a storm of praise, hype and media exposure'. But this adulation is largely down to her filling a gap in comedy with a finesse that appealed to a wide audience. Success did not come overnight. It took a decade of hard work and ploughing on regardless through rejections that got her to this point. She feels that this is just the start of her career, but has said she already feels tired with the amount of work and emotional strength it took her to get here. In the heat of the moment at the British Comedy Awards, she did pay tribute to those closest to her: 'I'd just like to thank my friends and family, really, for supporting me in the 10 years while I was gigging and didn't get a job basically and for persevering with me. Thank you very much.'

The 2011 BAFTA Television and Television Craft Awards did not provide *Miranda* with any further gongs, although the show earned three nominations. At the Television Awards on 8 May, Hart was in the running for Female Performance in a Comedy Programme (though Jo Brand would win the trophy thanks to her lead role in the hospital sitcom *Getting On*), while the programme itself was nominated in the YouTube-sponsored Audience Award, voted for by the public, a category won by the startlingly successful ITV2 series *The Only Way is Essex*. At the Television Craft Awards later in the month, *Miranda* director Juliet May was up against the directors of *The X-Factor*, *Strictly Come Dancing* and *Coronation Street*. Though May lost out to the *Street*'s Tony Prescott (for a special live episode of the serial), its association with three such well-established TV institutions underlined that, in a short space of time, *Miranda* had become appointment television.

Miranda Hart continues to be recognised for her talent and it appears that she is no flavour of the month, but a writer and performer with the ability to keep delivering. But where did this comedy star come from and what made her want to make people laugh for a living?

2

THE EARLY YEARS

*'Being told "Don't be silly" as a child really pissed me off,
so I thought, OK, I'll be silly for a living then.'*

— Miranda

The comedy stork delivered Miranda Katharine Hart Dyke to her parents in Torquay on 14 December 1972. She was joined by her sister Alice Louisa in 1975. There is a 'laughs as therapy' school of thought that believes comedians have usually suffered a troubled childhood they are trying to cope with. In many ways, Miranda's upbringing was a privileged one: her father was naval captain David Hart Dyke, commander of the HMS *Coventry* during the Falklands War, and her mother Diana Margaret Luce, daughter of Sir William Henry Tucker Luce (former British Governor and Commander in Chief of Aden). Speaking on Frank Skinner's TV series *Opinionated*, Miranda seemed coy about her aristocratic heritage, commenting, 'Well, I suppose strictly I'm from an upper-class background but I wouldn't say I'm upper class. The family goes back to the 12th century and my aunt and uncle live in a castle, three rooms of which they can't afford to run – that's how posh I am!'

Miranda's uncle, born Richard Luce, is in fact The Rt Hon. The Lord Luce KG GCVO PC DL – all those letters at the end marking him as a member of the Order of the Garter (a 'Sir'), the Royal Victorian Order, the Privy Council of the United Kingdom and Deputy Lieutenant of West Sussex. After working as a Conservative MP, Lord Luce served as Governor of Gibraltar and then Lord Chamberlain to Her Majesty The Queen until 2008. Most recently, in March 2011, he succeeded Douglas Hurd as High Steward of Westminster. So, not your average uncle then, but, as a former Minister for the Arts (1985–90), it must be quite a delight for him to see his niece Miranda flying the flag for female comics in the field.

The family moved to Petersfield, Hampshire, where Miranda spent the majority of her childhood, except when, like her comic counterpart, she was sent off to boarding school. But her comfortable upbringing suffered disruption at the age of nine when, in the spring of 1982, her father's ship was sent out to protect the troops in the Falklands War. He was in command of the Royal Navy Type 42 destroyer HMS *Coventry*, one of three ships sent to ward off aircraft and protect the troops, 20 miles ahead of the fleet. He found it hard being away from his wife and daughters, the only contact being through letters, which arrived by helicopter and were quickly distributed around the ship. The men on board had to write swift replies in time for the second chopper that would take them away. Captain Hart Dyke sent sketches of the ship in action and received letters and drawings from his daughters in reply. He later recalled a particular drawing Miranda did of *Coventry* to give to his Petty Officer Steward. The man in question, Mick Stuart, was very touched by the gesture and pinned it up on the pantry wall.

His main consolation during this difficult time was that his wife and family weren't the only ones in the area going through it. Miranda's mother Diana – known affectionately as 'D' – played an important role supporting other families in Hampshire who had husbands or sons fighting in the Falklands. But David kept a stiff upper lip throughout the operation. As he wrote in his memoirs, *Four Weeks in May*, 'The captain could not be seen by his sailors to be moping.'

But after one of their sister ships, *Sheffield*, sank, things were looking bleak for the brave father. His wife was understandably worried, doubled with the weight of other families looking to her for comfort, including the wife of Sam Salt, the ship's captain. Meanwhile, his daughters had their mind on other things. Miranda wrote to him about her upcoming cycling proficiency test and some new shoes she had acquired, with only one brief sentence referring to the sinking of *Sheffield*, which she described as 'very sad'.

Letters continued to be a source of reassurance for Captain Hart Dyke. He received one from his brother-in-law, Richard Luce, after he had been to visit D and the girls. He reassured the captain that they had overcome the shock of HMS *Sheffield* and were getting along well, and that he even played some duets with Miranda and her mother.

His mother wrote to him saying the girls were being wonderful – 'Miranda especially helpful and understanding – and looking so pretty with gorgeous liquid brown eyes like Devon pools'. Here, she was referring to a stretch of the River Teign where he used to play when staying with his grandparents when his father was away at sea. He says, 'Those deep brown pools, with their golden shingle which shone through to the surface in the sunlight, were magical, and they perfectly evoked Miranda's eyes.'

As things became more stressful on board, the captain found the letters something of a distraction. In a 2007 BBC documentary largely based on his memoirs, he remembered, 'I was very keen to get a last letter to say everything was well at home, the children were all right, and then I wanted to forget home. Put it behind me, on a sort of happy note... You really have to concentrate on the people you are leading and the matters in hand.'

His crew certainly needed him. HMS *Coventry*'s fate went from bad to worse and, eventually, on 25 May 1982, the destroyer was hit by Argentinean aircraft. The crew were prepared for a day filled with action as it was Argentina's national day, and emotions were going to be high. They fired a Sea Dart to ward the enemy off, but it flew straight into the hills. The nearby *Broadsword* had a technical hitch with their missile, so were unable to shoot the Argentinean aircraft down. They opened fire but, once out of missiles, with machine gun fire desperately firing, were reduced to waiting in silence. Two 1,000lb bombs fell on the ship, their explosions letting off a flash and unbearable heat. Many on board suffered severe flesh wounds; Hart Dyke himself sustained burns to the face, hands and wrists. While the ship's company attempted to escape, the captain awoke to a near-empty cabin and, suffocating from the smoke, felt near to admitting defeat. He recalled seeing severe devastation, figures on fire, and began to calmly accept his fate: 'There was no alternative but to die and so I prepared myself accordingly. Suffocation begins with a welcome calming effect, yet it is only one small step away from collapse and death. I was not far from it... I had thought of home and, ridiculous as it seems now, wondered who was going to mow the lawn in my absence. Then my mind had gone blank.'

Although he has no memory of how it happened, the captain found himself in clearer air. Despite the ship having no power and being in the process of sinking, he ordered Lieutenant-Commander Mike O'Connell to send the ship east into safer waters. But it was clear that the ship was going nowhere. Captain Hart Dyke felt helpless but, with help from the ship's company, finally managed to escape.

On that fateful day, 19 crew members were killed and 30 injured. Some were sent to a hospital ship, while the less serious cases – including Miranda's father – received first aid on the nearby *Broadsword*. Officers and public figures paid tribute including the then prime minister, Margaret Thatcher: 'Our fighting men are engaged on one of the most remarkable military operations of modern times... Our hearts go out to all the families who had men in those ships. We in Britain know the reality of war. We know its hazards and its dangers. We know the task which faces our fighting men.'

It was important to all men – and families – involved to know they had not been fighting in vain.

But when the news was announced on the BBC's World Service, the name of the ship was not mentioned and, even when it was, families had to wait hours to find out if their loved ones were safe. It caused severe worry back at home. In the first letter he received after the incident, D told David how difficult that night had been, how she had tried to distract herself by making up beds and sorting clothes.

Eventually, the call came and D knew her husband was safe. It was what she described as 'the most wonderful moment [she] can remember'.

During that time of uncertainty, D decided it was best not to tell Miranda and Alice that their father's ship had sunk, and so she sent them off to school as normal. But people at school had heard about the ship and were naturally concerned for the children's welfare. Miranda recalls one teacher asking how she was and her response – being something of a hypochondriac at the time – was 'I've got a bit of a cold, but I'm fine, thanks.'

When the children got home, their mother told them the terrible news. In interviews, Miranda has tended to put a comic sheen on the experience, saying she responded, 'Oh dear. Can I have a flapjack?', but her father's memoirs paint a more serious reaction. '[Miranda] sat down, went very red in the face and kept repeating, "Oh dear, oh dear, poor Daddy, oh dear."'

When David Hart Dyke was finally reunited with his family, it was an understandably emotional moment. His wife and daughters were led up to his cabin on the *QE2* when it came in to berth, and he and D had a tearful embrace. Once back in Petersfield, his life regained some normality, but he refused to speak publicly about the traumatic event for 25 years. In 1990, he retired from the armed services and now lives with D in Hambledon, Hampshire, near to Miranda's childhood home.

During its time in service, HMS *Coventry* brought down more enemy aircraft than any other ship in the Falklands, in its order to entice the enemy away from and protect British troops in San Carlos bay. Years later, he spoke pragmatically about the realities of conflict: 'That's war. It's like a game of chess. You've got to give up some pieces to get checkmate at the end. I was one of those pieces'.

Captain Hart Dyke was made an aide-de-camp to the Queen and was stationed in the United States. In the meantime, Miranda was sent away to boarding school in Berkshire. It doesn't seem that her father's ordeal affected the future comic any more than the small changes she experienced in her home life – a lot of women coming round for tea and the anxiety of cycling proficiency tests. Maybe she was to find distress waiting for her at boarding school, that she would have to therapeutically work out on the stage of a comedy club at a later date.

Or maybe not, for Miranda has described her school days as the happiest of her life. She attended Downe House boarding school in Berkshire, an independent girls-only place of learning. Karl Simpson, the current Director of Admissions, says, 'Downe House is not so much an independent girls' boarding school, it is more a school for independent girls.' This maxim seems to be reflected by the success of the school's alumni.

Miranda aside, former pupils at the school have included award-winning comedian Laura Solon, BBC sports presenter Clare Balding (who was head girl while Miranda was there), Sophie Dahl (and her mother Tessa), actress Geraldine James OBE, and even the possible future Queen Kate Middleton, who attended for one term before moving to Marlborough College. In an interview on *The One Show*, Balding – who Miranda remains friends with – reminded her of the school ethos: 'You know what we were taught at school – stand up for yourself, be independent in thought and deed, pull your socks up, don't pull your sleeves down, don't fiddle with your hair, don't spend more time trying to make your classmates laugh than you do concentrating on lessons and, above all, don't show off. Sad to say, you've made a living out of doing just that. And rather successfully.'

Indeed, rather than it being a nasty experience to forget, Miranda has huge fondness for her days at Downe House. Despite sporting a head brace and retainers for some of her time there, she was always popular: 'I flitted between gangs; it was a deliberate choice. If you were good at sport, then you were popular, and I was very good at lacrosse, if I say so myself. I played for Berkshire. I'm a lean, sporty woman trapped in a fat body.'

Hart has used her school days as inspiration for her comedy. In an interview on the red button following the first episode of the second series of *Miranda*, Downe House's Clare Balding said that she recognised the character of Tilly, played by Sally Phillips. Phillips is a well-respected comedy actress and writer who made her mark on Lee and Herring's TV series *Fist of Fun* in the mid-1990s, though she is probably best known for her performances in Channel 4's *Smack the Pony* and the *Bridget Jones* films. Her character Tilly is introduced in the first episode of series one, 'Date'. Miranda dreads meeting up with her old boarding-school friends for lunch (including Fanny, played by Katy Wix), but she gives in. 'As Tilly says, when you're dumped in a boarding-school dorm aged nine, you all bond for life. Even if you hate each other'.

Miranda wrote the series herself and says Tilly's language is based on the sort she heard during her time at boarding school. 'They do that thing of making English words sound a little bit European by going, "Marveloso!"' In the first episode alone, Tilly conjures up such classically quotable lines as 'Utmost cooliosity, kissingtons, marvelismos, brillo pads', and variations on Miranda's nickname Queen Kong: 'You're the Empress of Kong! You're Kongdeliza Rice!' It also introduces her recurring catchphrase 'Bear with... bear with...', used whenever she pauses conversation to look at a message on her phone. When she has finished, she returns to her reluctantly patient company with 'Back!'

Throughout the series, Miranda is referred to as Queen Kong (because of her height, of course), among the other ridiculous nicknames cited. Miranda admits this actually happened at Downe School – she knew a Tilly, Fanny and Podge, and in the series refers to Milly, Bella, Bunty, Hooty and Pussy. Claire Balding (aka 'Balders' or simply 'Head Girl') remembers her friend Sarah who everyone called Piffle ('because she talked such piffle all the time'). Viewers are left wondering who Tilly is referring to when she says, 'Stinky was the best head girl ever! Do you remember when she immac'd a squirrel?!'

On her blog for the BBC during the show's broadcast, Miranda said that, by the third week of rehearsals, the cast had all taken to speaking in Tilly's language. 'It's very contagious. Patricia Hodge will leave a rehearsal room saying "missingtons".'

In an interview for the *Sunday Times Culture* magazine, Miranda suggested that these characters are exaggerated versions of those at Downe House. 'My school didn't have lots of moneyed, King's Road Tilly types, so I got lucky, as boarding schools go.'

Miranda vividly remembers the first time she made someone laugh – doing an impression of her primary school's headmaster. By mimicking his bizarre idiosyncrasies, Miranda made her mum and sister laugh hysterically. From then on, little Miss Hart got the bug. On ITV in 2010, she told the *Loose Women* panel: 'I wasn't aware I craved the laughter, but I wanted to be on stage. I just love silliness and I find life quite boring. I don't like the responsibility of being an adult – I want to be making fun and lightness out of things. Being told "Don't be silly" as a child really pissed me off, so I thought, "OK, I'll be silly for a living then."'

Destined for comedy, Miranda was always the class clown and, as she told Alan Carr on Channel 4's *Chatty Man*, 'I always thought I was hilarious, whether I was or not.' In her formative years, Miranda got her kicks performing silly pranks and practical jokes, whether staying in a cupboard all lesson, only to reveal herself two minutes before the end with a 'Sorry I'm late', or going through the hassle of getting a sheep from the nearby fields and putting it in her dormitory, just to hear their teacher say, 'Who's put a sheep in here?' Very silly indeed.

She has recalled one particular classroom prank, although denies performing it herself. Once in class with a certain Mrs Thwaites, who had a very long, thin plait, one of her classmates cut it off while she was facing the blackboard. It's this sort of carelessness, common in childhood where there's little awareness of any consequences, which is replicated throughout *Miranda*.

There are several moments in the series which hint towards those sorts of classroom antics. In the third episode of series two, a flashback shows the young Miranda galloping down the school corridor. A teacher shouts at her, 'Hart! Don't run in the corridor!'

She replies confidently, 'It's a gallop, miss. I think all businessmen should do it, and one day I hope to tell the nation via a TV show.'

The teacher humours her. 'Oh, Hart. With that naïve optimism, you gallop, girl. It's the only you you'll ever know.' That (presumably imaginary) teacher could not have been more wrong.

In an interview with the BBC's Writersroom website, Miranda confesses that she has wanted to be a comedian as long as she can remember, to the point of wanting her own show on the BBC. Aged only six, she had seen Tommy Cooper, and knew even then that making people laugh was what she wanted to do. She has mentioned other comic greats as inspiration – Morecambe and Wise (Eric Morecambe especially), French and Saunders, Tony Hancock and Joyce Grenfell. And there are similarities between Hart and all of her comic heroes:

She and Hancock both star in eponymous sitcoms playing exaggerated versions of themselves. The audience feel warmth through the failure and ineptitude of Miranda's character the same way they did for Hancock. The same feeling could be said to be elicited by Tommy Cooper and his charmingly flawed magic tricks. Like French and Saunders, she isn't afraid of being a female clown – whether it be dressing in unflattering outfits, or falling fantastically arse over tit. She's got the well-spoken inflections of Joyce Grenfell. But perhaps most of all, she is the modern, female incarnation of the late Eric Morecambe. When she turns to camera with *that look*, we get a mischievous feeling we're part of something the others on the screen aren't. We're in on the joke.

Miranda has said that, when she saw Morecambe's looks to camera on TV, she thought, 'Ooh! He's looking at me; I want to do that.' And do it she has, with great aplomb.

She has that peculiar British brand of comedy – a combination of self-deprecation, sarcasm and slapstick. She blames being away at boarding school for missing out on seeing much of the alternative comedy scene of the 1980s but her influences have brought to the public a much-missed brand of humour: the light-entertainment style of the 1970s, a nostalgic kind of reminiscence for some of us, and something fun and new for others. Our beloved Miranda Hart was always destined to be a star of the comedy world – and wanted it more than anything – but, as we shall discover in the following chapters, it didn't come easily to her.

3

GROWING PAINS

'When I see a tall woman, I'm always slightly like, woah, it looks weird, but that could be because of my complex about it, my worry over whether it's womanly to be that tall.'

– Miranda

Actress and comedian Miranda Hart is the star of *Miranda*, but her alter ego in the series – joke-shop owner – is the butt of most of the jokes, lots of them revolving around her appearance. There is much speculation about how autobiographical the sitcom is, and how similar Miranda is to her on-screen persona. What is clear is that her appearance has played an important part in how she feels about herself, as well as being a source of comic material. Self-penned jokes about her size stem from a dark time in Miranda's life. 'In terms of my character, I did very much start from myself. Then I'd get too sad and morose and angry, so I had to find the fun side of my teenage angst.' Unlike her happy-go-lucky schooldays of galloping around corridors and being a popular lacrosse player, her teenage years and early twenties were pretty low times.

After winning the People's Choice Award, the comic expressed her surprise at her new-found popularity. She had been so busy that she regarded the viewing figures abstractedly as mere numbers, and she hadn't read any reviews. Why, though? Miranda hates the way she looks and journalists seem to fixate on her appearance almost as much as she does. 'People are obviously going to mention what I look like, but it's a shame it has to be a key part. I can't just be Miranda.' And who can blame her for avoiding reviews when papers have described her in such unflattering and even unpleasant terms as 'lady-mountain Miranda Hart', 'a human stegosaurus' or 'huge and hugely unfanciable'. 'One of those comments is OK,' Hart has argued, 'you can deal with it, but, if you read 60, even the strongest person would start feeling low.'

While Miranda remains understandably sensitive about certain comments regarding her appearance, she is still dedicated enough to comedy to courageously send herself up so frequently in her act, with so many laughs reliant on her size and clumsy nature. She is mistaken for a transvestite, addressed as 'Sir' by a delivery man and constantly called 'Queen Kong' by her old boarding-school friends. Now, Miranda is happy in herself, but still avoids reading reviews as it takes her back to unhappier times. 'I'm quite a confident person in many ways, but there's only so much you can hear about being compared to Hattie Jacques. For the record, she was a comedy goddess, but she was 25 stone. I hope I'm right in saying I'm not in any way nearly 25 stone.'

And she doesn't appear to be embarrassed by her body, willing to bare all for a laugh. Social awkwardness and being naked in public seem to go together for her comic creation, and the big-knickered Miranda does it so brilliantly and in such a typically English fashion. Her dress getting stuck in a taxi door and being ripped off wouldn't be nearly so funny if it revealed a supermodel figure in sexy matching undies, rather than the looming figure in galumphing pants we are treated to.

In one newspaper interview, the journalist is interrupted by the comic's PR saying that they need to start make-up. Grimacing, Miranda says, 'They probably looked at the state of me and thought, We'd better get her over there as quickly as possible.' It seems that, despite being branded 'Crush of the Week' in another paper, and her immense popularity across the nation, Miranda still hates the way she looks. 'I'm happy socially and I've got good friends, but everyone has got their thing, haven't they? And mine is I don't like looking in the mirror.' She has also said that she can't imagine anyone finding her attractive. This insecurity came from years of feeling she was different and being told by casting agents she did not fit the mould of the business they call show.

At 16 years old, she was already 6ft 1in and was very thin. People laughed at her gangliness and clumsiness. 'I was always tripping over and knocking into things, because I didn't realise how wide my wingspan was.' She wasn't too worried about her height, but family and friends kept reassuring her that it was OK to be tall, people kept referring to it, and she started to feel different. They would encourage her to embrace her height, and tell her that models were tall, but she started to feel uncomfortable with herself and the more it bore weight on her mind, the more it was mentioned, the more ill at ease she felt. Despite fitting in well, she never felt happy in her own skin. 'Perhaps that's being tall,' she reflected later, 'not being comfortable with men until my mid-twenties.'

And, although she was happy at the time, Hart reflects that going to an all-girls' school may have affected her confidence and approach to men: 'I think, for a shy person – and I was very shy until my mid- twenties – having been to an all-girls' school is not brilliant on the boyfriend front later.'

She had reached her full height by the time she was in the sixth form, but looked different to the Miranda we know today: 'I was also very, very thin, and people used to laugh at the gangliness rather than the precipitousness.'

Everything in Hart's life pointed her to comedy and performing, and she applied for stage-management courses but, under parental pressure, she went to Bristol Polytechnic (now the University of the West of England) to study politics. There were new people to meet, new experiences to be had and opportunities ahead of her. But being so image conscious held her back. 'It was definitely like meeting a new species of people. Suddenly, at age 19, I was thinking, Can you speak to these people? I was very, very nervous.' She was worried about not being attractive to men or, as she puts it, 'of not feeling like your stereotypical girl'. But it is exactly this aspect of her personality that people find attractive. It is her truth that people relate to when they watch the show's character – on-screen Miranda is very 'warts 'n' all' – or the endearing honesty and humility of the lady in interviews. She has said that, in retrospect, she realises she was 'God knows how many stones lighter' and that friends she was at university with have since told her that they thought she was sexy and wanted to make a move. She wishes she could stop thinking of herself negatively, but it seems a weakness she can't rid herself of. 'It's such a waste of energy, I know. And I still do it now. I'm an idiot.'

She graduated with a 2:1 in politics from Bristol by 'pretty much winging it with what amounted to a photographic memory'. But then she reset her sights and enrolled on a postgraduate acting course at the Academy of Live and Recorded Arts in London (ALRA) in London. She told the *Sunday Times* how even the tutors couldn't overlook her appearance. In ballet classes with her teacher Betty – 'We called her Betty Ballet, which I thought was hilarious' – her height was an issue. 'She used to say, "A metre apart, please, at the barre," and, with no sense of a joke, she added, "And two metres apart if you are next to Miranda."'

Miranda could see the funny side the first time it was said, but, as it was mentioned every lesson, the novelty quickly wore off. It set a precedent for the attitude of casting agents in the future. 'Nobody would cast me as a lead in a sitcom and nobody would cast me as the girlfriend or the daughter. I was 6ft 1in and not of televisual frame.'

Miranda found some solace writing sketches at university, but, after graduating, any work she could find was on the mundane side. Her first job was cleaning student flats, what she says is the worst job she ever had: 'One flat's sink was blocked and they were doing the washing up in the bath. Oh yes.'

She went back to Hampshire to live with her parents and, as she had to cope with the alien world of growing older, life became a little trickier. 'I was getting used to being tall. And then in my mid-twenties I ballooned in size. Then I was tall and big, and that I found difficult.'

Miranda was struggling with agoraphobia, anxiety and panic attacks, and it didn't help that the anti-depressants she had been prescribed added to the weight gain of some five stone. 'It all happened after university,' she told the *Guardian*. 'I think I was just very anxious. I thought the world was a bit scary. Some people get depressed for six months and then pull themselves together. I just hid in a room and didn't go out for two years.'

Although university and negative comments contributed to her depression, she has described it as her natural disposition. 'It's just bad genes, bad luck, really. I'll always have to force myself to see the positive, because I'm wired badly, I'd say. I'm just naturally a bit under, a bit depressed.'

This manifested itself as agoraphobia, but, rather than a fear of open spaces, it was more people and crowds that Miranda feared. Now, Miranda loves to visit the countryside. When she had finished filming the first series of her sitcom, she went on a road trip around Wales, Cumbria and Yorkshire. 'I love being in the middle of nowhere and looking up at the stars – it gives me this incredible feeling of peace.'

She said that people are often surprised that she enjoys being among these vast expanses because of her former agoraphobia, 'but the condition is nothing to do with a fear of open spaces. Agoraphobia goes hand in hand with crowds, so I'd have a panic attack in the theatre when I felt I couldn't get out, or in a supermarket queue.'

During one appearance on *Have I Got News For You*, they asked her if her agoraphobia was the reason she choose to do the sitcom *Not Going Out*. 'Now that's funny. And may I congratulate you because you are the first one to make said joke. How satisfying for us all. Oh and no, it's not the reason.'

But it turned out there was some pertinence to the question. 'Although I have to say, on a more serious note, when I did still have agoraphobia, I found a theatre or a TV studio total bliss to be in – dark, soundproof, total escapism from the world.'

It seems that some good came out of this unhappy situation: Miranda began to write. 'I started writing comedy around that time because it was more fun inside my head than in the real world.'

There is a theory that putting one's problems down in words can help you overcome them. Speaking at the Edinburgh International Book Festival in 2008, author David Lodge said, 'I find most writing therapeutic,' and Graham Greene famously said, 'Writing is a form of therapy; sometimes I wonder how all those who do not write, compose or paint can manage to escape the madness, the melancholia, the panic and fear, which is inherent in a human condition.'

'The Hills Are Alive' was Miranda's attempt to put the situation to bed by telling her story. Broadcast in October 2006 as part of BBC Radio 4's series *Inner Voices*, it was a character monologue, written with the help of her sister Alice, and was inspired by her time of suffering from agoraphobia. The description, 'Imprisoned in a bedroom, you can only dream of going on a *Sound of Music* coach tour', suggests that her sense of humour about the situation meant she had moved on to some extent.

'I've been there and done that,' she has said. 'I'm not a Stephen Fry, it's not going to be with me forever.'

Fry is one of four million people in the UK with bipolar disorder, which has affected him throughout his life. He attempted to break the social taboo of discussing mental health with his BBC Two documentary *The Secret Life of a*

Manic Depressive, talking to other sufferers of the condition. He says that, when he was diagnosed at the age of 37, 'I had a diagnosis that explains the massive highs and miserable lows I've lived with all my life.'

This idea of the sad clown is one that echoes throughout comedy history. The list of comedians who have suffered from depression is a lengthy one, and includes Robin Williams, Jim Carrey, Woody Allen, Groucho Marx, Lenny Bruce and Tommy Cooper. Other sufferers of bipolar disorder who went on to be comedians include Tony Slattery, Russell Brand, Bill Oddie, Ruby Wax and Spike Milligan.

Milligan's co-star in *The Goon Show*, Peter Sellers, was probably one of the condition's most famous sufferers. The film *The Life and Death of Peter Sellers* (based on Roger Lewis's book) was devoted to his struggle with his mental health. The pressure of Goon deadlines and a sick wife became too much for Milligan, as he later recounted: 'One day I was with Peter Sellers when something inside me snapped. I tried to kill him with a potato knife. Either that or I just wanted to peel him.'

Tony Hancock was another comic hero who was consumed by a sense of despair. He took his own life in 1968, aged just 44. Years later, Spike Milligan said that Hancock was a 'very difficult man to get on with. He used to drink excessively. You felt sorry for him. He ended up on his own. I thought, He's got rid of everybody else, he's going to get rid of himself, and he did.'

Even Miranda's hero Eric Morecambe was prone to bouts of mild depression.

Across the pond, outspoken comedian and broadcaster Sara

Benincasa developed a one-woman show in 2009, documenting her experiences with agoraphobia and panic attacks. This is now being made into a book called *Agorafabulous!* to be published by William Morrow, an imprint of Harper Collins.

Regarding her own experience of agoraphobia, Miranda is honest about her experience but prefers to keep it below the radar, prefacing answers to interviewers with: 'I won't bore you with it, because it wasn't very nice...'

And, unlike many of these cases, Miranda's was a temporary condition that she has moved on from: 'Though I'll always be a fairly anxious person,' she admits. 'I have a good old cry at bad news and get rather down. Pessimism is my default setting.'

In 1993, Miranda picked herself up and moved to Scotland – to Edinburgh. She lived there for a year, writing comedy and preparing herself for the 1994 Festival. This wasn't cosy Hampshire at Mum and Dad's house. It was a challenge. 'I went to live in Edinburgh for a year and forced myself out of feeling sorry for myself. I had no heating, so that's enough to wake you up.'

Coming out as a comedian to her parents was a turnaround moment. She had been working as a PA in the charity sector when she told them what she really wanted to do. 'They weren't discouraging,' she told the *Guardian*, 'but they weren't fully encouraging – which they are now – and that helped in a way. They just said, "Why don't you stick with being a PA, you're good at it," and that made me, in a teenage way, go, "You just wait then, I'll try and prove you all wrong."'

Determination combined with resilience meant that, no matter what people told her, or however few people turned up to see her, she carried on trying. 'There must always have been a sense of "I've got enough to carry on". You know, however much I'm terrified and think I look and sound ridiculous, there is a confidence that keeps me going. Every comedian has to be like that. You wouldn't get on stage if you didn't think that you were good.'

She even managed to accept the way she looks. Or, at least, she found a way to make the most of her height by adopting a certain Python's style of slapstick. 'Anyway, look at John Cleese. Why not use those limbs if you've got them? If he contained himself, he wouldn't be nearly as funny.'

Still, she says she would like to be a little less tall. 'I'd like to be 5ft 10in. That would be very nice, because then you can wear a heel and not look like a transvestite.'

Of course, this is not the case. As well as old university chums, many fans have admitted to finding her very attractive. When one newspaper even named her 'Crush of the Week', her response to the *Guardian*'s Kira Cochrane was typically self-deprecating: 'Shut up! That's very worrying. But I can guess what they would say – something like, not the obvious choice, not the conventional choice, but for some reason Crush of the Week.'

Charles I, a user of Digital Spy's, was one smitten fan. He asked his fellow discussion-board friends: 'Does anybody else find her attractive? I think I'd like to sit on her lap.' We should probably leave it there quoting Miranda's fans' fantasies, but it proves a point. Hart told *Stylist* magazine that, since she has become famous, men's reaction to her has changed: 'I was out for the first time recently and there was definitely a palpable difference in response, which was lovely, but I haven't had time to reflect on any offers of marriage yet. I'm bound to get more...'

Miranda has been single for three years because she's been working so hard and hasn't had time for a relationship. 'I'm much keener to be with people than I used to be and I can definitely see myself sharing my space in future... perhaps finally I'll go on a road trip with someone apart from Peggy – I'm open to offers, write in!'

But this tongue-in-cheek invitation came with a caveat: 'The relationship will only work if my partner understands I need the odd day on my own from time to time. I'll be the perfect wife: "Of course, darling, please go and have a weekend with the lads at football. Please get out of the house!"'

So who's the perfect husband for her? She told *Stylist* magazine that the main thing she looks for in a man is funniness. 'I don't need to be the funniest in a relationship; in fact, it would be really nice to have someone entertain me.'

In the main, Miranda has conquered her appearance complex and has put her above-average height to good use, entertaining the nation with her fabulous pratfalls. But before she got there, she had to conquer Edinburgh and the radio. It was quite a struggle for the Queen of Comedy.

She went from contented schoolgirl, showing off in class for laughs, to disaffected twenty-something, desperate for affirmation and a career in comedy. She is a strong woman and a role model for many young women, but who are the sisters of comedy that came before her? And is she alone in her suffering?

4

HERE COME THE GIRLS

'Men find funny women threatening. They ask me, "Are you going to be funny in bed?"'

– Joan Rivers

All set to throw off her worries and find her fortune at the Edinburgh Fringe Festival, what did Miranda Hart, as a woman, face when she put herself out there in the male-dominated world of comedy? Many female comedians insist there is no difference, but it is a discussion which dates back many years. Comedian Kerry Godliman told a *Guardian* interviewer that, when she was at the Comedy Store, she was looking at press cuttings they have on the wall at the back. 'There's bits and pieces there from 1984 about women in comedy and you think, Nothing's changed! We're still having that conversation!'

As we know, one of the main reasons Miranda doesn't look at reviews is because they mention her looks, whereas she doesn't think it is the case for men in the business: 'A fat male comedian isn't a "fat comedian", he's just a comedian. It's really frustrating... People are obviously going to mention what I look like, but it's a shame it has to be a key part. I can't just be Miranda.'

While men do get this same journalistic treatment about how they look – one recent article described Tim Minchin as 'kohl-eyed, poodle-haired, ivory-tickling' – with women, it does seem to get more personal about looks. This has even affected how some comics choose to represent themselves on stage.

Isy Suttie says that she never wears a skirt or tight top when she's performing stand-up: 'I never want them to be thinking about me as a sexual object of any kind.'

Some might argue, though, that doing so only perpetuates the myth that good-looking women can't be funny, and funny women are only so to make up for their lack of looks.

You might assume this attitude is dead and even consider it laughable, but, only in 2007, the late Christopher Hitchens wrote a piece for *Vanity Fair* called 'Why Women Aren't Funny'. Although he offers the disclaimer 'This is not to say that women are humourless, or cannot make great wits and comedians', he does go on to bring up the archaic theory that women feel no need to be funny as 'They already appeal to men, if you catch my drift'. The thrust of his article is best summed up by the following extract: 'My argument doesn't say that there are no decent women comedians... Most of them, though, when you come to review the situation, are hefty or dykey or Jewish, or some combo of the three.'

Ouch! Sexism in comedy is gradually going out of fashion but, as with any sociological change, it takes its time. The term 'comedienne' is being phased out, and it will only appear in this book inside quotation marks.

Giles Coren, restaurant critic and Gary-from-*Miranda* lookalike, wrote that he was looking to buy a stand-up comedy DVD as a Christmas gift: 'So, what to choose? Looking at the comedy chart shelf, it went: John Bishop, Kevin Bridges, Lee Mack, Frankie Boyle, Michael McIntyre, Dara O'Briain, Rhod Gilbert, Bill Bailey, Jimmy Carr, Peter Kay, Dave Allen, Billy Connolly, Sean Lock, Stewart Francis, Lee Evans, Karl Pilkington, Rob Brydon...'

He was astonished that there is not one female present in the list, not even one token girl. Coren cannot fathom why this is. As I looked at hmv.com's stand-up comedy DVDs section when writing the first edition of this book in 2011, only 18 of the 378 titles listed showcased female comedians. That's not even 5 per cent. These included: four Victoria Wood DVDs; three French and Saunders' live sketch shows (not really stand-up); *Grumpy Old Women* (stage show); and Pam Ayres (who, although funny, is primarily a poet). I considered including the two Lily Savage shows to bring it up to a nice round 20, but that would hardly be accurate. One year later, we've managed to push 4.76 per cent up to 5.39 per cent, with 24 appearances out of 445 DVDs. While this is a tiny improvement it shows that, despite the recent success of the likes of Sarah Millican, the truth is that women in comedy are heavily outnumbered.

It's not much better on the live circuit. Performer Lucy Porter says, 'Backstage at a gig, I occasionally realise that I'm the only woman in a dressing-room.' This brings female comedians closer, as Miranda herself has confirmed: 'I've made some really nice friends – mainly women. There's definitely a sisterhood.' There is a strange attitude that seems ingrained in our society that female comedians are separate. Sometimes, the compere gives them a discouraging introduction, whether through a simple mistake or brazen rudeness.

In his article, Giles Coren explains what happened to a female stand-up friend of his. She was appearing at a gig compered by Michael McIntyre, and pleaded with him before going on not to describe her as 'gorgeous': 'Men always do that when they're introducing me and it makes it very hard to perform – it means the women in the audience hate you before you even open your mouth, and the men are just sizing you up and going, "She's not all that."' But, probably out of habit, he brought her on with: 'This next act is the absolutely gorgeous... oops, she told me not to say that, but she is.'

In this case, McIntyre most likely said it by accident, but some male comperes are less innocent. Stand-up Tiffany Stevenson received the following patronising and rude introduction: 'Ladies and gentlemen, it's time for another act. Now, it is a girl, so be nice because she could be a bit... well, crap.'

The comedy community has tried to overcome this by putting together gig nights with a female-only line-up (Miranda has, in the past, hosted such a gig called 'Lipstick and Shopping'), or with an occasional 'token male'. But this can have the opposite effect of highlighting the very issue they are trying to solve. Nina Conti has said that it made her 'notice I was a female comic, rather than a male one'. Isy Suttie feels similarly: 'For me, stand-up is my job and the thing about women-only gigs is that they become like a pat on the back and I don't understand why people are patting my back.'

There was controversy in April 2011 when Funny Women, founded by Lynne Parker and which seeks to promote and develop new female comedy talent, announced that it would be charging a registration fee of £15 to those entering its annual competition. Comedians used Twitter as their soapbox and said what they thought of this 'Pay-to-Play' system. Sarah Millican offered: 'Advice to any budding female comedians: no need to pay to play by entering Funny Women. Just be funny, write loads & work very hard.'

Bethany Black added: 'If Lynne hasn't been able to raise the money to cover the costs then that's her failure. Why should comics who are at the start of their career pay for that failure?'

Shappi Khorsandi was equally dismissive: 'Aspiring comics! Never pay to enter a competition! Buy a new hat instead!'

Funny Women's website responded: 'So, potential female comedians of the future, you have been presented with both a choice and an opportunity: you can either take comedian Shappi Khorsandi's advice and do what's expected of you as a *girl* (namely take your registration fee and go shopping for a new hat), jump on the bandwagon and perpetuate the stereotype of the bitchy irrational female comedian who's more interested in gossip than developing a professional profile; or you can rise up and act with the strength and poise of a *woman*, join us in making a statement, and be a fundamental part of taking female comedy beyond this silliness and on the next level.'

This only inflamed the situation, and comics joined a Facebook group to boycott the competition. Jo Caulfield, whose picture was used by Funny Women in its publicity material to justify the fee, said: 'As the website face of Funny Women Pay2Play I advise all new young female comics to AVOID us like the plague.'

The next day, the blog post was deleted from the website, and replaced with an apology from Funny Women's head, Lynne Parker. 'I would like to apologise for yesterday's blog post. I was so shocked at the responses to the introduction of the £15 registration fee and have been hugely hurt by what's being said on Twitter and Facebook.' To try to make amends, she continued, 'I am a great personal fan of some of my worst critics and just so sorry that this has all been taken out of context. I really hope that we can all get past this and move on.'

When the 2012 competition was launched, Funny Women prompted a debate after choosing to keep the £15 entrance fee, even though they had secured sponsorship from the cosmetics company Benefit. It also has a variety award which honours character, speciality or sketch acts, which is sponsored by Blue Nun wine.

Female acts can find a similar fight on television, where panel shows dominate the comedy listings. Suzanne Moore, columnist for the *Mail on Sunday* and the *Guardian*, is critical of such formats. 'Every so often, someone like Miranda Hart or Josie Long comes along and reminds us that yes, women can be hilarious too, but panel show after panel show now consists of what we used to call DOTs (Dicks on Tables).' It's a rare panel show that features as many female guests as male ones – but the playful *We Need Answers* on BBC Four (on which both Hart and Long appeared) was one, and a world away from DOTs.

Rising star Holly Walsh defends the panel-show format. 'I really enjoy doing panel shows. I love writing jokes and I love the fact that you can't rely on your old material – you have to come up with new stuff.' She also points out that they are a good way of showcasing new comedians, as stand-up shows tend to only use 'tried and tested people'.

Germaine Greer, author of *The Female Eunuch*, had stirred up the debate in 2009 when she said on television that women weren't as funny as men. To try to stop the furious response, she published a piece in the *Guardian* beginning, 'I should probably not have said, in so few words on television recently, that women aren't as funny as men. Put so baldly, the observation sounds like deliberate provocation, as if I was baiting feminists, or looking for some kind of knee-jerk response.'

Her explanation, however, did not placate those who disapproved. As one blogger remarked, 'Germaine Greer regrets saying, "women aren't as funny as men" in so few words – so she says it in many, many more words.'

In the article, she makes further provocative statements such as 'they have not developed the arts of fooling, clowning, badinage, repartee, burlesque and innuendo'; 'Women famously cannot learn jokes. If they try, they invariably bugger up the punchline'; 'Put her in an improvised situation along with male comedians, and she is likely to be left speechless'; and 'Men do the inspired lunacy; women do droll.'

Tiffany Stevenson, who runs a gig with Zoe Lyons called Girls with Guns, was left feeling frustrated by Greer's article. 'The window of opportunity is already narrower for women on stage, as audiences and promoters come with prejudged notions about a woman's ability to be funny. Germaine Greer simply perpetuates the myth that we're not.'

Britain has a rich history of female comedians, so it is hard to understand why this entrenched attitude has not shifted that radically over the years. Miranda Hart says, 'As a female viewer, I've never felt like I needed women on the telly but actually maybe one does. Without French and Saunders or Joyce Grenfell, I wouldn't have thought it was possible to be a female comedian.'

Dawn French and Jennifer Saunders were one of the biggest comedy double-acts of the 1980s and 1990s, starting off at The Comic Strip, a London comedy club that also saw performances from the likes of Adrian Edmondson, Rik Mayall and Nigel Planer. In 2009, they were jointly awarded the BAFTA Fellowship, which led Miranda to tweet, 'Bafta fellowship for French and Saunders totally deserved IMHO [In My Humble Opinion]. Their influence [has] been extraordinary and [is] often unrecognised in industry elite.'

Other female British comedy greats over the decades have included Joyce Grenfell, Hattie Jacques, June Whitfield, Sheila Hancock, Jo Brand, Linda Smith, Jenny Eclair, Helen Lederer, Kathy Burke, Meera Syal, Morwenna Banks, Catherine Tate, Victoria Wood and Julie Walters. Miranda met Walters briefly at the 2009 BAFTAs. Although it wasn't a perfect encounter – Julie didn't recognise her and Miranda became flustered – she was excited enough, telling an interviewer, 'I've just met one of my heroes, Julie Walters… It wasn't the best of meetings to be honest. I was gunning that she might go, "Oh, I've seen your work," but she hasn't, and that's fair enough.'

Today, Victoria Wood and Julie Walters tend to restrict their collaborations to Christmas specials, French and Saunders have officially split, performing their last show on Drury Lane in 2008 (though they have reunited recently for occasional radio specials), and Catherine Tate is taking serious acting roles, often alongside David Tennant. The award-winning Channel 4 series *Smack the Pony* (1999–2003) played an important role in showcasing female character comedians and writers such as Sally Phillips, Doon Mackichan and Fiona Allen. Since it ended, a handful of female sketch shows have come and gone, such as *Tittybangbang*, *Little Miss Jocelyn* (both for BBC Three) and E4's *Beehive*.

It is now time, though, for a new generation of female comics to emerge. After lying dormant on the circuit, they are now getting opportunities to appear on television. People are calling the double-act Watson & Oliver the new French & Saunders, though they enjoy playing more male parts and offer a more surreal brand of humour. Meanwhile, Emma Fryer, who showed her worth as the stoned kleptomaniac Tanya (to be pronounced 'Tanyaaah') in Johnny Vegas's *Ideal*, has since written and starred in the BBC Two sitcom, *Home Time*. Elsewhere, Sharon Horgan's series *Pulling* brought attention to her deliciously dark and filthy sense of humour, while *Lizzie and Sarah* by Julia Davis and Jessica Hynes was a pilot that many loved and thought should have been a full series. For Miranda, one of the rising stars of TV comedy is a fellow comedy actor renowned for her *Big Ass Show* on ITV. 'I think someone like Katy Brand's incredibly brave because she makes herself ridiculous, she makes herself beautiful, she does everything.' And there are plenty of other promising figures who are gradually establishing themselves via panel games, stand-up and sitcom, Sarah Millican, Roisin Conaty, Pippa Evans, Holly Walsh, Laura Solon, Joanna Neary and Andi Osho among them.

One of the most noteworthy female stand-ups hitting the mainstream is Sarah Millican, the successor to Miranda's Queen of Comedy title from the British Comedy Awards. Her BBC Two show, *The Sarah Millican Television Show*, began in March 2012 and got a good critical reception as well as being a ratings hit. A second series was promptly commissioned.

Over many years, American female comedians – from Roseanne to Sarah Silverman – have become popular in Britain, where their sharp brand of self-deprecation and sarcasm has found enthusiastic followings. A recent import of note has been Kristen Schaal, probably best known as Mel in *Flight of the Conchords*. After performing at the Edinburgh Festival and clubs across London, she has made an impression on Britain's audiences, and her show *Penelope Princess of Pets* was shown as part of Channel 4's *Comedy Lab* strand.

The lady of the moment is, without doubt, Tina Fey. She stamped herself on the international consciousness with her impression of former Alaskan governor Sarah Palin on *Saturday Night Live*, during the 2008 presidential election campaign. Since 2007, she has been a writer and lead actor (as Liz Lemon) on the sitcom *30 Rock*, but some have tended to load this talented woman with the responsibility of representing funny women. Adam Frucci, who runs a comedy blog, believes: 'She is in a tough position. Not many comedians are forced to represent their entire gender when all they are just trying to be is funny.'

Inevitably, you can't please everyone and some think that Liz Lemon conforms to the stereotype of the lonely woman, desperate for a man. Others believe she has only got where she is because of her looks. Jill Filipovic, founder of a blog called

Feministe, says, 'If Tina Fey were ugly, then she would not have the career that she has had. We still don't see a lot of unconventionally attractive women on TV.'

But Fey also receives her fair share of nasty comments about her looks. She took the opportunity of a newspaper article she had written to publicise her autobiography *Bossypants* to have her say, explaining, 'When people care enough to write, the only well-mannered thing to do is to return the gift, so please indulge me as I answer some fans here.'

So, rather than avoid reviews, Tina Fey confronts them and hits back with sassy remarks. To someone posting, 'When is Tina going to do something about that hideous scar across her cheek?' she sarcastically replied, 'The trickier question is what am I going to do? I would love to get your advice, actually. I'm assuming you're a physician, because you seem really knowledgeable about how the human body works.'

Someone calling themselves 'Centaurious' sent the following missive to one site in the small hours: 'Tina Fey is an ugly, pear-shaped, bitchy, overrated troll.' Some would ignore such an attack, others would be affected by it, but Fey faced it with comedy. 'To say I'm an overrated troll, when you have never even seen me guard a bridge, is patently unfair… As for "ugly, pear-shaped and bitchy"? I prefer the terms "offbeat, business class-assed and exhausted", but I'll take what I can get.' And she can't help but sign off with a dig of her own: 'Now get to bed, you crazy night owl! You have to be at Nasa early in the morning. So they can look for your penis with the Hubble telescope.'

Just as Miranda Hart followed on from the British comic traditions of Joyce Grenfell, French and Saunders and other female performers, so Tina Fey had a foundation of American

TV comedy to build on, which dated back nearly 60 years to Lucille Ball. Ball, the star of *I Love Lucy* in the 1950s, was a popular female lead whose physical comedy had audiences in hysterics, but she was a relatively non-threatening character. It took characters like Carla, the barmaid in *Cheers* played by Rhea Perlman in the 1980s and 1990s, to show that comic females on television could 'grow a pair'. Carla was a smart ass who gave as good as she got, just as crude and biting as the boys. It could be a popular trait in stand-up comedy too – notably through the work of Joan Rivers – but the woman who led this trend on to the small screen was a certain Roseanne Barr. Transferring her stand-up character to television, Roseanne co-wrote her own show and her unyielding matriarchal voice made a huge social impact on the cultural landscape. After Roseanne, Ellen DeGeneres and Brett Butler had their own sitcom vehicles (respectively, *Ellen* and *Grace Under Fire*), while there were strong co-starring roles for Julia Louis Dreyfus (*Seinfeld*), Jane Kaczmarek (*Malcolm in the Middle*) and Jane Krakowski (*Ally McBeal*, *30 Rock*) as the strong women of American sitcom.

So, while Tina Fey is the ruling female in American TV comedy, perhaps Miranda Hart will end up flying the flag here in Britain. Hers is a softer, less aggressive style, and fits well with the national outlook. So, as she developed a stand-up persona for Edinburgh and the ultimate goal of television, what was Miranda hoping to achieve with her act? 'A lot of women seem to be either very laddy in their stand-up, or don't want to break their pretty, feminine look.' Instead, she aimed to avoid being pigeonholed by looking for something more spontaneous. 'I think it is a shame that more women don't act the fool and let go a bit – that is what naturally appeals to me but maybe that is just my personality.' And this isn't comedy for or about women that she is aiming for. Again, it's that universal appeal. 'I think as a comedian you've got to be free and you've got to have a confidence and you've got to be completely free to be laughed at. I see myself as a performer, not as a woman performer or woman writer. I just think of what is funny.'

Before television came calling, Miranda did what so many comedians did before her – she packed her bag full of gags and headed up to Edinburgh, the place where you can make it, where you can get taken seriously, if people notice you at all. But as a female comedian? The Edinburgh Festival is still very much a man's world. But it wouldn't be nothing without a woman, eh?

5

FRINGE BENEFITS

'I'll get drunk. I'll get laid. I'll get spotted. I'll get paid.'
– Arthur Smith on the four main ambitions
of performing at the Edinburgh Fringe

The Edinburgh Fringe Festival, or the Fringe, or Ed. Whatever you call it, it's the world's largest arts festival and undoubtedly the highlight of the live comedy calendar. Every August, the entire London comedy circuit heads up to the Scottish capital to be discovered by the comedy producers and promoters... of London. It's a funny old system, but it's one that was established in 1946 and, well, if it ain't broke... Of course, this isn't entirely true. Performers don't come *just* from London to take part, but from all over the world, whether they're seeking fame or recognition, or simply just to have a go. In 2010, there were an overwhelming 2,453 shows to choose from in the Fringe programme alone, not to mention numerous related festival events: the Edinburgh International Festival, Edinburgh Jazz and Blues Festival, Edinburgh Book Festival, Edinburgh Internet Festival, Edinburgh Swing Festival, Edinburgh International Television

Festival... There were so many offshoot events that the Edinburgh International Film Festival was shifted from August to late June in 2008.

For punters, it's a fantastic experience – there are shows to cater to every taste and there's nothing quite like sauntering into a pub and discovering something new and exciting. For residents, well, they're split: some love that their city becomes the centre of culture; some see it as an invasion. For the comedians, however, it's all part of the job – where your job involves nocturnal hours, drinking far too much, and leaving financially far worse off than you arrived. But it's the *spirit of the Fringe* and most embrace it.

For years, many acts performing at the Festival were battling for the Perrier Comedy Award. The inaugural winners were The Cambridge Footlights in 1981, whose Cellar Tapes show was directed by future *Dead Ringers* star Jan Ravens and was performed by Stephen Fry, Hugh Laurie, Emma Thompson, Tony Slattery, Penny Dwyer and Paul Shearer. Other big names who would win the award included Jeremy Hardy, Frank Skinner, Steve Coogan, Lee Evans, Jenny Eclair, Dylan Moran, The League of Gentlemen, Al Murray, Rich Hall, Daniel Kitson and Brendon Burns. When Perrier withdrew their sponsorship in 2006, it moved through various deals, rebranding as the if.comedy awards (the if.comeddies), but now seems to have settled on the less fussy Edinburgh Comedy Awards.

Winning or receiving a nomination for the main award is a big deal for comedians and can come as quite a shock. Russell Kane, the 2010 winner of the main award, can remember where he was when he received his nomination by voicemail.

'I was in a disabled toilet changing into a costume for a play and as I played the message I fell sideways and pulled the distress cord.'

Some feel that the very idea of an award is anti-Fringe. Richard Herring, who at the time of writing has written and performed in 30 Edinburgh shows since 1987, was once asked by a BBC interviewer what his one Edinburgh wish would be. He replied, 'If I could only have one, I would wish that the Perrier Award would be banished from the Festival in perpetuity. I think it creates an unpleasant atmosphere of competition in something that shouldn't be a competition and gives lazy TV execs and punters a shortcut way to see what are supposedly the best six acts without having to do the leg work themselves and discover that there are at least forty other shows that are equally deserving of their attention.'

We were taught as children that it's not about winning – it's the taking part that counts. Though, in 2008, the awards were accused of wimping out by giving the Spirit of the Fringe to 'Every comedian on the Fringe for making it happen'. After that year's ceremony, performer bars were full of talk, comedians threatening to put 'Spirit of the Fringe winner 2008' on next year's posters. I failed to spot any in 2009, but it's this sort of camaraderie and ethos that embodies the Fringe for so many performers and tempts them back year after year.

When asked about memorable Fringe moments, comedians paint a picture of a mischievous, debauched and frankly bizarre August. Jason Byrne said his favourite moment was when an audience member left his show to go to the toilet and he convinced the rest of the crowd to hide: 'I got 169 people to leave the venue via the exit door by the stage, and we all hid there while we watched the woman come back from the toilet. She came back and sat down, and we all jumped out and shouted, "Surprise!" The girl nearly died, it was great fun.'

Rhod Gilbert paints a romantic picture, fondly remembering spending the last night of the festival with good friends: 'Watching dawn break on the city that had been our home for a month, my flatmates and I quietly contemplated what had passed, while Steve Hall from We Are Klang played the recorder with his anus. It was as fitting a soundtrack as one could hope for.'

It's not just the comedians providing the bum notes (sorry), they also stumble across it themselves. Richard Herring recalled a very special and curious Edinburgh sight: 'I was once walking back to the Pleasance from the old Gilded Balloon quite late at night when I saw a couple having sex, quite openly, on a small stretch of grass by the road. They then both waved at me as I passed. And I waved back.'

For Miranda Hart, the Edinburgh Fringe represented a chance to put her depression and agoraphobia behind her, and to dip her toe into the world of comedy. It would be an inauspicious beginning: 'I first went to the Edinburgh Festival in 1994 with a terrible show called Hurrell and Hart and said to myself, "If I get an OK review and one night with more than 20 people in the audience then I am going to try to do this for a living."' Although, as she confessed years later to Fern Britton, they had to cancel most nights because no one turned up, one evening they performed to 21 people. In addition, what Hart describes now as a 'very OK three-star review in *The Scotsman*' made her determined to continue.

It would, however, be six years before she returned to the

Festival, this time in 2000 with Charity Trimm in the double-act the Orange Girls. The reviews were varied, from the dismissive ('The Orange Girls really are taking the pith. And that's the quality of much of their material') to the more considered ('The duo's show includes some nice sketches... as well as the aforementioned byplay, and the girls work equally well together in either mode'). Making good use of their disparate heights led to one review comparing them unfavourably with Little and Large, but another critic was more encouraging: 'It's a good start for a comedy double-act, and the Orange Girls make much of it; a couple of times Hart literally tucks Trimm under her arm and carries her across the stage.'

Despite a modest press reaction and humble audience numbers, they must have made some waves. Later in 2000, they contributed sketch material to the schools science series *Scientific Eye*, made by Yorkshire Television for Channel 4. In the programme, they demonstrate thermometers and how to make ice cream. You can still dig it up on YouTube.

Hart and Trimm worked together at Edinburgh again in 2001, but this time, instead of putting on a sketch show, they took part in *The Sitcom Trials*, a show devised and hosted by the Scottish comedian Kev F. Sutherland. Anyone can apply, and the shortlisted scripts are performed in front of a live audience who vote for which they like best. They then only see the ending of the chosen sitcom. The show had started out at The Comedy Box in Bristol in 1999, before playing at three Edinburgh Festivals, and leading to a series on ITV1 in 2003, and tours including Hollywood in 2005. It has now settled in its new home at the Leicester Square Theatre in London.

It was at Edinburgh 2001 that Miranda's eponymously titled sitcom began life. *The Sitcom Trials* site sums it up: 'It features Miranda, working in a joke shop that sells penis pasta, with a diminutive blonde sidekick, originally played by Charity Trimm, and the love interest in the cafe, played here by Gerard Foster.' The way in which Hart and Trimm fight over Sebastian (a character very similar to Gary) is much like the way Miranda and Stevie (Sarah Hadland) bicker and compete in the BBC sitcom. Even the character of Clive was present, played by Daniel Clegg. Ironically, James Holmes, who took on the role for television, performed in *The Sitcom Trials* the very next year. In February 2002, the show was restaged at the Leicester Comedy Festival, after which Miranda concluded she would have to go it alone for her next show.

The Edinburgh Fringe Programme for 2002 described her solo show, *Miranda Hart... throb*, as 'Character comedy from an up-and-coming comedy actress, formerly half of The Orange Girls double act. Miranda Hart-Throbs is in understudy rehearsals for a show – she is a wannabe, desperate for fame, but will she make it?'

In the show, she interacted with the crew as well as the audience themselves. Margaret Cabourn-Smith played the director and the technicians were Daniel Clegg and Anne-Marie Draycott. Hart borrowed £7,000 from a friend to put the show on and, unlike with Hurrell and Hart, she got a good audience, but still ended up losing money. Such is Edinburgh. But talk was beginning to spread and reviewers were taking notice. Ian Shuttleworth wrote for the *FT*: 'We should see more of Ms Hart, although at 6'1" there's quite a lot of her already. This hour showcases well her brand of silliness.'

Shuttleworth went on to describe one of the key things that people find appealing about Miranda: 'I usually have trouble with comedy of embarrassment, because I keep sympathising with the embarrassed party. One of Hart's strengths is that she can put herself in awkward situations without generating that kind of uneasiness.' Arguably, she still adopts this key skill in her current work, having spent several years developing her likeable alter ego.

However, the show wasn't perfect, and other critics picked out where they saw room for improvement. Comedy website Chortle gave it a three-star review and, while content with her performance, expressed concern for the sections when she is on stage alone: 'These stand-up sections are easily the weakest – sub-standard observations, a bar-room gag about an inflatable school and a recurring joke about the household hints found in women's magazines that are surely beyond parody, thanks to *Viz*.' While warmer towards the sketches, the same reviewer suggested that they might have been improved by being shortened, and that Hart's finest moments occurred when she interacted with the other characters, 'an insecure, sexually confused director, a safety-obsessed techie and the nervous work experience girl – producing some fertile comic friction. These running gags help make the whole a great deal more than the parts, thanks also to some neat callbacks and some likeable unscripted banter.'

All in all, the reviews concluded that, while Hart was an endearing performer, and was certainly getting noticed, there was room for improvement in *Miranda Hart... throb*. And at Edinburgh, there's always next year. So Hart returned in 2003 with *It's All About Me*: 'Unique character comedy from a delightful, talented and funny performer. Come and see why this comedy actress is raved about. A mix of unique character comedy, stand-up and there are attempts to sing and dance'. Prior to the Edinburgh run, the show played at the Finborough Theatre in London and, for the first time, the press releases could use references to last year's sell-out run. In *It's All About Me*, Hart played an aspiring but talentless actress trying out a show that she hopes will be discovered by Sean Connery and taken to Broadway. Audiences were treated to the physical prowess that would later attract millions to the BBC – her dance was of course clunky and clumsy and she decided to combine speech and mime (and call it "smime") as her movements weren't speaking for themselves. Miranda was brave enough to shave off the extra cast members, but retained just one technician, played by Anne-Marie Draycott. Draycott, ironically, later joined up with Charity Trimm to form the sketch group 3 Girls in a Boat. They were originally a trio but, as they put it, 'the third girl jumped ship'.

Once *It's All About Me* reached Edinburgh, Chortle gave Miranda another middling three stars, claiming there wasn't enough originality. 'The character of the theatrical, show-off madam convinced she's onto a fast track to adulation despite negligible skill seems to be to the aspiring comedienne what *Star Wars* and masturbation is to the stereotypical male standup.' There was little criticism of Miranda's performance, however: 'Hart pulls it off with aplomb, though. The semi-autobiographical character is utterly believable and the enthusiasm rubs off as she encourages us all to celebrate her poshness.' This is another quality that matured and is still a prominent theme in the *Miranda* sitcom.

Word started to spread about Hart during the 2003 Fringe. There was even talk of her as a potential contender for the comedy awards. Writing for the *FT*, Ian Shuttleworth listed her among Sarah Kendall, Lucy Porter and Nina Conti as one of the funniest females on the Fringe: 'Miranda Hart is now delightfully accomplished at self-parodic character work: imagine Dawn French at her best, but shaped like a classical caryatid.'

There was even talk of her as a potential contender for the Fringe's comedy awards, though she would be unsuccessful on that front. That year, Demetri Martin got the main gong, while Gary Le Strange (Waen Shepherd's eccentric Rock character) got best newcomer. But to be considered at all shows that she was stepping up to the challenge. Commercial success couldn't be too far away.

Miranda took a year off solo shows to work on her act, hone her stand-up and refine the character. Back in London, she performed a run of *It's All About Me* at the Soho Theatre in October 2003 and started hosting a regular comedy night for female performers called 'Lipstick and Shopping', at the Albany on Great Portland Street. Each night would accommodate one male performer. Stewart Lee was to become a near-regular – in January 2004, his newsletter read: 'These nights are ace and full of all-female talent, except for the token man, which I am now for the third time running.'

Miranda's 2004 Edinburgh found her in two daily productions: *Dogman*, a children's play based on the book by John Dowie, and *Finger Food*, written by and starring Helen Lederer. With one beginning at 2.15pm, the other at 7.45pm, the lifestyle of going to bed at 6am and sleeping into the early evening (standard for many Edinburgh comics) was not an option for her. She told the BBC what she planned to do with her time not spent performing: 'When I'm not working I will be seeing as many shows as possible. Plus for Helen's show I'm turning into a bit of a chef as I have to prep some nibbles and other food stuffs for her show where we cook on stage.'

Finger Food was a spoof cookery show, where Helen Lederer's wannabe presenter character gets her chance to fill in as the regular host is stuck in Paris. Miranda played the floor manager who is more concerned with her relationship woes than the situation in hand. The Fringe programme description sums it up as 'Three women in search of a nervous breakdown meets *Noises Off*!'

The reviews varied wildly from a one-star thrashing from Chortle, to a glowing review on EdinburghGuide.com: '[Their] verbal interplay is worth many chuckles on its own, and the script is rich with gags, too – and, to cap it, there's an admirable turn at the end of the show towards slapstick and the surreal.'

Dogman, meanwhile, was adapted for the stage by Leisa Rea, whose production is described in the programme as 'off beat, with daft physical comedy, a ukelele, toy piano, swanee whistle, accordion, clarinet, melodica and guitar'. Miranda was joined by Janice Phayre, Margaret Cabourn-Smith, Richard Vranch and Tom Price. One happy audience member logged on to Chortle to leave the comment: 'I took my five-year-old daughter to see dogman last week at the Gilded Balloon, we both enjoyed it. It is a fantastic show and I would recommend it to anybody.'

An audiobook CD was later released in 2005, narrated by Phill Jupitus and with songs from Neil Innes.

After that busy Edinburgh, Miranda took the 'Lipstick and Shopping' showcase to Stratford-upon-Avon in October 2004, as part of the Royal Shakespeare Company's second 'Week With Laughter' festival. Also appearing were Paul Merton's improv group The Comedy Store Players, as well as Jimmy Carr, Mark Thomas, Pam Ann and Al Murray. Throughout the year, she perfected her stage skills and really got to know her character.

Looking at the programme synopsis for her 2005 Edinburgh show, *Miranda Hart's House Party*, we see a pretty precise description of a Miranda who will, in not too much time, be on our screens: 'Miranda doesn't fit in! She was born into an upper-class background she can't relate to; she is 6'1" and finds it hard to feel feminine and fit in with the "girls"; she is single but has no flirting skills; and has always been a liability at social functions.' The show sees her holding a party to help her meet new friends, complete with a timetable of how the evening will run. She's desperate to please and cater for every taste, as she has Tennent's Lager, After Eights, Quality Street and a bowl of Es. The audience play a game of pass the parcel while Miranda tells them about her middle-class friends.

Also in the cast for *House Party* was Neil Edmond, who played Miranda's cousin. Edmond was a member of sketch group The Consultants with Justin Edwards and James Rawlings, and they had won the Perrier Award for Best Newcomer in 2002. More recently, he has appeared in such series as BBC7's *Knocker*, and in TV shows such as Jack Dee's *Lead Balloon* and indeed *Miranda* itself. In the Edinburgh run of *House Party*, as her cousin, Edmond fills in for Miranda while she changes into costume for the various party guests she plays. They include Poo, her 'jolly hockey sticks' horsey friend; the guy she had a crush on at university; and the girlfriend who tells gushing tales about her fiancé, undercut by her denial of sadness at his not marrying her.

Theatre Guide London praised Miranda's performance and understanding of human despair: 'Like Joyce Grenfell, Hart walks such a knife-edge between comedy and drama that at times you don't know whether to laugh or cry. But laugh all the way through the audience does.' Its impressed reviewer Nick Awde continued: 'I've rarely witnessed such a brilliantly pulled-off piece as this, one that touches every soul in the audience (and manages to get most of them onstage by the end).' *Three Weeks* echoed this opinion, urging potential audience members not to miss out: 'Hilarious... delirious fun, go!'

Once again, despite such acclaim for *House Party*, Miranda still lost out when it came to the Edinburgh Comedy Awards. Laura Solon, who by coincidence had also attended Downe House school some years after Hart, took home the main award. But at least *House Party* would eventually transfer to radio – in early 2008, BBC Radio 4 broadcast a four-part adaptation in its high-profile 6.30pm evening comedy slot. This came about when Abigail Wilson, a producer for French and Saunders, saw Hart's 2003 show, and suggested she pitch to the BBC. After working on the format and making such improvements that gave her critical acclaim, she did a readthrough of her script for BBC executives. Miranda remembers the pitch: 'People were crying with laughter at her crying with laughter. You could see commissioners thinking, Well, she's laughing. So we got lucky.'

So Edinburgh delivered Miranda her dream. It may have been 11 years after her debut trip but, in *Miranda Hart's House Party*, she had a hit. Despite the hard work, once she learned to take the pressure off, she enjoyed it: 'I've learned that a show is just a show, not life threatening or a world changer, and, as long as you don't really care out of proportion about it, then Edinburgh is brilliant and I love it.'

Now, her first commission had arrived and Miranda had the chance to take her character to a bigger audience via a new medium – the radio.

6

RADIO DAYS

'Doctor Radio has fully kicked in.'
– Miranda on BBC Radio 2 with Jon Holmes

Many of today's modern comedians made their way to television via the radio. It is often seen as a testing ground for talent before it is transferred to the small screen. The BBC is particularly considered the master of nurturing talent on the airwaves. Shows that started out on BBC Radio include *Hancock's Half Hour* (which made the leap to television as long ago as 1956), Alan Partridge in *Knowing Me Knowing You*, *Goodness Gracious Me*, *The Mighty Boosh*, Mitchell and Webb, *The League of Gentlemen*, *Flight of the Conchords*, *People Like Us*, *Dead Ringers*, *Little Britain* and, of course, *Miranda Hart's Joke Shop*.

Radio is also a fantastic way for budding comedy writers to get their break through shows that are open to submissions. Most notably, there was the long-running satirical series *Week Ending*, broadcast on Friday evenings on BBC Radio 4, between 1970 and 1998. It welcomed material via post, fax or email, and held open writers' meetings, making it a great entry point for budding writers and comedians. Among the now-familiar names who wrote for the show during its run were Andy Hamilton, David Renwick, David Baddiel and Rob Newman, Andy Riley, Kevin Cecil, Richard Herring, Stewart Lee, Harry Hill, Al Murray, John O'Farrell and Peter Baynham. Between them, they gave us *Old Harry's Game*, *Outnumbered, One Foot in the Grave, The Mary Whitehouse Experience, The 99p Challenge, Hyperdrive, On the Hour, Fist of Fun, Time Gentlemen Please, Jerry Springer – The Opera, Harry Hill's TV Burp* and the film of *Borat*. Its many producers, who included John Lloyd, Griff Rhys Jones, the late Geoffrey Perkins and Armando Iannucci, would also nurture numerous writers when they later worked in TV on programmes such as *Not the Nine O'Clock News, Spitting Image, The Day Today* and *Friday Night Armistice*.

Another radio hit with many writer submissions was BBC Radio 2's *The News Huddlines*, a topical show with a studio audience, and with a regular cast of Roy Hudd, June Whitfield and Chris Emmett. It ran from 1975 to 2001, and in doing so outlived *Week Ending*, with whom it shared many contributors (including Hamilton and Renwick). It also gave early work to Paul Kerensa, who would later work on one-liners for *Not Going Out* and *Miranda*.

More recently, James Cary devised *Recording for Training Purposes*, where new and experienced writers submitted material, an experiment which unearthed so much fresh talent that established contributors were taking a back seat by its second and third series. Now BBC Radio 4 Extra (formerly BBC7) has *Newsjack*, hosted by Justin Edwards and supported by a regular cast of Lewis MacLeod, Margaret Cabourn-Smith, Pippa Evans and Cariad Lloyd. These sorts of opportunities are exclusive to radio and mean that talented writers and performers can improve and grow, rather than being thrown straight to television and lambasted by critics.

Writers have affection for radio because of its intimacy. James Cary says, 'If TV is like being yelled at, radio is like a pleasant side-by-side conversation. It's more like reading a novel, where the pictures are in your head – where the special effects are so much better, and far more memorable.' There is also far less red tape, and it's usually a team of far fewer people: the writer, the producer and a broadcast assistant. The live audience give that same instant gratification for performers and script feedback for writers that are associated with television studio sitcoms, as Miranda would discover as she honed her sitcom on BBC Radio 2.

But *Miranda Hart's Joke Shop* wasn't the comedian's first foray into the world of radio comedy. One of Miranda's first acting jobs was in BBC Radio 4's *At Home with the Snails*, a bizarre comedy written by and starring Gerard Foster in the lead role of Alex. The show, which ran for two series in 2001–02, follows the post-uni life of Alex, whose unhealthy obsession with snails helps alleviate his depressive disposition. He individually names them, usually after celebrities (there's a Janet Street-Porter, a Paul Daniels and his favourite, Laurence Llewelyn-Bowen).

Alex's father, played by Geoffrey Palmer, is delighted at the situation, using his son as a source of material for the book he is writing. Miranda plays Alex's sister Rose, who lives away from the parental home and runs her own sweet shop. She is greedy for money and has a strange condition. Her heart is quite literally in the wrong place, right up under her armpit – an unusual affliction which means she could die at any moment. Wikipedia succinctly sums up the show's unique appeal: 'The humour is politely and subliminally obscene.' Years after its making and broadcast, Miranda was pleasantly surprised to be reminded on Twitter about the series, responding to @SaliWho: 'I had forgotten all about *Home with the Snails*. Geoffrey Palmer and Angela Thorne as your parents as a first job pretty cool.'

Between Edinburgh runs and appearances on the comedy circuit, while holding down office temp work, Miranda found more radio offers trickling in after *At Home with the Snails*. In October 2002, she appeared on BBC Radio 4's long-running panel game *Quote... Unquote* alongside chairman Nigel Rees and fellow guests Louise Doughty, Christopher Brookmyre and Chris Neill. By 2004, she was in with the cool kids, on *The 99p Challenge*, which was well liked and renowned for having only the best guests – there was no filler here. Hosted every week by Sue Perkins, Miranda was billed alongside Armando Iannucci, Marcus Brigstocke and Nick Frost. Other regular contributors to the show were Simon Pegg, Peter Serafinowicz, Peter Baynham, Bill Bailey, Rob Rouse and David Quantick. Even the writing credits were high calibre: Kevin Cecil, Andy Riley and Jon Holmes supplied the script. She later rejoined Iannucci for the last episode of *Armando Iannucci's Charm Offensive*'s fourth series in September 2008, where Quantick and Chris Addison were her fellow panellists. Meanwhile, in 2005, David Tyler, the producer of both *Charm Offensive* and *The 99p Challenge*, had also cast her in a guest part for Marcus Brigstocke's sitcom, *Giles Wemmbley-Hogg Goes Off*.

Hart's first self-penned work for radio came in 2006 with *The Hills are Alive*, a 15-minute character monologue broadcast on BBC Radio 4 as part of its 'Inner Voices' strand. There were five episodes in total; the other comedians in the series were Julia Morris, Pauline McLynn, Laura Solon and Joanna Neary. Miranda's younger sister Alice co-wrote the piece inspired by the comedian's agoraphobic phase.

But it was the radio adaptation of her 2005 Edinburgh show which firmly established Miranda in her own right. *Miranda Hart's House Party* began on Radio 4 on Tuesday, 1 January 2008. The BBC's blurb for the show revealed a new supporting cast: 'Miranda Hart serves up a cocktail of standup, sketches, song and dance, aided and abetted by Sharon Horgan, Kim Wall and special guests.' While Miranda wrote the show herself, she did have some assistance from additional writers John Finnemore and Tony Roche, as well as members of the cast.

The first episode was transferred almost directly from the stage show, where she tries too hard to be the best host she possibly can. Across the four episodes, though, Miranda explores new ways to entertain her friends. She holds a pre-clubbing party, desperate to claw back her youth; she gets bored with her flat, so decides to take her friends out for a picnic; and she tries to impress with a celebrity guest.

Prior to *House Party*'s run, in May 2007, the pilot of *Miranda Hart's Joke Shop* had kicked off a series of half-hour comedy pilots for BBC Radio 2. Some of the characters were played by different actors to the subsequent full series: Stevie was played by Morwenna Banks and Penny (Miranda's mother) was played by Alison Steadman, while Katy Brand, Jim Howick, Charlotte McDougall and Vincenzo Pellegrino took supporting roles.

Miranda told the BBC's Writersroom of the changes within the show during the writing process: 'There were initially three people who worked in the shop. One woman was incredibly nervous, screamed a lot... And there were three boarding-school friends and now there are only two. Small changes.'

One listener, enjoying a repeat on BBC7 in March 2010, was confused by the differences, not realising it was the pilot that was being broadcast. On Digital Spy, a user called Check_it posted on the forum: 'Hi, has anyone noticed that they're running this on BBC 7, and saying that it's the original, but it's been completely re-recorded with most of the actors replaced, with no mention of it. Does anyone know why they've done this?! ... Oh and Gary isn't a chef anymore, he's a travel agent!!! It's really bizarre!!!' You'll be pleased to hear that Check_it was put out of his or her misery and the situation was explained.

Joke Shop was commissioned for a four-part series, beginning in August 2008. Patricia Hodge took over as Mum, Sarah Hadland was cast as Stevie and Tom Ellis became Gary. The stories are very similar to those in the subsequent TV series.

Episode one, 'What A Flirt', sees Gary back from his travels in Malaysia. Miranda runs into him, discovering that he is the chef at the restaurant next door to her joke shop. She makes a fool of herself, telling him that she's an Olympic gymnast and pretending to have trapped wind. When he asks her out for a drink, she goes clothes shopping in an effort to impress. Finding nothing at Big and Long, she chooses an outfit from another store and returns to the shop to show it off to Stevie, who exclaims, 'Miranda! Why are you dressed as a transvestite?' While at dinner, Miranda and Gary discuss how they are not interested in having children, despite their mothers' pleas for marriage and kids. Things are going well, and Gary follows Miranda up to her flat. When they switch on the light, though, they discover masses of baby clothes and toys strewn on the floor – Stevie's revenge. The next day, Miranda tries to convince Gary it was a mix-up, and all is well again. But then, he spots her with her old school chums, trying on wedding dresses and runs away. She chases after him while screaming, 'I'm not desperate.'

This sounds very similar to the plot of the TV series' very first episode, although there are key differences. The script was, in fact, initially written for television, but, when Miranda was offered a radio show instead, she had to find some workarounds. Of course, the look to camera wasn't possible on radio, so Miranda tried a different approach: 'What we did do on the radio was occasionally whisper to the listener which didn't really work. It's a perfect example of why radio's so much harder to write – I've got to write a joke there because I can't look to camera.'

James Cary, a writer on the show, backs this up, talking about the importance of the script in radio comedy. 'There's no hiding in radio – and so, as a radio sitcom writer, you learn fast. If the show misfires, it's unlikely to have been a technical fault. Most likely, it's a script error, a string of duff jokes, a confusing plot turn or a badly defined character, i.e. your fault.'

Another of radio's restrictions on Miranda's style was the slapstick element of the show. Speaking on *Loose Women*, she said, 'It was quite hard doing the falling over on the radio. There was a lot of "Oh! Mind those boxes, Miranda…" "Oh! Ohhhh nooo!" BANG! Sort of doesn't sound very good.'

Episode two of *Joke Shop* sees Miranda trying to prove she can get a real job, but ends up singing 'The Greatest Love of All' to her interviewers, claiming, 'I didn't realise I knew so many verses.' In the television version, one prospective employer quips back, 'I didn't know there were so many,' but this must have been added in Miranda's rewrite or by one of her gag writers, as it isn't in the radio show. Instead, the scene finishes with a joke that could only work on radio. She asks him if he thinks she would look sexy in a power suit and he replies dryly, 'Anything's better than the pirate outfit.'

'What A Wife', the third episode, is the most radio-friendly of the four. While some jokes and the idea of Miranda being Gary's safety wife made it through to the TV series, the main storyline would not feature. When an entrepreneur goes into Gary's restaurant, he assumes that it is a family business and he lies that it is. So when he hosts a charity gala event, Gary needs to take a fake wife with him. Controversially, he asks Stevie instead of Miranda.

The final episode of the radio series is 'What An Excuse', in which Miranda desperately tries to find a reason not to attend her mother's *Pride and Prejudice*-themed party, which Penny says will be 'totally thrillybots'. In the end, she resorts to saying she's a lesbian just to get out of being set up at the party.

Interestingly, in this episode, Stevie refers to her boyfriend Phil who was scrapped for the television series, allowing for more competition and bickering when Miranda is trying to impress men. On her BBC blog for series one of the TV version, Miranda talked about rewriting this episode for television: 'It was very useful having written episodes for the radio before writing the TV [series] – but I used a lot less from them than I thought I would, as in a way, it is better to start from scratch... I became stuck on material from the radio that had worked in front of the live audience, and tried to force it in to a story. That is often harder than starting a draft from scratch.'

The radio show got a decent reception. Martin Hoyle of the *Financial Times* wrote: '*Miranda Hart's Joke Shop* is likeably silly, the maladroit heroine engagingly self-destructing.'

In the spring of 2009, it was even nominated for the prestigious Sony Radio Academy Award for Comedy but Count Arthur Strong's Radio 4 sitcom, written by and starring Steve Delaney, took the accolade. Hart was gracious in defeat, posting on Twitter: 'Back from Sony awards. Count Arthur won – yay! Although firmly believe awards are bollocks. And yes would say that even if I had won.'

Writing in *The Times*, Chris Campling stated that 'Miranda Hart is shaping up as the Big Lady of the future', and argued that 'Hart's new sitcom (so much a trailer for a TV version that they are already filming the TV version) trades on her not only being big, but very tall and extremely posh.' Indeed, a pilot of *Miranda* had been made for television while *Joke Shop* was still being broadcast on Radio 2, but BBC executives were so sure of the show that they commissioned a full series.

Before the TV series started and her popularity rocketed,

Miranda was known for the sitcoms *Hyperdrive* and *Not Going Out*, and so appeared on radio panel shows as a relative unknown. But her wit and likeable persona made her the perfect guest and, in April 2009, she appeared on *The Unbelievable Truth*, hosted by David Mitchell. Her fellow guests were veteran panel-show performers Arthur Smith, Sue Perkins and Sean Lock. She had to sneak truths past the others about cricket, but the team managed to spot most of the facts among her nonsense, including the following: 'Cricket took place between England and Australia in a series of so-called pest matches. The winners were traditionally awarded the Ashers – Jane and her brother Peter. Jane has catered for cricket teas since its invention, but was sacked in the 80s when Ian Botham became too fat to run.'

She only managed to smuggle one truth in, which is that Prince Philip sometimes hides a radio in his top hat when he goes to the Ascot races, because he likes listening to the cricket. She ended up in third place with minus one point.

Her next big radio gig came in March 2011, at the peak of Miranda hype. Fresh from awards season, she returned to BBC Radio 2 for three nights presenting with Jon Holmes. Jon usually hosts the Saturday afternoon 'drive time' show on BBC 6 Music, and has described it as being broadcast 'on a day when no one's driving home from work on a digital radio station that you can't get in your car'. Previously, he had worked for commercial stations XFM and Virgin Radio, but parted company from both after various stunts and pranks. Virgin received a record taste and decency fine of £75,000 for Holmes's feature 'Swearing Radio Hangman for the Under-12s'.

In recent years, Holmes wrote for and appeared on *The Now Show* and *The 99p Challenge*. He won his sixth Sony Award for his work as a writer on *Armando Iannucci's Charm Offensive*. Before their stint on Radio 2, he and Hart worked together on *2009 Unwrapped*, a fictional review of the year show for BBC Two that Miranda hosted. The fake and re-edited archive footage was in a similar vein to Jon Holmes's radio show *Listen Against*.

So, in 2011, the very tall lady and the not very tall man were reunited when Mark Radcliffe and Stuart Maconie were leaving their mid-evening Radio 2 show for the new pastures of BBC 6 Music, and Jo Whiley from Radio 1 was about to take their place as a regular host. Hart and Holmes bridged the gap with three two-hour shows, for which they were joined by studio guests Stephen Fry, Will Young and David Baddiel.

The Head of Programmes at Radio 2, Lewis Carnie, told *Radio Today*, 'The opportunity to pair two of the UK's best-loved comedy talents was irresistible to us and I'm very much looking forward to hearing their shows.'

Miranda was overjoyed. 'I am full of childish excitement to have the honour of joining the wonderful, and my favourite, Radio 2 for a few nights. Can I call myself a, what I call, disc jockey now?'

Jon, on the other hand, didn't take things so seriously. His statement took the opportunity to gleefully spread some wild rumours: 'Miranda and I have been conducting a clandestine affair for many years, so what better way to announce our union than by becoming broadcasting's latest romantically linked couple after Richard and Judy, Radcliffe and Maconie, and Bernie Winters and Schnorbitz.'

One of the features on the show was a 'getting to know you' segment, where existing Radio 2 DJs asked Jon and Miranda questions as a sort of welcome. Jeremy Vine (whose brother, comedian Tim, appeared with Miranda in *Not Going Out*) asked Jon if he would like to be in *Miranda* and, if so, would he play the love interest. Diminutive Jon confirmed that he would like to do that, but Miranda interjected saying it would be quite hard to fit them both in a two-shot.

Die-hard Radcliffe and Maconie fans were upset at their departure. 'Someone at Radio 2 obviously thought throwing a successful sitcom star and a Radio 6 DJ/comedian together would be the perfect radio show dreamteam to replace Radcliffe and Maconie,' wrote Ricardo, a blogger on *The Word* magazine's website. He concluded, 'Maybe it looked better on paper.'

But many thought the show a triumph. Clare Heal, writing for the *Express*, said, 'Their banter was only with each other and it felt a little like a party to which we weren't invited. Miranda and Jon had games that the audience could get involved with, as well as a jovial chemistry with each other, Miranda's unashamed goofiness making an excellent foil for Jon's sarcasm.'

For the *Guardian*, Elisabeth Mahoney wrote that they were 'sharp, funny and properly disgusting... an instant presenting yin-yang hit', and made special mention of Miranda's leftfield asides: 'Holmes suggested that Radcliffe and Maconie are actually a pantomime cow off-air, but didn't know who was at which end. "Jeremy Vine might know," said Hart, quick as a flash, "because he milks them."'

The twosome reunited Christmas 2011 with a special, 'Jon

and Miranda's Secret Santa'. Jon and Miranda said at the time, 'We're delighted to be sharing some mulled Radio 2 with listeners over Christmas and promise to both ding and dong merrily – not just on high either, but all over the place. It's our Christmas gift to the nation. Although we have kept the receipt, just in case.'

So, radio had been a good friend to Miranda during her years of stage performing, TV bit-parts and office temping. It laid the foundations for her big TV break in *Miranda*. She had only been able to give up temping in 2005, thanks to landing a co-starring role in a new sitcom for television called *Hyperdrive*. But her TV career extends further back than that.

7

OPPORTUNITY KNOCKS

*'I think dreams are better achieved with a fight –
in retrospect of course!'*

– Miranda

Miranda's first memorable television appearance was alongside Arabella Weir in a 'Nourishment not punishment' Alpen advert, in which she famously ate cat food. Getting her foot in the door in TV was something of a battle, though. As well as putting herself out there at the Edinburgh Festival, Miranda was proactive, and she recalls sending 'embarrassing letters to important people to persuade them to come and see me'.

Before her big break, Miranda was working as a temp in London to pay the bills. She was keen not to be seen as the posh girl who had it easy, so used to play down her upper-class accent. She told Dominic Maxwell in *The Times*: 'I used to fear that people would think I've not had a problem in my life, that people would think: "Oh, Daddy's bankrolling her." And that wasn't the case.'

In 2002, she was PA to the grants director of Comic Relief

and once took the minutes of a meeting when its co-founder Richard Curtis was present. Seizing her opportunity, she approached him, asking, 'I really want to be on Comic Relief, have you got any advice?' He gave her the contact details of the casting director and was very supportive, but it was some time before Miranda would be doing 'something funny for money'.

When Miranda appeared on Fern Britton's Channel 4 chat show in March 2011, Fern suggested, 'But that's the wonderful thing about having a slow burn on a career is that you can learn so much while flying under the radar.'

Miranda agreed, saying that she 'wouldn't have it any other way now'. So, how did this slow burn go?

Smack the Pony offered Miranda Hart her first comic acting role on the small screen. In 2001, she appeared in three episodes as part of its third series, most famously as part of the regular video-dating sketches. These saw singletons talk to camera about themselves, hoping to inspire someone to get in touch and take them out. Miranda's most memorable speech was this: 'I'm very, very experienced. I've had men. I've had a lot of women. I've done plus-60s; done a lot of Saga holidays. I've done under-21s. All the in-betweens. Oh, and I've done some animals. I mean, to be honest, I've got a fanny as big as a bucket.'

Appearing in *Smack the Pony* was a real coup for Miranda. It was a hugely respected show within the industry, was a big success internationally and was seen as something of a showcase for Britain's comedy actresses. It was written by and starred Doon Mackichan, Fiona Allen and Sally Phillips, with regular appearances from Sarah Alexander (*Coupling*), and with Darren Boyd (*Kiss Me Kate*) taking many of the male parts.

Other early TV cameos for Hart included the BBC legal sitcom *Chambers* (starring John Bird, James Fleet and Sarah Lancashire) in 2001, and, two years later, the BBC Three series *This is Dom Joly*. But it was in 2004 that Hart began to make more regular appearances on TV. She played Penelope, a small part in the second series of *William and Mary*, an ITV comedy drama starring Martin Clunes as an undertaker and Julie Graham as a midwife. She was more of a leading character in *Mothers and Daughters*, a black comedy written by David Conolly and Hannah Davis, and with Lynda La Plante as executive producer. It looked at the relationships of families in different situations, 'a dilapidated North London council house, a middle-class dinner party in a Fulham mansion block and an expensive psychiatrist's couch'. The synopsis of the show asked: 'Drug-fuelled sex with a vicar and lustful longings for other women, are there some things a girl shouldn't share with her mother?'

As we already know, Miranda's first solo Edinburgh show in 2003 had impressed Abigail Wilson, a producer who worked with Dawn French and Jennifer Saunders. This eventually led to her appearing in the Christmas special of Saunders' *Absolutely Fabulous*, broadcast on Christmas Day 2004. In this episode, 'White Box', Eddie is desperate to find the right interior furnishings for her new kitchen. With Patsy, who's typically more interested in the free champagne than the furniture, she visits Terence Conran (who plays himself) and another designer called Kunz (played by Nathan Lane). Hart played his assistant, an eccentric girl called Yoko who wears an elaborate outfit and a crudely drawn-on monobrow because, as she explains, 'I'm Japanese.'

Just a week later, she appeared alongside Saunders' comedy partner Dawn French in a New Year's Day special of *The Vicar of Dibley*. Her character, Suzie, was a small role in an episode celebrating Geraldine's 40th birthday. The villagers buy the vicar a ticket to a speed-dating event, but when she arrives they turn out to make up most of the available dates. The episode also guest-starred the gorgeous Cristian Solimeno, best known as Jason Turner in *Footballers' Wives*.

This stamp of approval from two of the biggest names in British comedy did wonders for Miranda's profile. More speed-dating laughs were on the way via a *Comedy Lab* pilot for Channel 4 in May 2005 called *Speeding*, which was based in the upstairs of a pub. A bit-part in BBC sketch show *Man Stroke Woman* followed, and then she proved she could embrace the darker side of comedy by appearing as Beth in the second series of Julia Davis's *Nighty Night*. Miranda, speaking in 2005, said it was her favourite job to date: 'I had a very small part but was in Devon (where it was filmed) for a couple of weeks. It was beautiful weather, amazing location, and I had the most wonderful company in Georgie Glen, Julia Davis, Mark Gatiss and Ruth Jones – we just laughed constantly.'

Nighty Night contained some extremely black humour. Davis's character Jill is a beautician whose husband Terry is dying of cancer. In response to this news, she proceeds to abandon him, chasing after her neighbour Don (played by Angus Deayton), whose wife Cath (Rebecca Front) is suffering from MS. The British Comedy Guide website points out that episode one of the first series alone features '...suicide, asthma attacks, multiple sclerosis, cancer and some horrible put-downs by the monstrous Jill (who makes David Brent look like an angel, seriously she is pure evil – you'll hate her). Don't let this put you off though, it's well worth watching if you can stomach the bleak premise and Jill's painfully embarrassing behaviour.'

By the end of *Nighty Night*'s first series, Jill has committed mass murder, but manages to frame her new boyfriend Glen (Mark Gatiss) who gets put in a mental institution. The second series sees her chasing Don and Cathy, who have moved away and are trying to patch up their marital difficulties. The series has achieved cult status, with die-hard fans even meeting up for a *Nighty Night* Night, on Great Portland Street on 8 December 2010. Attendees were treated to a screening of series one, DJs and 'A celebration of all things dark, moronic and hilarious'.

The show was produced by Baby Cow, a production company set up by Steve Coogan and Henry Normal, which also made Rob Brydon's *Marion and Geoff*, *The Mighty Boosh*, *Gavin & Stacey*, *Saxondale* and the animated comedy *I Am Not an Animal*.

As well as her television appearances, Miranda developed her career by appearing in a stage play called *Cruising*. Written by Alecky Blythe, it ran at the Bush Theatre, London, in the summer of 2006. Miranda took the lead role, Maureen, a geriatric looking for love. All the characters are played by actors some 30 years their junior. The show's website described the play thus: 'After 33 blind dates, 12 cruises and one broken heart, she is still determined to find Mr Right. But when best friend Margaret beats her to the altar, Maureen has her doubts

– is Margaret just on the rebound and, more importantly, will she lose her pension?'

It received great critical acclaim. *Time Out*, which made it a Critics' Choice, praised its 'gloriously idiosyncratic dialogue, which even the most skilful writer would struggle to devise', while *Metro* called it 'a heart-warming piece of theatre'.

British Theatre Guide reviewer Philip Fisher praised its innovative style: 'All five actors, playing numerous parts in *Cruising*, have expensive looking Sennheiser earphones on throughout the play. Rather than broadcasting to the hard of hearing or even listening to Gnarls Barkley or Sandi Thom, they are listening to the original speakers, whose lines they are delivering, verbatim, seconds later.'

That same year, Miranda appeared in a short film called *Don't Even Think It!*, written by the novelist Jasper Fforde. She plays Ginny Singleton, an upper-class lady who, along with her husband Neville, stops to pick up Boz, a hitchhiker with a certain talent. Boz is a medium who can read the thoughts of her drivers. She thinks they're snobs, so gets her own back by revealing the secrets the couple are keeping from one another. The short was screened at at least five international film festivals and is the only filmed Jasper Fforde script to date.

When it arrived in October 2006, Jack Dee's sitcom *Lead Balloon* was often seen as the UK's answer to Larry David's *Curb Your Enthusiasm*. It stars Dee as Rick Spleen, a stand-up comedian grappling with life's petty annoyances. It later transferred to BBC Two, but the first series was initially broadcast on BBC Four. The very first episode finds Spleen needing to find a christening gift for a friend's baby,

Trixiebelle, and so visits a posh shop stocking baby clothes and gifts. Miranda played the shop's owner, Maureen. Astonished by the shop's exorbitant prices, Rick settles for a pewter christening cup and tries to haggle with Maureen over the cost of engraving, because it costs an extra £5 for any name longer than eight characters. She insists she can't change the policy very politely, but, as he keeps hassling her, she snaps and barks at him, 'I won't do it!' Through a mixture of spite and frugality/meanness, he settles for the engraving of the shortened 'Trixie', but, when his partner insists he take it back to get the full name, he tries to engrave the remaining letters himself. Of course, he makes a botch job of it, and passes the blame.

As well as these high-profile parts, Miranda took on most things that came her way. This included *The Everglades*, a 20-minute comedy short for a planned series which was ultimately never commissioned, despite BBC Comedy asking for a half-hour script and a rehearsed reading of the script. The premise of the show was to follow the lives of people shopping and working in a South London mall called The Everglades. The cast also included Ruth Jones and James Corden, who would soon write and star in *Gavin & Stacey*.

Miranda's debut film role came in the form of 2007's *12 in a Box*, written and directed by John McKenzie. The film is set in a remote country house, where a dozen people attending a school-reunion dinner are offered the chance of a million pounds each – all they have to do is stay closed off in the mansion for 96 hours.

The synopsis teases what transpires: 'They were only 96 hours away from collecting a fortune. It was as simple as that.

Then someone dropped dead – and things started to get a bit more complicated.'

Miranda plays Rachel, the fiancée of Barry, one of the 12 due to cash in a million, but they are due to marry within those designated 96 hours, and so, when she arrives and goes berserk at the suggestion of postponing the wedding, he locks her in one of the bedrooms.

Producer Bruce Windwood explained that he and the writer were aiming to return to the British film industry's glory days. 'We are fans of the classic Ealing Comedy movies, and felt that it was time to revisit that style of movie; a style which simply sets out to entertain.'

And entertain they did. The *LA Times* called it 'a nicely calibrated romp peppered with more than a few genuinely funny moments. The cast performs with comic aplomb as McKenzie ratchets up the stakes before going for broke in the final reel. It's jolly good fun.' *12 in a Box* went on to win Best UK Feature Film at the Los Angeles British Film Festival 2009, Best Original Screenplay at the 2009 Boston International Film Festival and the Audience Award at the 3rd Zurich Film Festival.

Miranda's silver-screen CV also expanded with bit parts in Mitchell and Webb's *Magicians* and *I Want Candy*, starring Tom Riley and Tom Burke. Also, in 2007, she appeared in Tim Plester's short film *World of Wrestling*. She played Klondyke Kate, a wrestler who was known as 'hell in boots'.

Meanwhile, her television career continued to thrive. She took a role in *Rush Hour*, not the Jackie Chan/Chris Tucker martial arts romp, but a BBC Three sketch show set among the traffic of the trip to and from work. With the likes of

Charlie Brooker and Adam Buxton involved, comedy fans' hopes were high, but many believed it did not reach its potential. One user, tigers_hungry, commented on IMDb: 'Instead of utilising the potential of the show's set up... for sharp observational humour, the premise is reduced to little more than a gimmick through which the show defines itself against the legion of mediocre British sketch shows. I do fear that I may be judging the show too harshly, but I feel like a disappointed teacher that expected better of her pupils.'

Other voices disagreed, such as John Beresford at *TV Scoop*. 'Like a cross between *The Fast Show* and *Little Britain*, *Rush Hour* is assured a place in the nation's psyche, once it finds its way out of the digital backwater that BBC Three still is.'

Still, the bad reviews dominated and BBC Three decided not to recommission the show for a second series.

Miranda's return to terrestrial TV exposure came with a small role (as a casting director) in BBC Two's *Roman's Empire* (2007), the writing debut of brothers Harry and Jack Williams. The series starred Mathew Horne as Leo, the ex of Nikki, the daughter of businessman Roman Pretty. He tries to win the family's favour and ultimately get the girl by attempting to reveal her new boyfriend's dodgy past.

That same year, she also got a part in *Angelo's*, often considered a hugely underrated sitcom on Five, written by and starring Sharon Horgan. It got low audience ratings and the channel has stopped developing scripted comedies, so it is unlikely to return. However, critics loved it. The British Comedy Guide says of it: '*Angelo's* is a warm, subtle comedy with the characters right at the heart of it – something many recent sitcoms have neglected... Miranda Hart as the taxi driver, Simon Farnaby as the mime artist, and Kim Wall as the unemployed Russell are our favourites – they don't even need to speak to raise a smile – their characters' backgrounds and mannerisms are enough alone to do this.'

Hart portrayed illegal minicab driver Shelley, who is man-desperate and who has founded a club for virgins called 'The Promise Keepers'. She tells her clients that she is waiting for 'the one' to pop her cherry, but in reality she's waiting for 'anyone'. In an attempt at wooing, she plays romantic music when she has male passengers and even set up a blind date with one who left his wallet behind.

Writing in the *Independent*, Gerard Gilbert said of the show's creator: '"The funniest woman you've never heard of" and "late starter" are two tags that have followed the Irish comedian Sharon Horgan ever since the riotously and filthily funny *Pulling* attracted just enough critical attention to ensure that it didn't become the most underrated sitcom of the Noughties. (That dubious honour arguably goes to Horgan's later Channel 5 series, *Angelo's*.)'

The Abbey for ITV in 2007 was yet another pilot, this time made by Baby Cow, with a cast including its writer, Morwenna Banks, plus Russell Brand, Omid Djalili, Reece Shearsmith and Liz Smith. Banks plays Marianne Hope, who goes to rehab to cope with a celebrity relationship break-up. When she comes out, she start up a money-making sanctuary which attracts drugged-up DJ Terry (Brand), a nymphomaniac geriatric called Elsie (Smith) and Helen (Hart), the suicidal wife of an MP.

Miranda didn't stop. Even when recording her radio shows in 2008, she voiced Miss Much, a pompous rabbit in *Tales of the Riverbank*. Alongside such revered voice artists as Stephen Fry and Peter Serafinowicz, this was a huge honour for the actress. She also took a part in *Hotel Trubble*, a children's comedy drama for CBBC. Miranda plays Mrs Lily Lemon, mother of one of the lead characters, Lenny. Lenny has told her that he is the manager of the hotel when in fact he is only a porter. The episode revolves around the team trying to convince her he is the boss. Other guest stars on the show have included Josie d'Arby, Les Dennis, Phil Cornwell and another cast member from *Hyperdrive*: Stephen Evans (aka Vine).

As she built herself up towards the broadcast of her sitcom in late 2009, there was still plenty of Miranda to be enjoyed elsewhere, such as in the film *A Very British Cult*. The lead character, David, was played by Richard Herring, who described the film on his daily blog, Warming Up, as follows: 'The film is about a rubbish cult of which my character is the leader. They are all threatening to rebel and go and join a rival cult that seems to know when Jesus is returning and which has a glossy TV advert which makes their own cult look about as shit as it is.'

Herring's character dreams some numbers, what he believes to be the date of the second coming. They turn out to be very exciting indeed, but perhaps not in the way he expected. Other members of the cult were played by Emma Kennedy, Jim Barclay, Margaret Cabourn-Smith and Gus Brown.

Fans of Tom Ellis from *Miranda* may have already seen *Monday Monday*, the 2009 ITV drama also starring Fay Ripley and Jenny Agutter. If not, they certainly should. He plays a flirty office worker in a secret relationship with the boss (Agutter). They all work at the head office of a supermarket called Butterworth's, which has relocated from London to Leeds as a result of downsizing. *Broadcast* magazine said the show aimed to 'shed light on a world of alcoholic HR bosses, power-crazed managers and sexually unfettered PAs'. Miranda played the small part of Tall Karen, an office assistant who works in HR. When the show was first broadcast on 13 July 2009, she tweeted, 'ITV 9pm Monday Monday, have a tiny regular part in it. So small in 1st ep don't be blinking.' And then, as an afterthought, she added, 'P.S. not seen it yet so no idea what it's like. Great cast though. Tom Ellis who is in my show is the main man.'

In the light of *Miranda*'s first series, broadcast in late 2009, and with her popularity gathering momentum, the BBC gave her a high-profile presenting job: *2009 Unwrapped with Miranda Hart*. The festive show was a round-up of the year's events, but using spoof news stories because, as Miranda quipped, 'We're filming this in April. I hope we get the events right – we're just guessing.'

Celebrities 'remembered' such memorable moments as 'Arthur' on *Britain's Got Talent*, who had a trumpeting penis. Sally Phillips commented, 'How romantic is that? It would be so romantic to be serenaded in that way.'

Unwrapped is reminiscent of *Time Trumpet*, a BBC Two show from 2006 set in the future in which Armando Iannucci interviews celebrities about stories from their pasts, but pasts which are still in our future. (Clear? Good.) It also has similarities in style to Jon Holmes's *Listen Against*, a Radio 4 show. This is largely because Holmes wrote for all three shows. The tradition of authoritative spoof news as we know it, however, dates back to the days of Armando

Iannucci and Chris Morris's *On the Hour* for Radio 4 in the early 1990s, which spawned *The Day Today* on television, as well as various vehicles for Steve Coogan's sports reporter Alan Partridge.

Unwrapped was revived for the end of 2010 with clips including a spoof of Professor Brian Cox's programme called 'Wonders of the Stoner System'; the year's must-have gadget, the iTurd; and the Scandal League, which sets footballers up with others' girlfriends. And one for the fact fans: both episodes were produced by Alex Walsh-Taylor, who also produced *Hyperdrive*.

In that Christmas TV season of 2010/11, old and new were united in a one-off special, *The One Ronnie*. Corbett, the surviving Ronnie, one of the country's best-loved comics, performed sketches alongside today's stars to celebrate his 80th birthday. It was a stellar cast including Matt Lucas, David Walliams, Harry Enfield, Catherine Tate, Rob Brydon, James Corden and, of course, Miranda Hart.

Earlier in 2010, however, Miranda had another shot at the big screen, playing Mrs Keyes in *The Infidel*. She had the honour of breaking some rather shocking news to Omid Djalili's character, a salt-of-the-earth East End Muslim named Mahmud Nasir – who turns out to be Jewish. The film, written by David Baddiel, brought Hart to a wider audience, but her most significant performances outside of *Miranda* were as Barbara in *Not Going Out* and Teal in *Hyperdrive*, two shows we'll return to shortly.

What this roll call of film and TV appearances has proved is the drive and resilience of Miranda, and her commitment to her dream. As she says herself, 'I think, however much I worry it's all going to stop, that someone else much better will come along. Ultimately, there's always been a percentage of me that believes I'm funny. I think I just kept going, like tunnel vision.'

Miranda Hart is no overnight success, but a hard-working woman with the ethos: 'If you commit to it, you commit to it.'

8

GOING INTO HYPERDRIVE

'I know NOTHING about science fiction. NOTHING!'
— Miranda

When Miranda Hart was offered the role for the BBC Two sci-fi sitcom *Hyperdrive*, she finally gave up temping, and became a full-time professional comedy actress, over 10 years after her first appearance at the Edinburgh Fringe. She had achieved her dream, but there was still room to grow. As she said in an interview for *Hyperdrive*'s fan website: 'I have always wanted to be a comedy actress. That has been and still is my dream. There is SO much I would still love to do. I feel like I am just at the beginning of my career really.'

The writers and creators of the show, Andy Riley and Kevin Cecil, have explained how the idea first came about: 'We were stuck in a windowless office in LA and started musing about what a British space force would be like. There'd be a lot more arguing and a lot of meetings and a lot of biscuits.'

In the show's development, its title changed from *Lasers* to

Stun, then to *Lepus*, and then *Full Power*. It was under the last title that an untransmitted pilot was filmed, directed by Armando Iannucci. Aside from Sanjeev Bhaskar (as Henderson) and Mark Gatiss (as York), the cast – including Hart – remained the same as for the eventual series.

Finally, BBC Two commissioned a full series of the show, now called *Hyperdrive*. Bhaskar and Gatiss were replaced in their respective roles by Nick Frost and Kevin Eldon. 'We've always had this burning ambition to do science fiction and the chance doesn't come round that often,' co-writer Kevin Cecil admitted. 'The BBC decided the time was right, though.'

In a making-of documentary called *Hyperdrivel*, star of the show Nick Frost joked about how he got the part: 'They came to my big Malibu house with a big case of money, and they said, "It could all be yours – we need you for eight weeks." So I came out of retirement and I did the gig.'

By the time the first episode of *Hyperdrive* was broadcast, on 11 January 2006, sci-fi was deemed to be cool again, primarily because of the revival of the BBC's *Doctor Who* the previous spring. Christopher Eccleston had been replaced as the Doctor at Christmas 2005 by David Tennant, whose first episode was the festive special, 'The Christmas Invasion'. Science-fiction fans were anxious to see how the tenth doctor would progress under Tennant when the new series was due to start in April 2006. This actually put *Hyperdrive*'s creators under some pressure, as producer Alex Walsh-Taylor explained: 'When you're dealing with sci-fi comedy, you've got a huge fan base of the genre, that are watching, not only for science fiction, but the comedy as well... We all had to create this world that we were very certain of, that played within the rules that have kind of been set by this 40-year history of TV and film sci-fi.'

Co-writer Andy Riley thinks the potential audience for such a show extends beyond fans of science fiction. 'It would make me enormously pleased if people that didn't normally like science fiction would give this a go. Hopefully it's got this Croft and Perry effect of having lots of characters from lots of different social classes thrown together in a situation where they have to do things.'

The writers had rules though. While writing the series, they had a sign on the office wall that said, 'No time travel', and another which ordered, 'No teleporting'. They wanted to avoid parody and create a believable science-fiction world for the characters to inhabit. Within reason. Of course, sci-fi isn't sci-fi without an alien or two. Riley explains how this became inevitable. 'We had to have aliens. We had aliens arriving on about page three of the first script! In the very first episode, there's about three alien species, so we start as we mean to go on.'

As big science-fiction fans, Cecil and Riley were keen to educate the cast of its history. The set became something of a DVD lending library – not that many of the cast members were that enthusiastic. Miranda has bravely admitted to the show's fans: 'I know NOTHING about science fiction. NOTHING! I approached *Hyperdrive* as a sitcom that happened to be set in space and often have to ask the boys about the sci-fi references.'

Nick Frost is partial to science fiction but decided to steer clear. 'I didn't watch much other sci-fi while I was doing it, because I didn't really want it to inform how I did it. But I know that sounds twatty.'

In the Venn diagram of science fiction and British comedy, only a small number of shows lie in the middle segment: *Come Back Mrs Noah* in 1977, starring Ian Lavender and Mollie Sugden; *Astronauts*, a 1981 series created by Graeme Garden and Bill Oddie; *Goodnight Sweetheart*, where Nicholas Lyndhurst time travels to the 1940s; *My Hero*, with the superhero played by Ardal O'Hanlon; *The Strangerers*, a Rob Grant comedy shown in 2000; and the most successful of all, *Red Dwarf*, a megahit with Chris Barrie, Robert Llewellyn, Craig Charles and Danny John-Jules.

As a sitcom set on a spaceship, *Hyperdrive* was inevitably compared to *Red Dwarf* but the writers were keen that it should be seen on its own merit. 'The differences with *Red Dwarf* are in the writing, the acting style and the level of performance,' Andy Riley asserted. 'It's got a different look too. It's got more in common with *2001*.'

Writing partner Kevin Cecil added, 'Also the situation is very different. With *Red Dwarf* they're answerable to no one; they're free agents. In ours, they're very much not. They're the crew of a vessel that is part of the British Space Force and they have to follow orders.'

Miranda Hart concurred, 'As for *Hyperdrive* being the new *Red Dwarf* – I think they are totally different shows and should be viewed as such.'

Hyperdrive is set in 2151 on the HMS *Camden Lock*, a space crew on a mission, not to discover new worlds, but to act as salesmen for Britain and persuade alien businesses to relocate to Peterborough, extolling the virtues of the nearby Lake District as a holiday destination. But, as with any comedy, the show is really about the characters and their relationships. Executive producer of the show Jon Plowman explained, 'The show is really about them trying to persuade aliens to relocate to Britain, while the Americans offer Florida, and partly about a group of people being stuck together in a confined place for a long time.'

The first series (of six episodes) aired on BBC Two from 11 January 2006, with a second run following from 12 July 2007. Miranda Hart auditioned for the pilot and so impressed the writers that, when they wrote the series, they wrote the character of Diplomatic Officer Teal with her in mind. Director on the series John Henderson has commented, 'She was just absolutely perfect because she completely epitomised the Teal we were after and the boys wrote for her... I couldn't imagine anyone else ever playing that role.'

Hart too felt an affinity with the character, telling the Camden Lock fan site, 'I am not sure how many people went up for the part at that stage, but I am delighted to say they still wanted me for the series as I just fell in love with the character of Teal.'

Diplomatic Officer Chloe Teal is a perfectionist who is more comfortable arranging her pens than dealing with social situations. Miranda describes her as a 'conscientious, slightly prudish, home counties girl. She sticks to the rules and regulations and her efficiency and organisation mean she is seen as the school swot of the team. She is much better at her job than at social interaction – and doesn't really understand how to flirt or to relax socially.'

She shares a forces background with the character, but it is about there that the similarities end. 'Teal continues to enjoy and live by the regimented, emotionally uptight elements of that background,' Miranda explains. '[I] am much more informal and slobby than Teal.'

Miranda impressed the crew, too. The producer, Alex Walsh-Taylor, said, 'Physically she's very funny. She's very tall and she's developed this great galumphing walk for Teal, which looks really funny.'

Miranda has joked that it wasn't just her acting which turned heads on the set, saying during *Hyperdrive* that there was some tension with some of the male cast members. 'They all, bar none, fancy me. I know that... I had to make it clear that I wasn't going to mount them at lunch – they all offered. Every day for two weeks, initially. Once we got that out of the way – it wasn't going to happen – it's been good ever since.'

Andy Riley quipped in kind. '[She's] very physical. Sometimes I look – particularly when she's in the costume – it gets me going. Purely in a professional way and I wouldn't possibly cross that line. But I'd like to.'

The character of Teal was unlucky in love. She fell for Space Commander Michael Henderson, played by Nick Frost, but didn't know how to cope with it. Director John Henderson liked the dynamic of the relationship: 'It's really nice because an upper-class lady with a crush on Henderson is a great dynamic to have. There's a whole sort of *To the Manor Born* thing going here which is really, really nice.'

Captain Henderson, however, has no idea how Teal feels about him. 'She fancies him and he just sees her as a mate,' commented Nick Frost. 'I think, because he doesn't see it, that drives her all the more crazy.'

Miranda has said of Teal's feelings for Henderson: 'Someone suggested the other day that it was lust. It's not lust, let me correct you there. It's simple adoration and love. I reckon she's probably fallen in love with him as her first love. She doesn't know quite how to deal with it.' She has also said that she would like to see Teal find happiness in a reciprocal relationship but concluded, 'I don't think it will happen!' Her hunch was correct.

Nick Frost has compared the bond between the two characters with another in classic comedy history. 'It reminds me a bit of Kenneth Williams and Hattie Jacques in the *Carry On* films – that same dynamic where they really like each other but every now and again she comes on a bit strong and he pulls back.'

Space Commander Henderson, leader of HMS *Camden Lock*, values his job but sometimes takes a risk with his superiors for the good of his team, seeing his orders as 'open to interpretation'. Frost describes his character as 'very well meaning, he's very nice… he cares if they don't like him'. Of his character's back story, he reckons Henderson got lucky: 'He's been through a war, I think. But I think more by luck than judgement he made it through. I like to think maybe he was knocked unconscious and lay there as they scoured the battlefield for the dead and he just went unnoticed.'

It's his enthusiasm and compassion that makes Mike Henderson such a likeable character, along with his everyman quality. *Hyperdrive*'s director John Henderson regarded the character as key to the group's dynamic: 'He becomes the centre of the group because he's the audience and his reaction to things is kind of what the audience's reaction to things would be. It's everybody around him that has a slightly more eccentric quality.'

The other characters certainly cover a wide spectrum of personality. As well as the amiable Commander Henderson and the fastidious Chloe Teal, there is the strict, borderline sociopath First Officer York; Navigator Vine, who is so nervous it seems impossible he ever got the job; Jeffers, the geeky but layabout Technical Officer; and Sandstrom, the enhanced human who acts as Pilot. Writer Andy Riley commented, 'Hopefully, there's one person in the mix that any person could identify with.'

York is played by the actor Kevin Eldon, a familiar face to comedy fans as he has featured in numerous shows over the past 15 years including *Fist of Fun*, *I'm Alan Partridge*, *Big Train*, *Brass Eye* and *Nighty Night*. In 2010, he did his first full solo stand-up show at the Edinburgh Festival, which received great critical acclaim. Bruce Dessau, comedy critic for the *Evening Standard* and the *Guardian*, gave him five stars. He concluded by saying the show's only fault was that 'it could have been longer. Give this man his own TV show right now.'

Playing Henderson's right-hand man, Eldon is cold-hearted and pragmatic, seeing the rest of the crew as amateurs and really believes he should be in charge. The British Comedy Guide sums up his character by pointing out that he is 'still the only trainee at Space Force Academy to have killed someone in a role play workshop. Apparently he was "just trying to make it realistic".'

Nick Frost was delighted to be able to work with Eldon for the first time. 'I've known Kevin for quite a while but we've never worked together before. I had a tiny part in *Big Train* which he was in and he had a couple of days on *Spaced* but we didn't have any scenes together, so it's nice to work so closely at last.' Off-screen, though, Frost reveals the hierarchy was reversed: 'Off the set it was a different matter, as it was definitely Kevin who was in charge!'

On the show, their relationship is ripe for comedy: Henderson thinks York is his best friend, while York has little but contempt for his commander, as he believes he would do a much better job. Occasionally, there are tender moments of camaraderie – not that York would admit to it.

Stephen Evans plays Navigator Vine. Of all the cast, Evans is the biggest sci-fi fan in the cast, described by Riley as a *Doctor Who* obsessive. Vine is a depressive sort, who only seems happy when collecting 1990s paraphernalia, or 'antiques' as he calls them. He believes it to be a simpler time, as we discover when Henderson and York trespass into his subconscious, and find his only dream is where he owns a pub in 1995 with his wife, who looks suspiciously like Sandstrom. He is usually rather detached from the group, unable to bond and too nervous to stand up to any of them, but he shares a tender moment with Jeffers when they visit the planet he buys on a whim on an auction website. He calls it 'Vineworld' and, as he and Jeffers traverse the derelict mess, names areas Vine City 1 and Vine Ridge.

Jeffers is played by the stand-up comedian Dan Antopolski, who was nominated three times for the Edinburgh award. He won the BBC New Comedy Award in 1998 and was awarded the honour of Best Joke at the 2009 Edinburgh Festival Fringe, given by the channel Dave. The winning one-liner was 'Hedgehogs. Why can't they just share the hedge?', which featured in his show *Silent But Deadly*. Punslinger Tim Vine took the title in 2010 with 'I've just been on a once-in-a-lifetime holiday. I'll tell you what, never again.'

Antopolski's character has something of a devil-may-care attitude, charming his way out of trouble, or simply covering his tracks. 'Jeffers is pretty geeky, he knows his computers,' Dan ruminates, 'but he's also a bit of a naughty schoolboy. He's a bit arsey and has got a problem with authority.' But he cares about his work and eventually does what he's told, albeit reluctantly. 'He's basically me, I think. Or me as I was in school.'

In *Hyperdrive*, the making-of programme, Dan explains how he got the part in a style that epitomises his surreal style of stand-up: 'Me and the writers first got in touch online, unusually. It was a chat room. I was posing as a 12-year-old girl. Obviously they've rewritten the part a bit; it's been adjusted. But they know what jelly babies I like – I'll tell you that much.'

The member of the HMS *Camden Lock* family who it might be easy to neglect is Sandstrom, the prototype enhanced human who pilots the ship. She stands among bright poles that she strokes in a bizarre performance reminiscent of Reeves and Mortimer's performance artist characters. This is unsurprising as she is played by Petra Massey, a member of the physical theatre company Spymonkey, who have toured all over Europe and the USA. As the series progress, it becomes clear that both Vine and York have a soft spot for Sandstrom.

The cast aside, *Hyperdrive* had a fantastic start with its creative team. The writers, Andy Riley and Kevin Cecil, had previously collaborated on the BAFTA award-winning third series of *Black Books*. They didn't simply write the script and then leave it to the production team; instead they took a very hands-on approach to filming. Miranda Hart commented, 'They are on set every day which is great. A real help. They are making minor adjustments right up to the last minute and are very open to suggestions and lines that come out of improvements and rehearsals. It is a genuine pleasure to work with such generous writers.'

Kevin Cecil describes the process in more detail on the making-of documentary. First the actors rehearse with no one in the room but the director, in a relaxed environment, and then rehearse in front of the crew and writers. 'At that point,' he explained, 'if we think a line's not working, or if we've got on an idea, or if the actors are worried about a line, we'll go into a little huddle and we'll work on the scene.'

Riley says that they've usually made the relevant changes within five minutes while the cameras are being set up. 'Then everyone will go and have a cup of tea, and then it's time to shoot it.'

The love-in extended right across the group, as many were very excited to work with John Henderson, the director. He was the oldest member of the crew, approaching 60, but he brought wisdom and experience with him. His first directing job was on *Spitting Image* on ITV, for which he won a BAFTA.

With such credentials, *Hyperdrive* was bound to work. Critical reaction, however, was mixed. Many comedy fans loved the show. Jay, a user of the British Comedy Guide website, said that it was 'funny, clever and engaging' and 'destined to be a classic'. Fellow forum-member Ben said, 'Kevin Cecil and Andy Riley have a pleasingly absurdist bent to their writing... and *Hyperdrive* is agreeably quirky as a result.' The show's biggest fan was 'Captain Helix', named after the show-within-the-show sci-fi hero whom Henderson idolises, who said that he was disappointed at first, but, once he managed to get other shows out of his mind, he was 'able to enjoy it for itself, forgetting comparisons with *Red Dwarf* and other TV shows, and judge it on its own merits'.

Some couldn't forget though – Daniel O'Rourke wrote, 'I thought this show was absolutely abysmal, it is just a rip-off from *Red Dwarf*.' And die-hard science-fiction fans were the hardest to please. One magazine dedicated to the genre, *SFX*, gave it only 1.5 stars. Reviewer Dave Golder said, 'This new sci-fi Brit-com may as well have been called Black Hole, because that's where most of the humour seems to have been sucked into.' He continued, 'The creators appear to be aiming for a hybrid of *Red Dwarf* and *The Office*. In practice, it's a car-crash mix of styles that actually work against each other.'

But *Hyperdrive* embraced its sci-fi heritage, introducing a set inspired by *Blake's 7* and guest aliens that recall the more comic episodes of *Doctor Who*. In the first episode, we meet the Glish, who have some bizarre customs as Nick Frost describes: 'The Glish are a strange race who like to lick people as a form of greeting. They lick your hands and sometimes your face so I had to make sure my hands were clean and smelling of Imperial Leather that day!'

The meeting doesn't go quite as the crew of the *Camden Lock* intended and the Glish leave a man-eating parasite as a parting gift.

Frost says that episode two was good fun to film as they leave the spaceship. 'We go down to the planet to meet the aliens...

It's been a long time since they have had any contact with humans so they are very excited.' Henderson ruins their chances when he falls in love with the King's daughter and Teal becomes so jealous she causes quite a scene. They try to escape but Vine has been led astray by Jeffers, who has taken advantage of the empty ship to have a race with his friends.

The episode 'Weekend Off' is one where Miranda really shines. The whole ship takes time off for Gary Neville Day, celebrating 'the 21st-century footballer and inventor of artificial gravity'. While Vine and Jeffers go to explore Planet Vine, Teal gets overexcited about the Officers' Dinner. She rigs it so that no one can attend except her and Commander Henderson – by any means necessary. She serves up a meal of Wotsits, clumsily trying to instigate flirty chat. Of course, the captain is oblivious and immediately dismisses the thought that people may talk. This desperation to be liked is a trait that would also appear in the sitcom *Miranda*, but Teal is a totally different character that Hart pulls off brilliantly. In the fan-site interview, she told mega-fan 'Captain Helix', 'If I met Teal in real life (bizarre idea!) then I would probably not dislike her, but she wouldn't be on top of my list to go to the pub with. She wouldn't be quite as free and silly as I would like a drinking companion to be. She's a bit too uptight for me.'

There was one joke on set that will already be a familiar theme – teasing Miranda about her appearance. 'I am sure my kind and loving nicknames Queen Kong and Big Truck will stick – a couple of those got into the show, which really made me laugh.' Queen Kong, as her old school friends call her in the BBC sitcom, doesn't appear in the show. At one point, where the cast are improvising at the beginning and end of scenes, though, she gets called 'Big Truck', and it survives the edit. Miranda admitted that it's at times like these that she can't keep in the laughs. 'I would say I am probably the worst at corpsing. If at the end of a scene the director didn't shout cut straight away, we would improvise and I would always be the first to laugh.'

One episode – 'Clare' – also reunited Miranda with Sally Phillips, who she had previously worked with on *Smack the Pony*. Phillips played Clare Winchester, an Ellen McArthur-in-space figure who travels the galaxies solo. When he spots her flying near them, Henderson gets excited at the thought of meeting a celebrity and visits to attempt to make friends and cheer her up. It's a fantastic performance of cabin fever – Winchester refuses to talk at first, is erratic and has an unhealthy relationship with Mr Cup, who is literally a cup.

The overriding feeling of the show, both on- and off-screen, is one of camaraderie. Nick Frost summed up how well the cast bounced off each other: 'We're all really different people and we come from different backgrounds but it worked. I think that comes through in the dynamic of the ship's crew as well; because we got on well off-screen, that gave us a nice shorthand on-screen.'

The credibility of the characters and the performers came across to viewers, and it led to Hart receiving added recognition: she received her first British Comedy Awards nomination in November 2006 as Best Female Comedy Newcomer. She was up against Katherine Parkinson from *The IT Crowd* and singer-turned-talk-show host Charlotte Church. Church won the award at the ceremony in December, but nevertheless, the nomination helped to raise Hart's profile some more.

9

NOT GOING OUT

'It had to happen sooner or later. BBC One has finally found a sitcom worth staying in for.'

– Jane Simon, *Daily Mirror*

So Miranda was now a familiar face to comedy fans and many were praising her work, but it was BBC One's sitcom *Not Going Out* that made her, if not a household name, then at least a household face. Everybody loved her character, Barbara. Lee Mack, who co-created and starred in *Not Going Out*, says of her performance in *Miranda*, 'She plays an extension of herself. She's a true comedian, putting herself into the part, rather than an actor changing to fit it.' But Mack spotted her potential early in the run of *Not Going Out* – after she played a bit-part in a series-one episode, he created the role of Barbara the cleaner specifically for her.

BAFTA-winning comedian Lee Mack created the sitcom with Andrew Collins, who had previously won a Sony Award for BBC Radio 1 show *Collins and Maconie's Hit Parade*. It came together when Avalon, the comedy production and management company who were developing the show with

Lee, put the two in touch. Collins had already collaborated with another Avalon act, Simon Day, for *The Fast Show* spin-off *Grass*. He told the British Comedy Guide that initially he was brought in as a 'straight man' writer: 'I feel I am more instinctively better at story, structure and character than actual gags and punchlines, although I've written comic stuff for myself on the radio before.'

Collins, however, discovered that both Day on *Grass* and Mack on *Not Going Out* were keen to work on structure and story, while he could add some strong gags to the respective shows. He found that Lee's vision was for an old-fashioned style of show, in front of a studio audience and thick with gags: 'At that stage, it should be noted, we were developing *Not Going Out* with a view to showing it on BBC Two, not BBC One. So our ideas were a little edgier than something like *My Family*. I realised that this would be a challenge, and relished working with someone new. You only improve by trying new things with new people, and I liked Lee from day one.'

It was Lee Mack alone who came up with the premise for the first series. Lee and his housemate Kate have an easy-going friendship that is moving towards a will-they, wont-they? situation. Hence the title *Not Going Out*. What makes it a real problem, though, is that Kate's ex is Tim, Lee's best friend. The relationship between Lee and Kate came from a sketch show Mack did in Edinburgh. Andrew Collins explained the character's origin: 'The character of Lee is a big layabout with big dreams. The real Lee is a bundle of creative energy, and not a layabout at all. But he cracks jokes all the time, and so does the character Lee.'

Lee (the character) meanders between jobs, relying on the goodwill of others to support him. But, while Kate (Megan Dodds) is doing her best to motivate Lee, Tim (played by Tim Vine) has trouble coping with how close they are becoming.

A non-broadcast pilot was made at Teddington Studios at the end of 2005 with Catherine Tate playing Kate, as she did in the original Edinburgh show, *Lee Mack's Bits*, in 2000. As well as being a stand-up, Mack appeared in ITV's *The Sketch Show*, running for two series between 2001 and 2003, and even transferred to American TV, scheduled next to *The Simpsons* on the Fox network's Sunday line-up, and with a cast featuring Kelsey Grammer. Mack also starred in *The Lee Mack Show* on BBC Radio 2 (nominated for a Sony Radio Award) and hosted the final series of *They Think It's All Over*. Most recently, he has become a popular team captain on *Would I Lie To You?*, sparring with David Mitchell under the watchful eye of hosts Angus Deayton and, in later series, Rob Brydon.

Tim, eventually played by master of puns Tim Vine, is Lee's best friend. He's an accountant for the local council and, compared with Lee, he's rather uptight and sensible. Vine also starred in *The Sketch Show* and has also worked as a presenter, hosting and devising *Fluke* – a Rose d'Or Award-nominated Channel 4 show – as well as presenting the quiz show *Whittle* in the early days of Channel Five. He is probably best known for his unrelenting one-liner style of stand-up. He holds the Guinness World Record for 'Telling The Most Jokes in an Hour', fitting in 499 jokes – that's roughly one every seven seconds.

Despite Vine's close relationship with Mack, the part of Tim wasn't written with him in mind. Lee said, 'I've worked with him for years on *The Sketch Show* and on the stand-up circuit, and it was the obvious thing to have him in *Not Going Out...* and yet I didn't really think about him at first. He certainly wasn't written for in the un-broadcast pilot.'

Tim's character was initially called Colin, 'a city boy with stubble and a leather jacket'. As Catherine Tate played Kate quite aggressively, they needed someone who would be believable as her ex-boyfriend. When they cast the full series, they held auditions in the usual manner, but Lee thought of his friend and asked him if he wanted to audition. 'Tim can sometimes be phenomenally laid back and he sort of went, "Well, I'm a bit busy tomorrow, but go on then." He came in, he read it, and it immediately made sense. Obviously we rewrote the show then to make the character more of a middle-class twit.'

As they changed this vital character, other characters had to adapt around him. Catherine Tate's ballsy Kate was rewritten into a kind, health-conscious Californian. Megan Dodds, best known as Christine Dale in *Spooks*, took the series one role. Tim's ex-girlfriend Kate is also Lee's landlady, who, despite the huge personality differences, finds herself attracted to Mack's character. Tim still had feelings for his ex, turning up at the flat with dubious excuses for seeing her. In one episode, he even invites her along to his grandma's funeral, hoping that pity might develop into something more.

Miranda first appeared in *Not Going Out* in series one episode four, 'Stress'. Lee gives Kate some driving lessons, which causes his stress levels to go off the chart. They try yoga – but he doesn't really enter into the spirit of things.

Exasperated, Kate makes Lee an appointment with an acupuncturist – played by Miranda. She gives a superb performance of a passive-aggressive woman who eventually turns to out-and-out violence. As he settles down into the chair, Lee asks, 'Is this going to hurt?' and she drily replies, 'Depends if I like you or not.' He goes on to infuriate her, giving wisecrack answers to her questions, but relations slide further when she asks him, 'Are you pregnant? Silly question', and he bats back with 'Are you pregnant? Silly question', looking at the character's bulging stomach (for which padding was used!). Unimpressed, she answers 'No', and proceeds to stab the needles into his skin.

As we have seen, Miranda's scene-stealing performance as the acupuncturist so impressed Lee that, for the second series, he created a new character for her: Barbara the cleaner. The writers did not draw attention to the connection in the programme, leaving it to eagle-eyed viewers to create Barbara's back story themselves.

Reaction to the first series was positive. The industry recognised its success: writers Lee Mack and Andrew Collins won the RTS Breakthrough Award – Behind the Screen – and the show itself was honoured with the Gold Rose D'or award for Best Sitcom.

Critics agreed. David Stephenson wrote in the *Sunday Express*, 'Telling jokes as we know it is almost a dying art in TV comedy but here Mack cleverly combines the traditions of sitcom with some classy production values. In short, it's funny.'

The *Mail on Sunday*'s Jaci Stephen said, '*Not Going Out* turned into one of the most laugh-aloud comedies on screen in aeons. The ubiquitous shots of buildings lend it a distinctly

American feel, but it is the tightness of the scripts with quite complex gags built up over conversations – particularly between Lee and his friend Tim – that make it so different.'

At the *Guardian*, meanwhile, Lucy Mangan wrote, 'This is a programme you can really savour.'

But, most importantly, it pleased the audience. Ratings gradually grew as word spread and viewers were impressed. A review on IMDb by the user stephenclayton calls it 'an absolute gem' and says, three episodes in, 'it just keeps getting funnier, although there appears to be a love interest developing between Kate and Lee it can only add to the laughter (provided it remains unrequited).'

Andrew Collins commented, 'Megan Dodds brought a lot to the first series. We hadn't even written Kate as an American, Megan just proved the best at auditions, and we went back and developed her character accordingly.'

Lee Mack said that some people found it hard to get used to having an American in British sitcoms. 'The amount of people that have said to me, "I didn't like the American girl at first, but, by the end, I really loved her – she got better and better."' But, as he pointed out, the episodes are filmed out of sequence, so it wasn't her that changed, just that people took time to get used to it.

At the end of the first series, Kate moves back to America and Tim needs to find a new owner for the flat. Lee battles for its ownership against Lucy, who is Tim's younger sister. Because of his lack of steady income, Lee loses but Tim makes it part of the deal that Lucy has to rent the spare room to him. Inevitably, he starts having feelings for her too, but Lucy is more interested in her new boss Guy, a suave older man. Lucy is played by Sally Bretton who comedy fans will recognise from her appearance in *The Office* as Donna, the daughter of Brent's friends, who comes for work experience at Wernham Hogg. Following this, Bretton landed roles in a number of sitcoms including *Green Wing*, *Absolute Power* and Ben Elton's series *Blessed*.

Bretton's character Lucy is an ambitious, career-focused young lady who spent a number of years as a successful businesswoman in Zurich before returning to England. There is sibling rivalry between her and Tim; she was always the favourite, while Tim is seen as something of a disappointment.

Kate's departure for America also gives Tim a new lease of life as he can finally move on. But he hasn't done quite as well with his new girlfriend, Daisy. She's a typical nice-but-dim girl, who is gullible and suffers from an intellect deficiency. It's a bit of a mystery why they are together, as Tim is clearly embarrassed by her. Daisy is played by Katy Wix, who later appears in *Miranda* as Fanny, one of her former boarding-school friends.

People looked forward to the second series after such a strong start, and the pressure was on for the writers. Andrew Collins said at the time, 'It'll be tough to get past the affection people always feel for a first series. But by bringing in new characters, while keeping to the basic set-up, we've mixed things up a bit, and it's given us a new dynamic to play with.'

In the second series, Lee has a new job as an ice-cream man, so the story focused less on him trying to get a job, and the writers concentrated on developing the characters' relationships. Lucy and Tim's sibling rivalry is pushed to the limit when Tim becomes suspicious of Lee's motives.

Ahead of series two's broadcast in the autumn of 2007, Collins said, 'We're all pretty pleased with the way the scripts have turned out. When the cast did live readthroughs in front of an invited audience at a small theatre in August, the results were excellent. This gave us a real shot in the arm.'

So, on 7 September 2007, the second series began. In the second episode, Lucy meets Guy. He's an entrepreneur, Lucy's new boss, and she takes a shine to him. But when a colleague tells her he's gay, she doesn't give up and attempts to turn him. She makes a joke that she's worried he might have interpreted as homophobic, so she tries to make it up to him. She invites him round for dinner to meet her gay flatmate. Of course, her flatmate isn't gay, so she convinces Lee to pretend to be. There follows a succession of hilarious misunderstandings – Guy reassures Tim he definitely comes across as gay, while Tim is oblivious and is upset Lee won't come out to him – but ultimately Lucy discovers Guy is actually straight and they end up kissing. Naturally, Lee does not approve and takes every opportunity, and also creates some, to take shots at Guy about his age.

As the series progresses, Lucy starts to worry about the age gap – especially when Guy brings his grandson to meet her. At the end of the series, the couple break up, which is a helpful twist as it leaves Lucy available, and raises the question of Lee finally making a move in series three.

Series two attracted audiences of 3–4 million and a third series was given the go-ahead. Mack felt positive about it. 'Well, hand on heart, it is definitely the best of the three series, if I do say so myself. I'm convinced of it.' This was reassuring after the risk of new characters, he believed: 'The last series we had to bring in a new lead girl, as well as introduce some new characters, so it was sort of like starting again. And people don't like change, especially people who like your show.'

The third series, transmitted from January to March 2009, went well and ratings continued to gradually rise, but, because they didn't quite match the same as other BBC One sitcoms, the channel announced that the show was being cancelled. The team did their best to convince the Corporation to change its mind. Lee Mack was in the back of a car after a recording of *Would I Lie To You?* when he was informed by his manager of the axing. 'He said, "I'll get to the point – the show's been cancelled." The third series hadn't even finished being on telly! I was very shocked by it.'

So Mission: Recommission began. Andrew Collins wrote on his blog: 'It all comes down to numbers in the end, even though the BBC is a publicly funded broadcaster and thus not reliant on advertising revenue and thus not really in the ratings game to the degree where, like American broadcasters, it cancels shows that aren't performing to a set of made-up targets.'

And then there was something akin to a call to arms. Collins joined in with a discussion on the British Comedy Guide's forum, answered some of the fans' questions and then concluded his post with the following disclaimer: 'I'm not going to say anything negative about the BBC, as I rely upon them for a lot of other work. That's the God's honest truth. Those of you who don't, however, can say what you like.'

And speak they did. More than 1,500 people signed a petition to save the show. The petition said, 'At its peak *Not Going Out* was reaching over three million people, and with a rising following these figures were sure to increase... Lee Mack is a comic writing genius and this show should be going down in history as a cult classic, and shouldn't be axed when viewing is on a high.'

Within the BBC, opinions were divided. A BBC spokeswoman said, 'We recognise that *Not Going Out* has a loyal fan base, and appreciate that the decision not to recommission the series for BBC1 will come as a disappointment. However, it is felt that the show has run its course on the channel and of late has not been performing as well as hoped.'

But one BBC producer, who wished to remain anonymous, told *The Stage*, 'I am just devastated by that decision. The last series was so assured. I don't understand the rationale. It's just a really good show.'

In the end, the BBC gave in to pressure and decided to revive *Not Going Out* for a fourth series, which aired from January 2011. However, they chose to move it from Fridays to Thursdays – and this coincided with Miranda Hart's decision to leave the show. Not because of the new slot, but because her own sitcom had become a hit and she was busy writing and appearing in its second series. When series four aired, she couldn't help but admit to feeling left out, as she tweeted: 'Looking forward to *Not Going Out* at half nine. Although v sad not to be in it.'

Although Barbara the cleaner's absence from *Not Going Out*'s fourth series wasn't referred to, most viewers' might presume that she had probably been fired. After all, she did everything she could to avoid work and, even when she did clean, she was so clumsy that she nearly always broke something. They carried on Miranda-free and the show achieved its highest figures yet (4.75 million for the first episode), and, despite rumours that Tim Vine was quitting the series, it was happily announced not only that he was staying on board, but also that a fifth and sixth series had been commissioned by the BBC. Mack commented, 'It's great news. I can finally get that extension finished.'

Good news also for fans and critics alike. The rest of the cast, also, would have been delighted. Lee had paid tribute to the good relations between them: 'Of the five main cast members – Tim, Sally Bretton, Miranda Hart, Katy Wix and me – there's genuinely not one relationship that's wrong in that five. It's brilliant. I couldn't be working with nicer people to be honest with you... and that makes a lot of difference, because I wouldn't be able to do it otherwise.' And as the fifth series was broadcast on BBC One at the beginning of 2012, it returned to its rightful spot on Friday nights at 9.30pm.

It's a rare British sitcom nowadays that lasts more than a few series, and so *Not Going Out* is set to be one of BBC One's long-runners, having survived against the odds. But Miranda Hart – central cast member for its second and third series – now has her own project to concentrate on. More than 15 years after her first performance at the Edinburgh Festival Fringe, Miranda was to finally realise her dream – to star in her own BBC sitcom. Now all she had to do was write it.

10

THE WRITER'S JOURNEY

*'Classical music helps when writing I am finding.
Makes me feel mature. *farts*.'*
– Miranda, on Twitter

Douglas Adams once said, 'Writing is easy. All you have to do is stare at a blank sheet of paper until your forehead bleeds.'

Miranda has made it clear that she doesn't enjoy the process of writing and she isn't alone. It's that classic image of the tortured artist at the typewriter surrounded by piles of crumpled-up paper. She started writing when suffering from agoraphobia because, petrified by crowds outside, she found 'it was more fun inside my head than in the real world'. Now that is no longer true and she prefers life to writing, but the process is simply a means to an end.

When no one was writing parts for her to perform, Miranda took the liberty of writing parts for herself and taking shows to Edinburgh. 'My heart wasn't in writing. My heart was really just in performing.' With a commission, though, came the commitment to write a sitcom which became *Miranda*. She looks back on her temping days and says, 'I'd much rather be doing that than writing a sitcom, but ultimately the writing is what gets the results. However naff it sounds, it's worth it to hear those laughs.'

With the first series of *Miranda* in late 2009, it seemed Miranda the writer had a head start. With a radio show in the bag, much of the material could be adapted for the screen. Those former issues with slapstick in an audio medium were no longer a problem, and so visual gags could thrive. An audience had already loved her show and had provided feedback in the most encouraging way – laughter. On her blog, Miranda said that she became 'stuck on material from the radio that had worked in front of the live audience, and tried to force it in to a story'. This was a process she found harder than starting from scratch. She also discovered that the characters had matured and the one episode she did transfer directly from radio (episode five) seemed a little dated. So, using a lot less from the BBC Radio 2 show than she thought she could, she had six scripts to write.

In conversation with television critic Grace Dent for a BAFTA comedy writing masterclass, Miranda revealed it was enjoyable to begin with, 'The first pilot was great fun because I didn't think it would be on telly. I thought it was brilliant, I'll just write what my dream job would be. It would be the sitcom in what I am the lead! That'd be nice! And let's be really bold with this, I want to look to camera like Eric Morecambe did.' With the dream-come-true opportunity, Miranda didn't want her chance to be wasted so she took her time writing the pilot, dedicating around 18 months to it.

After the success of the first series, expectations were high for the second. There were a few nuggets of unused material left over from the first series, but this was more of a challenge. As the first episode of the second series was about to air in November 2010, Miranda wrote on her blog, 'It's been really hard over the last eight months writing the second series – mainly I have been in a blind panic!'

And so it begins again. What are people expecting from *Miranda* for the third series? Is it like following up a hugely successful debut album?

Miranda has said that 'writing comedy is the equivalent of doing homework that's going to end up on national television'. And many writers feel the same, putting it off and leaving the work to the last minute. Speaking to Charlie Brooker on a special writers' edition of *Screenwipe*, Russell T. Davies says he's got stuck in a system that has to be punishing in some way. The former *Doctor Who* producer said of scriptwriting at the time that 'It's like homework for me. I'm due in a script now I should have started weeks ago and I keep putting off. If I leave here and start that script, I know my Christmas will be lovely and everything will be marvellous – but I won't.'

Davies's own creative struggle has been chronicled in *The Writer's Tale*, a book in which he wrote about one year as a *Doctor Who* writer. He has described it as like therapy in that he could see what he was doing wrong, but it hasn't helped. He sums up many writers' attitudes when he says, 'I love it, but I love it when it's made. Then I'm really proud, even though I'm critical of it. But I hate writing at the same time, I absolutely hate it.'

So, Miranda, join the club. But there is an added pressure.

Miranda is not only the main writer and creator of her sitcom; she plays the lead character who is present in every scene. There's no passing any blame here. In the first two series, she takes charge of the show, giving feedback and notes to cast members in the guise of a character she calls 'Anal McPartlin'. She is so passionate about this opportunity that she is incredibly hard-working in making sure everything goes to plan. She admits, 'I do have an element of the controller but I think most writing performers do. It's really hard to let go, to be in the rehearsal room and seeing flats going up around you and going, "This isn't my joke shop. This is not what I meant at all."'

With six to eight months of hard graft at the writing table behind her, the show's creator should be allowed the occasional diva moment.

One of the most common and obvious questions writers are faced with is 'where do you get your ideas from?' The usual answer, 'my imagination', doesn't seem to satisfy, as everyone relishes tales such as Basil Fawlty being based on a real hotel owner the Pythons encountered in Torquay. Everyone, that is, except Donald Sinclair, the poor chap himself. It has inspired Miranda to be playful with this in many interviews, telling one man on the red carpet of the First Light Movie Awards that she was looking for inspiration right now, and 'You never know, you might feature.' Talking to *Gavin and Stacey*'s Ruth Jones (Nessa), Miranda has said that some of the 'crazy, embarrassing, mortifying situations that happen to [her] are almost too ridiculous for a sitcom'. While Miranda always carries a notebook and says she gets on to buses and the tube just to eavesdrop, most of the stories are, as she puts it, 'all from my weird head'. For example, one day she was idling down a BBC corridor, sulking that she hadn't had any funny ideas that day, and then – out of nowhere – had an image of Stevie coming into the shop with a massive Great Dane and apologising for being late. It amused Miranda so much that she found a way to get it in and – tada! – in series one episode six, there it was.

Miranda occasionally goes to the BBC to write, but spends the majority of her writing time in her Hammersmith flat. She doesn't take on any other work so stays at home sat in a 'weird Mastermind-style chair'. To get away, she takes her dog Peggy for a walk twice a day or goes to the cinema. For other distractions, she says, 'I watch bleak, dark films to get away from anything vaguely funny.'

It takes a lot of hard work to make a show that looks effortlessly funny. *Peep Show* writer Sam Bain has said, 'It's probably that the more fun the writing process is, the less good the show will be and the more hard work the writing process is, the more funny the show will be.' This certainly seems to ring true with Miranda. Writing her hugely successful show, which caused such a reaction from the studio audience that it was accused of having a laughter track, was quite an ordeal.

Miranda admits that she has cried quite a lot during the writing process, turning to Peggy ('a fluffy cross between a shih-tzu and a bichon frise') for moral support. She has described herself during the process as 'lonely, frustrated, bored and stressed'. If you'd like a better picture, she usually wears stained tracksuit bottoms and trainers, and finds solace in cups of tea and plates of biscuits. She says of writing, 'It's not something I leap out of bed in the morning for. It requires patience (which I lack), discipline (which I lack), nerves of steel (which I lack), unending energy (which I lack) and hard-core tea drinking and biscuit eating (this is where I excel).' But she is disciplined, working a nine-to-six day. Miranda is not the type of person who gets an idea and will write into the early hours because, as she admits, 'frankly, I'm in bed at 10.30pm'.

The second series of *Miranda* was easier to write because she had learned, through experience. 'I did go slightly mental writing the first series,' she admitted. 'I know how not to write a sitcom now, which is to take five months out of your life and not speak to anyone, ignore your friends and your family, and think you need every single day and every single moment to write. It actually doesn't work.'

Everyone has their ways of cheering themselves up. As well as Peggy, Miranda used to get out a toy rubber duck when she was going through a bad patch. Miranda says that, ideally, it takes eight months to write six episodes of a sitcom. 'Two months to pace about for ideas and then structuring the storylines and then a month on each episode to really hone it.' All this graft, just so we can have a jolly good chuckle.

So what do we want from a sitcom? James Cary, one of the writers who helps Miranda structure the episodes, sums up the recipe for sitcom success as 'character + conflict + confinement + catastrophe + catchphrase + casting = comedy (except when it doesn't)'. That last bracketed disclaimer alludes to the fact that, however formulaic, sitcoms could fly or flounder. These essential elements make up a sitcom – it's not just gags about chocolate penises.

Getting the main character right in sitcom is crucial, especially when the show is named after them. Cary says they should have a basic flaw. One of the most common is a figure who thinks they should be doing better in life and don't know why they aren't (see also Mainwaring, Fawlty, Rimmer, Brent, Hancock). Similarly, Miranda tries desperately to fit in and cope with the high social expectations of the modern world. And most importantly, as we've seen previously, Miranda is so likeable that, when things go wrong for her (as they so often do), it makes us squirm. It's amused discomfort which occurs whether it's a simple dress-caught-in-taxi moment, or a heart-wrenching scene where she pours her heart out to Gary... only for us to realise moments later that the perfect monologue was in her head, and now we're going to see her make an epic fool of herself.

For conflict and confinement, the writers have to put their character into a situation they can't escape from. This could be a literal prison (*Porridge*) or the ties of a father–son relationship (*Steptoe and Son*). This is where they put the situation into 'situation comedy'. Miranda is stuck in the joke shop with Stevie, constantly visited by her mother and friends. Gary lives just next door which not only makes it easier to contrive stories, it also means it's impossible for her to escape her feelings for him. Talking to BBC Writersroom, Miranda says that it took a year and a half to decide that the joke shop was the right place, despite reservations at the time from the Head of Comedy. 'He was like, "What's it going to be all about? Fart sweets?"' recalled Miranda. It was suggested that the show could be set in an office, but Miranda stuck to her guns. Miranda is trapped in a world with her sitcom 'family', a dynamic played out through a well-written group of characters. She is at odds with her mother Penny, Tilly, Stevie and even Gary, but ultimately loves them all.

The family unit is often vital in sitcom, whether or not the characters are biologically related. Writer Graham Linehan has said of the 'family' in *Father Ted*, 'Sometimes you get lucky, I think. We accidentally created a bunch of characters who really spoke to each other... What we didn't realise was that these were separate people but, when you saw them together, they looked like a family.'

And then, hopefully, comedic cracks start to show in those relationships. James Cary says in his sitcom 'recipe'. 'After a while, your carefully blended ingredients should rise and then explode into amusing calamitous peaks, up to three times in half an hour, if you're lucky.'

This certainly happens in *Miranda*. It seems it can't go 10 minutes without the lead character getting caught, sometimes literally, with her pants down. These are the moments in sitcoms that live beyond the context of the show. Cary cites other examples like the 'chandelier in *Only Fools And Horses*; vicar and huge puddle in *The Vicar of Dibley*; Compo in bath on wheels in *Last Of The Summer Wine*'. Next to these, Miranda falling into an open grave fits neatly into this canon of clip-show fodder. Then there's the matter of catchphrases, and Miranda has plenty of those as we know: 'Bear with, bear with...', '...what I call...' and the very subtitle of this book.

The last ingredient in the sitcom 'recipe' is casting, and, with supporting characters played by the likes of Sally Phillips, Sarah Hadland, Tom Ellis, Patricia Hodge, James

Holmes and Tom Conti, there are fantastic performances to support Miranda's lead role.

Miranda begins the writing process on paper, firstly in her notepad. Before long, the walls of her kitchen are covered with flipchart paper in order to work out each plot. After that, she writes a scene-by-scene breakdown before sitting down to the first draft. While she knew her characters and was good with jokes and dialogue, Miranda didn't have much experience with story – something vital to sitcom – and so swotting up was necessary: 'I read loads of books, did loads of research and I had two people help me – Richard Hurst and James Cary – and I would present them with subject matters or big set pieces that I thought would be funny and vague ideas how that would work with scenes and they would help me structure that into a sitcom story.'

During the BAFTA comedy writing masterclass, Miranda told Grace Dent that occasionally this would all fit into place naturally. Referring to the scene where she meets the sexy American chef Danny, played by Michael Landes, and makes a fool of herself, she said, 'That, actually, was a rare example of a scene that was written like that and never changed. Curtseying in an awkward situation and then coming up and farting – I was just pretty sure that was funny. And then I just needed to find the highest status situation to do that in. So when I was thinking, "Right, now the hunky chef needs to come in, right, what can I do? Ah! Fart curtsey. Perfect!"'

Another satisfying moment was writing 'Just Act Normal', the fifth episode of series two, where Miranda and Penny spend the entire episode in a therapist's office. That came from an idea for a set piece but, as she developed it, became a whole episode. 'Initially that was terrifying but – although there was a bit of story in it, I had to pace it and there was a bit of a jigsaw puzzle working out which jokes are best where – it was very freeing to write. I think I wrote the first draft of that in three days. Loved it.'

But most of the time fitting the jigsaw pieces in their correct position was a challenge for her and she needed the help of graphs as well as Hurst and Cary. 'I think that writing comedy is incredibly technical,' she told Grace Dent, 'that's why it's so dreary.'

Miranda isn't alone here in finding the plotting tough. Award-winning writer Jesse Armstrong, whose credits include *Peep Show* and *The Thick of It*, has said, 'The plotting is by far the hardest bit. It feels like the bit where you need someone else in the room because you get an idea and it's no good or it's difficult to get to the next idea unless you've got someone else to bounce off.'

His co-writer on *Peep Show*, Sam Bain, added, 'It's sort of like engineering or building a table, just making sure it all works. It can be quite exhausting.'

Linking these strands of story and escalating them to a climax is the ultimate goal for sitcom writers and can be seen executed brilliantly in modern sitcoms such as *Curb Your Enthusiasm*. Every episode sees Larry David caught up in a web of deceit, awkwardness and anger, usually of his own making. Miranda was keen to get this pace into her own sitcom: 'It took a bit of persuading to have two or three stories going at once – because we're so used to American sitcoms, which are so fast paced – but I think everyone's reaction, even the producer, was there's too much going on here.' However, because the lead character is in every scene, there isn't the option to cut away to someone else, then cut back to Miranda in another situation. With a strong foundation in place, there is room for the show to race about chaotically and avoid the relatively pedestrian pace of certain British comedies. Miranda commented, 'Sometimes I watch six minutes of a British sitcom (naming no names) and I think surely forty minutes have passed, so I wanted to make it as pacey as possible.'

One way the writers maintained the show's pace was to imagine the climactic point of a plot, then place it in the middle of the episode, thus forcing themselves to go further still in the final minutes. Miranda could relate here to the writing methods of the man behind *Father Ted* and *The IT Crowd*: 'That's Graham Linehan's thing of: think of three set pieces for your characters, what would be a really funny situation for them, then connect them.' As with Stevie and the Great Dane, the gym montage with Miranda rolling on yoga balls and struggling with the cross trainer was initially conceived as a set piece and the story wove around it. It was meant to be the end of the episode but instead made up its beginning. She compares this sort of momentum to her past experience writing her stand-up act: 'You've got to kill them with the first one and then the last one's got to be good too. As Ken Dodd says, start good, end brilliant.'

Once Miranda has written the scene-by-scene breakdown to work from, she begins work on the lonely and arduous task of writing the first draft.

Writer of *Shameless* Paul Abbott has said, 'I think the first draft is always a drudge, and I wish there were elves that could sort of just lay down the canvas and stuff. Well, they can't. You have to do it and you have to bleed.'

It can take Miranda as little as five days to squeeze out her first draft out, but rewriting and honing the story to make it as credible and funny as possible can take a further three or four weeks. As a studio audience sitcom, *Miranda* needs to have as many gags as possible, to encourage the crowd to laugh out loud. Although Miranda's good at jokes, with so many 'laugh-out-louds' required, she enlisted some gag writers to become involved at the end of the process. One writer, Paul Kerensa, had already written for Miranda on *Not Going Out* and added that same gag-heavy tone which had made that show such a success.

Being a studio audience show in the 21st century, *Miranda* may be seen by some as old-fashioned, but, as well as sticking to the traditions of light entertainment, it deconstructs them. Miranda said that, while developing the show with the BBC, she was keen to create something that combined light entertainment with sitcom: 'A sitcom that can do the Eric Morecambe look to camera, I want to do that.'

Deconstructing sitcom is tricky to pull off and Miranda and her writers were careful not to overstep the mark. James Cary said, 'There are one or two lines delivered to camera in the middle of scenes like "This is like a farce", but these jokes have a law of diminishing returns, and we often write them, feel better and delete them before they get to the readthrough.' The knowing in-joke can be clever, but threatens to distract from the story and the characters the audience really care about. 'They have invested emotionally in the world that's been created,' said Cary, 'and they don't want to see behind the scenery.'

Interestingly, a similar sort of deconstruction is taking place in another contemporary studio audience sitcom: the BBC's *Mrs Brown's Boys*. It appears on the face of it to be an intensely traditional sitcom, but actually plays with the form. So, when an actor forgets their lines or a piece of set falls down, the blooper is left in. Some shows would shift the outtakes to the credits roll or a DVD extra, but not here. Never mind looks to the camera, the fourth wall is well and truly broken down there.

So with just the right amount of pratfalls, looks to camera, utterances of 'Such fun!' and escalating storylines, the script is ready. After a readthrough with the actors, pre-production starts, and Miranda meets with the crew to describe how she envisions what she has written: 'Suddenly you find yourself having meetings with costume designers about characters you have written, or the props department about how exactly you saw that "grapefruit you wanted to have befriended".'

Finally, an invited audience shows up at the studio to watch the show being recorded. No matter how meticulously the script is gone over to make sure there is a steady stream of jokes, the British public can be unpredictable. 'You can't go three minutes with a silent audience,' Miranda has warned. 'There were moments I thought that would get something and didn't, or I thought would be bigger.' But thankfully an incidental line can also be unexpectedly well received. One of the first lines in the show is where Miranda blames her lateness on the train commute, but, as Stevie points out to her, 'You live upstairs.' The audience laughs very loudly, which apparently wasn't expected. Miranda has said, 'I watch it slightly cringing going, "Oh, there shouldn't have been a massive laugh there. Let's crack on. It's not that funny."'

As we know, *Miranda* quickly became a huge success, but it was the standard of writing which particularly impressed some of Hart's peers. Friend and colleague David Baddiel congratulated the show: 'It successfully uses the model of letting small mistakes by the main character grow into enormous, comic disasters, normally operating at least two, sometimes three, plotlines that all skilfully come together at the end.'

So those weeks toiling over structure with James Cary and Richard Hurst were worth it in the end. Baddiel continued, 'There are fabulous one-liners – such as in last Christmas's show, when a glum, unhelpful Post Office worker at the collection depot tells Miranda, who is getting nowhere trying to pick up a package of presents, that his wife has just left him. She replies, "Did she leave a card so that you could collect her later?"'

Clearly, those extra weeks spent adding jokes, redrafting and creating gag-graphs were well spent. But then Baddiel saved further acclaim for Miranda's character, 'which blends her acutely modern delivery with a more classic sitcom clown to create a genuinely new type of comic hero – a woman who continually breaks through her crippling self-consciousness with large, liberating, anarchic gestures'.

With series one and two now firm favourites with audiences and critics alike, it seems that everyone is looking forward to the third series. BBC Writersroom asked Miranda how she would feel about someone else writing the show for her. She responded positively, but was concerned that other writers might not know the character well enough. 'It would be lovely if there was someone there that got me, could write for me, find my voice and write the show. But at the moment I feel like only I would know that'. At the end of it all, Miranda has realised that all her hard work is worth it for the end result. 'I'm beginning to think, Oh, hang on, I can call myself a writer now. That's exciting.'

11

MIRANDA ARRIVES AT THE BEEB

*'It just brings joy to the heart. It's just daft. I love the talking
to camera. I think it's a joy whenever she looks down the lens –
it's like Eric Morecambe.'*

– Kathy Burke

And so, on 9 November 2009, Miranda Hart achieved her lifelong goal – her own BBC television sitcom series. She told one newspaper, 'Since I can remember I have wanted to be a comedian and so to have my own show on the BBC is a total thrill, albeit slightly unnerving.'

The pilot version of Miranda had been recorded in March 2008 with a slightly different cast. Most noticeably, Patricia Hodge was absent; Penny was played by Elizabeth Bennett, whose long career included roles in the 1980s sitcom *Home to Roost*, Jimmy McGovern's *The Lakes* and the film *Calendar Girls*. Also appearing was *Hyperdrive*'s Stephen Evans. The pilot of *Miranda* was not broadcast, but sufficiently impressed BBC executives, and so a first series was commissioned.

Calling the show *Miranda* wasn't always the plan. Hart cheekily used it as a working title. 'When I was writing it, I didn't even think it would be commissioned. I just went with calling it my name because that was my absolute dream scenario, with no idea it would actually happen.'

In the end, it was the producer's idea to go with the eponymous title, and it made sense as the character appears in every scene and talks to the camera. It's very much about Miranda. It was a bold move, though, following in the footsteps of other performers (usually American) whose sitcoms had been named after themselves: (Jerry) *Seinfeld*, *Ellen* (DeGeneres), (Bob) *Newhart*, *Roseanne* and *Cybill* (Shepherd). As Miranda herself has acknowledged, 'It's got that "Who does she think she is?" feel.'

Unlike her US counterparts, though, Miranda didn't have anywhere near the level of fame that usually suggests a self-titled show. Very few members of the public tuned into the show because they already loved her – it was usually because their friend had told them to check it out. 'I have to call it "my show",' she said, 'rather than its title *Miranda* because that feels very weird, being my name an' all. In meetings I have to ask people to call it "the sitcom", otherwise I hear "the thing about Miranda is…" or "when does Miranda finish?"'

Being in the show's production office, and hearing people answer the phone with the greeting 'Hello, Miranda' will always be odd. It might have inspired the line in the third episode of series two when Miranda is trying to lie to her friend Tilly and claims she's making a programme for a production company called What's It Called, for a channel called Who For: 'Which is funny, because when people ring up, we say "Hello! What's It Called" and they say "Don't you know? It's your company we're ringing" and then they say, "Who are you making programmes for?" and we say "Who

For" and they say, "Yes that's what I'm asking you." And we all laugh, so very much.'

As we have seen, 'the sitcom', as Miranda prefers it to be called, started out in Edinburgh before being written as a TV pilot, then rewritten for BBC Radio 2 later in 2008 as *Miranda Hart's Joke Shop*. Then it was adapted back again for television. The radio show had received critical acclaim and was even nominated for a Sony award. *The Independent* called it a 'well-deserved TV transfer'.

Miranda was commissioned by BBC Two alongside two other comedies, a new show called *In My Country* written by Simon Nye, creator of *Men Behaving Badly*, and the return of Gregor Fisher as *Rab C. Nesbitt*. Lucy Lumsden, BBC comedy commissioner, announced: 'The return of a great character such as Rab C. Nesbitt, along with two new audience sitcoms, reflects the wide range of diverse, distinctive, quality comedy BBC Two continues to offer viewers.'

While *In My Country* failed to progress any further than the pilot, recorded in May 2008, the channel's audiences were glad to see the return of Glaswegian character Nesbitt in his first series for a decade. Meanwhile, there were rumbles in the media as Miranda and co. prepared for 'the sitcom'. Executive producer Jo Sargent was quoted by Chortle as saying, 'We are delighted to be working with Miranda – it is rare to find someone so uniquely talented.'

If many were excited about the planned series, others were a little more doubtful. While this show was very different from what had come before, it bore similarities to what had come before that. The light-entertainment attitude of the 1970s which Miranda embodied was not very fashionable, as we'll see later, but it had its supporters. *The Word* magazine would later write, 'It actually comes as a blessed relief, an antidote to the seemingly endless darkness that has enveloped comedy over the past few years. Perhaps to watch something so simple and light at 8.30pm on a Monday night is just the ticket.'

Writing in *The Independent*, Robert Hanks agreed, saying, '*Miranda*'s success reflects a certain public weariness with the comedy of   outrage... *Miranda* belongs with *The IT Crowd* and *Harry Hill's TV Burp* in a tradition of amiability and brazen silliness, a school of comedy that wants its audience to laugh not out of shock or a refusal to be shocked, but out of delight.'

So what *is Miranda*, and what makes it so special? Well, on the surface, it is a sitcom about a well-educated, socially awkward girl who owns a joke shop, trying to improve her life and get it on with the boy next door. She delegates all the work in the shop to Stevie, her self-important 'little friend', so she can set about the important task of ruining everything for herself. One reviewer described it as 'a girly *Black Books* with penis-shaped pasta instead of books, and no alcoholism'.

But it is much more than this. It has a potentially universal appeal. One reviewer for the *Independent* wrote, 'It is the first new primetime sitcom I can recall that unites the whole family, all laughing their socks off.' Slapstick spans age and even race – more about that later – so, in the same way all generations of the family can laugh at *You've Been Framed*, Miranda can provoke a giggle. One reviewer noted, 'I bet kids loved the bit in the first episode where she was on the dance floor with her handsome crush and her skirt fell down, or when she fell over piles of boxes for no reason other than her awkwardness.

Insecure girls, too, probably adore Miranda's refusal to be cowed by her prettier, more popular friends, a pair of screeching materialist harridans pixelated by thoughts of marriage and wedding dresses.'

And there's very little in the show to offend your nan. The rudest bit in the show is a reference to chocolate penises, but rather than being smutty it is just silly and there's no need for anyone to leave the room in embarrassment. As Miranda has said, 'It wasn't planned to put the series out at 8.30 originally, but I found that I loved that pre-watershed slot. So much so, that for the second series I decided to put no profanity in whatsoever. There's not even an "Oh my God"... The mainstream's where I'm at.'

Almost everyone can relate to something in Miranda – bossy mums (OMG, annoying right?!), unsuitable friends, a job you have little interest in, the guy you know you should be with but *just aren't*, perhaps even being mistaken for a man. With *Miranda*, BBC Two seems to have hit the jackpot with a show that attracts viewers of all ages, which just means higher viewing figures and lasting popularity.

There have been suggestions that the show would mainly, or even exclusively, appeal to women. There are even hints that, within the industry, there is this separation. *Not Going Out*'s Lee Mack has said, 'Miranda is naturally funny – BBC Two seems to allow itself one funny woman at a time, and, now that Catherine Tate has finished her show, that job is hers.'

This could be seen as a rather cynical view, but it's hard to argue against. Hart herself doesn't appreciate the distinction. She told the *Daily Telegraph*, 'I hate being called a "woman in comedy". I understand that men may possibly only watch it because they're persuaded to do so by their partners but I want to make sure it's for everyone. I don't want to write a show for women. Everyone feels they've been a bit of an idiot in social situations but no one likes to admit to it.'

This honesty is a large part of the character's – and therefore the show's – appeal. A lot of the show's social embarrassment stems from the neuroses of women... naturally, because the lead character is female, and so inevitably, the show appeals to women a great deal. Hart has said it's like having a 'friend you can laugh at... who does things you fear you might do, or have done'.

When Hart appeared on *Loose Women*, her popularity among the sisterhood was confirmed. Amid cheers from the studio audience, host Kate Thornton said, '*Miranda* is such a breath of fresh air. It's nice to see a female comic doing something on her own terms, you know... trailblazing again, because it's been a while since we had female comics on screen doing something that isn't just stand-up.'

Hart's most devout fans may be women, but many men also love the show – like the *Observer*'s Phil Hogan who wrote, 'There's always a sharp sensibility at work – in Hart's gleeful observations of Miranda's post-Bridget Jones victimhood, of girly fads and shibboleths ("Fabulasmic!")... So, yes, more.'

Hart's fellow comic Frank Skinner is also a fan. When she asked him if he thinks female comedy appeals to men, he replied, 'I think, Miranda, it's just, just funny. You can break it down into many categories, but if one of the ones it sits comfortably in is "funny", you're all right.'

Even *Miranda*'s opening titles do something to endear the viewer, male or female. The theme tune is cheerful, like the main character's disposition but, as the show's script editor James Cary points out, the succession of large childhood photographs Hart holds during the sequence 'begin the theme of family embarrassment and we're already beginning to invest in her emotionally'.

Everyone is on Miranda's side, and this is largely due to the clever way the character was devised and developed over a number of years. The *Guardian*'s Kira Cochrane has written, 'While the character is awkward, she is made admirable, even heroic, by her essential happiness. Miranda is one of the few single women in pop culture ever to truly enjoy their own company, constantly breaking into song while alone in her flat, or drawing faces on items of fruit.'

James Cary explains that, despite the character's delight in herself, she is really at odds with herself, in a constant struggle to fit in: 'Miranda reveals the truth that fitting in is a lot harder than it looks, takes a lot of effort and can lead you down any number of blind or embarrassing alleys (in a way that many of the audience identify with).'

We'll look at it in more depth a little later, but one of the key talking points around *Miranda* was the way it affectionately harked back to the sitcoms of yesteryear. Its old-fashioned style attracted some of the audience but put others off. It was definitely the marmite-esque ingredient of the show. Miranda said, 'I knew, before the first series went out, that the phrase "old-fashioned" would be levelled at me. But I regard that as a positive rather than a negative. The mainstream's where I'm at.'

So we already know and love Miranda, but what of the people around her – who makes up the sitcom family? Her best friend, shop manager and fellow conspirator is Stevie. They grew up together and generally enjoy each other's company despite huge personality differences. Stevie is uptight, business-like and takes pride in her work. She encourages Miranda to strive for success and has Heather Small as a sort of motivational spirit guide. Throughout the series, she pops the Heather mask over her face and asks Miranda – doing her best impression and in tribute to Small's hit of 2000 – 'What have you done today to make you feel proud?'

Stevie is played by Sarah Hadland, who previously appeared in TV series including *Moving Wallpaper*, *That Mitchell and Webb Look* and *How Not to Live Your Life*, as well as playing the small part of Ocean Sky Receptionist in the Bond film *Quantum of Solace*. Her smaller physical stature gives Miranda many opportunities to bite back with remarks about her size – a key aspect of the relationship since there had been a similar dynamic between Hart and Charity Trimm, in the Edinburgh Festival *Sitcom Trials* show in 2001.

The lady who gave Miranda's character many of her insecurities during her upbringing was her mother Penny. She sees her daughter as an enormous disappointment and embarrassment; she is desperate for her to find a husband and secure a more respectable job than playing around in her joke shop. Penny brought the sitcom one of its most memorable catchphrases. If it has momentarily slipped your mind, just recheck the front cover of this book.

Patricia Hodge plays Penny, as she did in the BBC Radio 2 version of the show, but she might not necessarily have been Miranda's first choice to play her on-screen mum. In April 2009, Miranda told her Twitter followers, 'Today I will be

David Hart Dyke with wife Diana and children Miranda and Alice,
11 June 1982.

Above: As frisky pensioner Maureen in *Cruising* at the Bush Theatre in 2006.

© *Alamy*

Below: Invited to No 10 as part of Sport Relief in 2010. From left, with Helen Skelton, Sarah and Prime Minister Gordon Brown, Christine Bleakley, Lawrence Dallaglio, Fearne Cotton and Jimmy Carr. © *PA Photos*

Cycling with, top, David Walliams and other celebrities, including Russell Howard (bottom, centre) and Davina McCall (front, right).

Miranda cast Tom Ellis, Patricia Hodge and Sarah Hadland join the star on the red carpet.

Left: Miranda and James Corden engage in unlikely Dirty Dancing for the Teenage Cancer Trust Comedy Night 2011.

© *PA Photos*

Right: Miranda and her on-screen hunk, Tom Ellis, at the British Comedy Awards.

© *Rex Features*

Above: Fooling around with fellow comic Rhod Gilbert on *Would I Lie to You?*

© *Rex Features*

Below: Miranda and *Would I Lie to You?* host Rob Brydon stand either side of cultural guru Melvyn Bragg at the South Bank Sky Arts awards.

© *Getty Images*

Right: At the 2011 British Comedy Awards, flirting with Duran Duran's Simon Le Bon.

© *Rex Features*

Left: Miranda with her mentor and comedy icon, Dawn French.   © *Rex Features*

Once a PA temp at Comic Relief, Miranda now warms up for a busy year of fundraising.
© Getty Images

penning a letter to Penelope Keith to persuade her to be in my sitcom. Think it unlikely but one can but try.' Getting in touch with the actress's agent, she kept her fans in the loop: 'Penelope Keith update – the letter is sent, but her agent says "it's highly unlikely". Think BBC2 not 1 was nail in coffin!' On receiving the bad news – 'Penny Keith can't do my show. Shame' – she asked for more suggestions from her followers. Many replies followed, and Miranda summarised the results: 'The funniest mother suggestion was Margaret Mountford. The most exciting suggestion was Julie Andrews. Imagine! Thanks team.'

But Hart didn't approach Sir Alan's former right-hand lady or Mary Poppins. Instead, she popped by the Noël Coward Theatre in London, during the run of *Calendar Girls*, to meet Patricia Hodge in her dressing room. A week later, it was confirmed that the former *Rumpole of the Bailey* star would play Miranda's mum.

Penny is one of the most popular characters in the show, perhaps because she is so familiar to us, or maybe because she's given so many fantastic lines, whether it's responding to a casual 'Good morning!' with the riposte 'Don't get emotional, we're not Spanish', or indeed her many utterances of her immortal catchphrase. One of my personal favourites to feature the latter would be: 'I don't know what I'm going to buy for such an ugly baby... Your father's suggested a balaclava. Such fun!'

Penny's biggest obsession is finding Miranda a man. Her first line in the series is 'Are you engaged yet?' and Miranda humours her with the reply: 'Not since you asked last night, no.' She does her best to set her daughter up with any man possible, even suggesting her cousin, as well as stopping to pick up hitchhikers but leaving them stranded on the side of the road at the first mention of a girlfriend. But there is one person she overlooks as a potential son-in-law – Gary Preston.

Gary (Tom Ellis) comes back into Miranda's life after some time travelling abroad. He has taken the job of chef at a bistro that just so happens to be next door to the joke shop. Miranda does her best to create romantic moments, but her yearning to succeed is about as powerful as the forces that make her fail. It even seems like Gary has feelings for her too, but it never seems to be the right time.

Clive is Gary's boss, the manager of the restaurant. The characters of Clive and Miranda obviously know each other well, though their backstory is never explained. He teases her like a good friend and always manages to get himself involved in her problems. James Holmes, who plays Clive, is the only member of the cast who manages to out-camp Miranda. Before the sitcom, he appeared mostly in the theatre, formerly playing Lady Bracknell ('a handbag?!') in *The Importance of Being Earnest*, as well as taking various roles in Catherine Tate's theatre comedy show. Before this, he was a stand-up comedian working the circuit and he took his solo show *Anorak of Fire* to the Edinburgh Festival in 1993 and 1994.

Tilly is a 'friend' from boarding school whom Miranda has failed to shake off. She is forever lying to be seen in Tilly's favour, despite the fact she doesn't even seem to like her. She is played by Sally Phillips, who had previously worked with Hart on *Smack the Pony*, and Hart felt honoured when Phillips agreed to appear in the series. The character of Tilly plays an important role in the stories of the show, as she represents a standard of achievement which Penny approves of, and then compares Miranda unfavourably to her. So the main reason Penny pushes her daughter to lying about a new job, and then seeking one, is because Tilly has just got a promotion. For Penny, it's all about keeping up with the Joneses, where Miss Jones is Tilly.

Another ex-school friend is Fanny, played by Katy Wix (Daisy in *Not Going Out*), and who plagues Miranda with screams of 'Aaaah! I'm engaged!' Plus, in the second series' Christmas special, there is a guest appearance from Tom Conti as Miranda's father, Charles. The Oscar-nominated actor and fellow RTS award winner has, among numerous other roles, played the lead in *Jeffrey Bernard is Unwell* at London's Garrick Theatre. More recently, he appeared in an episode of *Lark Rise to Candleford*, playing the role of Mr Reppington. In the Christmas episode, Charles shows where Miranda inherited her clumsiness from. He exceeds the show's usual quota of falling over, stumbling into furniture as naturally as his ungainly daughter.

In an interview on the red button, Miranda thanked Conti for 'joining the family' and he was just as happy to be there, telling Miranda, 'I'm shocked by the degree of your talent; the enormity of your talent – it's pretty damn stunning. You have the magic.' He continued to talk about how well the cast got on and the relaxed atmosphere: 'There's no – well, maybe you're all crazy, I don't know – but you don't show it. Maybe you just keep the crazy for when you get home and then your husbands or partners get it. Certainly, we don't get it in rehearsal – it's very good fun.'

Among other secrets revealed in this conversation with her

sitcom 'family' were that Patricia Hodge was the worst culprit of the cast when it came to corpsing. But then Sarah Hadland put Miranda in it by pointing accusingly at her and saying, 'I'd rather somebody corpsed than farted. It's literally like working in a wind tunnel actually, and I speak for all of us.' Hadland went on to reveal her favourite flatulent moment of the series to date, which came about when they were in a taxi filming the opener for series one: 'We had to have our make-up checks done, and the make-up ladies were on the outside of the taxi but for some reason they could only get the window down a bit. So I had my face like this, halfway through a window, leaning across you, and then you did a massive trump. I was trapped with my head halfway through a window and your wind rising up. We laughed so much, as quickly as they were putting the make-up on me, I was crying it off!'

There was a lot of fun to be had on set, but there was just as much work to be done. The shows were recorded on Sunday nights. Before this, there was the readthrough on Wednesday mornings and then rehearsals for the rest of each Wednesday and Thursday. Miranda told BBC Writersroom about the rest of the process: 'Friday at 2:00pm [we have] the producer's run to make sure we're not doing anything that upsets them. Then you might do final script notes that afternoon. Then Saturday you pre-record things in the studio that you can't do live, and then Sunday you start at 9:00am and rehearse on camera all day. And then do the show at 7:00pm.'

Recordings for series one of Miranda began in July 2009. After the first studio recording, Hart posted on Twitter the following message: 'I was terrified, but audience were brilliant and it couldn't have gone better. I am one happy lucky lady.' It all suggested that, when broadcast, the series could well become a success.

12

ADVENTURES IN A JOKE SHOP

'Hello to you and thanks for joining! This is exciting, isn't it?'
– Miranda

'So here we are. It's show time. Episode One tonight,' wrote Miranda on her BBC blog that Monday night in November 2009. All her hard work had built up to this moment, so it was unsurprising she was nervous about how it would be received. 'Hope you enjoy the show tonight. I can't believe it's going out (this has been years in the coming). My career either takes off or comes to a sad end tonight...!'

Miranda remembered the first day's filming was a location shoot for scenes for this episode – including Patricia Hodge fainting in a busy high street: 'So on the first day's filming it was "Hello Patricia, lovely to meet you, thanks for doing this, now we just need you to faint on to this grubby Hounslow pavement – ok, action..."' She saw someone sweeping the pavement ahead of Patricia having to lie there and was most impressed, telling her blog readership: 'I thought, that's nice, I do lots of falling over in this show, perhaps that will be a precedent. Let me tell you – I have yet to be swept for. I am still waiting.'

The first-ever episode sees Miranda excited about being reunited with her crush, Gary Preston, who she hears is back from travelling. She decides to give in and go to lunch with her old school friends, despite the fact that she hates them. It's either that or help Stevie unpack the chocolate penises and wrongly delivered baby stock. She goes to the restaurant next door and discovers Gary is working there as the new chef. Trying her best to impress, she at first tells him she has trapped wind, and then lies that she was a gymnast in the last Olympics... in the busty category.

After her girly lunch where she inadvertently agrees to go wedding-dress shopping, she lies to Gary again, saying that her two children (Orlando and Bloom) froze to death – children that of course have never existed. Gary doesn't mind, though, and asks her if she'd like to go to dinner, saying, 'Don't worry, it's not a date, it's just a thing.' She then worries about what to wear, so, after she 'tidies' away the boxes of stock (by putting them in Stevie's office), she goes shopping. Struggling to find something in her size, she unwittingly buys an outfit from a shop for transvestites. She feels proud when a customer compliments her, but less so when Stevie sees her wearing the outfit and asks why she is dressed as a transvestite. At this point, Gary walks in and Miranda rushes upstairs to change. Meanwhile, Stevie is furious to discover the boxes stored in her office.

Eventually, Gary and Miranda have a lovely dinner and things seem to be going well. But after he goes up the stairs to Miranda's flat, he discovers it is filled with all the baby stock.

He apologises the next day, but things go from bad to worse when he sees Miranda trying on wedding dresses with Tilly and Fanny. She runs down the street after him, shouting for him to come back.

Ratings were good for the first episode. The *Guardian* reported that it reached 2.5 million people in its 8.30pm slot (not bad considering its competition on other channels included *Coronation Street* on ITV). A same-week repeat, at the later time of 10pm attracted an extra 1.7 million viewers, and a 7 per cent share of the audience watching at that time.

The second episode ('Teacher') introduced a special guest star – Peter Davison, whose long career included a stint in the early 1980s as TV's *Doctor Who*. 'Yes, hark at me,' Miranda wrote on her blog, 'I only got a Doctor to stay in the show'.

The episode begins with Miranda agreeing to be Gary's safety wife. When he says that, if there was to be 'a moment', they wouldn't ignore it, Miranda then sets about trying to 'create a moment and do some wooing'. Stevie comes to stay with Miranda and convinces her to join her French evening class, but then discovers the teacher is Mr Clayton (Davison), her old teacher from school, and makes a quick escape. Meanwhile, Miranda tries to make it up to Gary for not appreciating his cooking by inviting him to a tango class – though, obviously, she has ulterior motives.

The next morning, Miranda is disgusted to discover Stevie has brought Mr Clayton ('Keith', in fact) home with her. She and Gary go to the tango class, but the teacher dances with Gary so Miranda tries to get in between them. When they get home, they argue because she says she prefers her kebab to his cooking. He insists that she let him give her a cooking lesson.

She thinks this could create a moment as she finds him sexy when he's angry. Of course, things don't go to plan. There is almost 'a moment' – they are about to kiss – but are interrupted by Mr Clayton bursting in saying, 'Has anyone seen my pants?'

Then Miranda's mother arrives and the regular 'You Have Been Watching' sequence at the end (in which each character in turn waves to the camera) is reminiscent of Morecambe and Wise's breakfast routine.

During the episode, Miranda talks about a sex-education video they were shown in biology about conception in which the egg was represented by a woman on a lilo, in the middle of a swimming pool; the sperm were represented by men wearing swimming trunks and caps.

It turns out that this came from real-life experience. It was completely true, Miranda revealed. 'No wonder it wasn't until my mid-twenties that I could talk to men without giggling shyly.' She also mentioned that it was not the first time that Sarah Hadland had kissed a *Doctor Who* star on-screen; before Davison, she had kissed David Tennant in the 2007 comedy-drama *Learners*, in which Tennant teaches Jessica Hynes's character to drive.

Hart added mischievously, 'I can also reveal that Patricia Hodge once sucked Tom Baker's toe – although she didn't say whether that was professional or personal. Either way, the image isn't ideal, let's be honest.' What younger viewers may not have realised is that Davison and Hodge had regularly worked together before – they had starred in early-1980s sitcom *Holding the Fort* for ITV.

Miranda's third episode ('Job') finds our heroine trying to prove herself as a 'career bitch', despite her unstoppable habit of singing during interviews. As part of her new fitness regime, she braves the gym but realises it's not for her – though rolling about on yoga balls is *so* Miranda. Hart revealed that filming the workout montage was very tiring, but points out on her blog that the sweat soaking her T-shirt was fake: 'I was sprayed with water under the pits etc – it was rather nice on a hot June filming day.' The yoga ball 'stunt' was inspired by a prank she had played while working: 'I had done it with very large rolls of bubble wrap in an office when I was an office manager. (We all get our kicks somehow.)'

Miranda tries her best to wriggle out of her membership contract with the gym but it is watertight, so next she threatens to escape via the loophole of anti-social behaviour: 'If you don't cancel my membership, I will... I will shit all over your towels.' When that doesn't work, she says she'll break the swimming pool by ushering in 'a mass of dirty dogs... and I will throw them in the pool along with a sheep covered in "pooballs"!' Now at her wit's end, she warns the gym receptionist that she will wee all over the ball pool – and it's at this point that her new employer walks in, and fires her before she's even started her new job. The receptionist says, if she stops her threats, she can have £5 off her monthly fee, and six weeks with a free instructor. She ends up falling for an extended 36-month contract when she discovers she'll get a free towelling robe.

It ends with a farcical sequence where Miranda is caught in a web of job lies, trying not to reveal to Tilly that she's a waitress at Conky's Grill, before insisting that she's working in the forces. But then Gary saves the day, turning up in his RAF cadet uniform after a reunion and addressing Miranda as commander, before whisking her off her feet and carrying her out of the restaurant, *a la Officer and a Gentlemen*. For once it all works out. As Miranda put it, 'marvelissa-Mussonlini!'

Episode four ('Holiday') was director Juliet May's favourite script and the one Miranda most enjoyed filming: 'That could have been something to do with the dancing to Billy Joel,' she said. It finds Miranda taking a holiday and included some more special guest stars. Dave Lamb, an actor who provides the sarcastic voiceover on *Come Dine with Me*, played Colin the businessman. Miranda described him as 'very funny and also one of the nicest men I know'.

Younger fans of the show were delighted, and possibly even went a bit giggly, with a cameo from the 20-year-old *Skins* actor Luke Pasqualino. The women on set were rather taken with him, as Miranda explained on her blog: 'In the studio for this episode we had a hotel room set, so there was a bed, and at various intervals I would see women unashamedly asking Luke to lie on the bed and have their photograph taken with them. I think that might have included Patricia Hodge. Not a way to treat a guest actor. Very bad form. (I have my photo on my bedside table.)'

In 'Holiday', to prove to her friends that she is spontaneous, Miranda tells them she is going to Thailand for a few days. But, hating travel and the unknown, she opts for the Hamilton Lodge, a hotel just around the corner. She makes the most of the facilities, watches films, orders numerous meals from room service and even orders 'company', which turns out to be an escort – and not just any escort, but Clive from the restaurant.

Penny discovers her daughter's true whereabouts when Miranda sneaks home to rescue all her trousers, and make the most of the Hamilton Lodge's Corby trouser press. One of Miranda's tactics to avoid being mistaken for a sad, lonely diner is to dress in a business suit so it looks like she is working. This ends up working almost too well, as Colin the businessman mistakes her for a woman called Amanda Barnes, whom he is expecting to present a seminar the next day. Miranda gets drunk and ends up giving away her whereabouts at the hotel to Gary who turns up there. She tries to convince him to 'do a bit of the sex', but she ends up passing out on top of him. On discovering the next morning that she has to lead the seminar for Colin, and discovers that Stevie is in the audience, she escapes out of the window. And she returns to something more her style – dancing in the restaurant to 'Uptown Girl' by Billy Joel.

Robert Epstein, reviewing the show for the *Independent*, said he found *Miranda* to be something of a grower and says that this episode had him in fits: 'Not for its originality of premise – taking on a self-improvement lecturer's persona and playing merry hell with it is not exactly mind-blowing – nor the farce (one of the friends she lied to turns up as an "escort" she mistakenly ordered) but perhaps because it is impossible not to warm to someone so at ease with their own inadequacies.'

In 'Excuse', the fifth episode, Penny is in her element, organising a *Pride and Prejudice*-themed party in order to set her daughter up with a man. But, when Stevie finds an online profile of Penny's planned match for Miranda, Miranda does everything she can to avoid the party – even accepting a blind date arranged by Tilly.

Dreamboat Charlie (Adrian Scarborough) turns out to be anything but dreamy; he's a super toff who calls her a nice bit of totty. Tilly informs Penny that the date didn't go well, so Miranda's attendance at the party is expected. Finally, Miranda comes up with the only way to stop her mum trying to set her up with inappropriate men – to come out as a lesbian. Penny is delighted and makes it a 'coming out' party. Miranda is devastated when another party guest, Edmund Dettori (Alex Hassell), turns out to be 'a handsome'. Miranda disappoints everyone by admitting she is actually straight, but then, when she hears Edmund speak (in an absurdly high-pitched voice), it's a different matter. She runs away from the party, batting away protestations with cries of 'Such fun! Such fun! Such fun!'

Adrian Scarborough, making the first of two appearances in the series as Dreamboat Charlie, told Miranda that he didn't mind being cast for parts on the basis of his looks: 'I'm very grateful for it because I've got a lot of money and made a career out of it. I'd much rather be short and fat and ginger with a big nose than a sort of rather dashing debonair... I'd rather be a character actor because I think you get much more interesting parts.'

The first series drew to a close on 14 December 2010. Miranda took the opportunity on her blog to bid farewell to her viewers. 'It has been a pleasure and thank you so much for watching and being interested. It means a hell of a lot,' she wrote. 'This profession is insecure breeding enough but putting a show out there with your name in the title, and playing "yourself", was always going to be a risk, so I am grateful for anyone who stuck by it. Thank you... Time to say goodbye. Come on, no tears.'

In the sixth and final episode of the series, 'Dog', Miranda and Stevie compete for the attention of Robert Husband (Philip Brodie), a man who left his wallet at the shop. They discover a card in his wallet advertising a self-defence class, which they decide to attend. They also discover a picture of a dog in the same wallet, which leads Stevie to get herself a Great Dane. When Husband turns up at the joke shop, he avoids the matter of whom out of Miranda and Stevie he would prefer to take out for dinner. He manages to escape, but Miranda is undeterred and decides to try to attract his attention by getting a dog of her own to rival Stevie's acquisition. But, while Stevie has an amusingly sized Great Dane, Miranda has a Chihuahua Titan.

Meanwhile, Penny is trying to give Miranda advice to make sure she doesn't embarrass herself at the Henley Regatta, while Clive persuades Miranda to tell Gary how she feels about him, in order to stop him going abroad to Hong Kong. She comes up with the perfect romantic speech and rehearses it in her head, but, when it comes to saying it, Gary and Clive are distracted by Titan, and Miranda muddles up its delivery. In the park, Robert 'wallet guy' Husband sees the girls with their dogs and – as Miranda has just run out from weeing in a bush, with trousers round her ankles – says he would prefer to take Stevie. He asks her if she would like to go for a drink and the two of them react with disgust.

At Gary's leaving party, he asks Miranda to dance, and as the music changes to a slow number he says he wants to talk to her, but Stevie honours a pact made earlier and swiftly changes the song, inspiring the whole room to burst into a rendition of the conga. Another chance blown for Miranda, and, with Gary off to Hong Kong, might it be her last?

Miranda wrote on her blog: 'As you will see in this episode I leave a little bit of a cliff hanger in terms of my relationship with Gary (Tom Ellis). Here's hoping I get a chance to write more episodes and finish the story, but, if I don't, it has been a real joy and experience to have done the series.'

Fortunately, it was clear that Miranda would return for a second series. Whichever way you look at it, it was successful. Fans, critics, fellow comedians and even her family loved the show. But it was the end of an exciting journey, and it's not surprising that she got a little emotional. 'Last show done,' she tweeted. 'Series over. I am not going to lie I've had a little cry.'

Hart was oblivious to reviews praising the show – she wasn't confident enough to read them first-hand – until others told her of the acclaim: 'People were saying, "You know it's going all right reviews-wise." Then, around episode four, they told me the viewing figures – three million. I was like, wow… that is good, right?'

Bruce Dessau, writing for the *Guardian*'s TV blog, cited his favourite moments as Miranda's now-famous looks to the camera: 'What made *Miranda* so memorable, apart from the sublime slapstick tumbles, was the way she constantly acknowledged the viewer, shamelessly mugging to the screen… The success of *Miranda* – one of the few recent sitcoms that is truly laugh-out-loud funny – demonstrates that whether one describes it as mugging to the camera like a demented vaudevillian, or gets all structuralist and calls it the apotheosis of self-referential po-mo dislocation, pulling a face on-screen will always be a hit.'

Her show seemed to have universal appeal. The gossipy towers of *Heat* magazine applauded: 'As we reach the end of the series, let's all acknowledge (yes, all of us) that this has been the flat-out funniest thing on television for ages, mixing silliness with smartness... Roll on series two!'

The respected industry weekly *Broadcast* was similarly smitten: 'She's a big lass... and funny. And I don't mean whimsical, wry, dark or clever, I mean fart gags, chocolate willies and ludicrous set-ups that deliver great visual gags!... I laughed, out loud, a lot.'

It seemed that many were grateful for this outbreak of innocent fun and laughter on our screens, rather than the dark, challenging material which had been fashionable in TV comedy. Marsha Coupe wrote in the *Sunday Times' Culture* supplement: 'How refreshing to watch *Miranda* (BBC Two), a half-hour show free of the hateful filth that usually passes for humour.'

But, as always, thanks to the subjective nature of comedy, what one person may love may be loathed by another. One reviewer for the daily freesheet *Metro* did not hold back, drawing comparisons with a controversial *Have I Got News For You* joke made at the expense of the royal family: 'Anyone tuning in hoping for some edgy "kraut Queen" jokes would have been sadly disillusioned. Chocolate penises (penii?) was as risqué as it got, which is fine if you find cacao-based genitalia intrinsically amusing. If not you had to suck on a lot of knowing asides to camera and the gauche charms of Miranda, which, after the umpteenth time she'd gone tongue-tied and bonkers in the presence of her dream man, wore pretty thin.'

But the *Guardian*'s Lucy Mangan is definitely a supporter of the show. She commented, 'I love it for exactly the same reasons many people seem to hate it – because it's not a high-powered, finely tuned precision piece of American sitcom engineering. Much as I love those too, there is room in my life for something gentler and more endearing – something in which you can immerse yourself as you would a warm bath.'

Hart's fellow comedian (and her Alpen advert co-star) Arabella Weir agreed, saying that she has a natural talent. 'She can't not be funny: everything about her – her expressions, her mannerisms, her pauses, even her silences – are funny. It is an unlearnable and rare quality.' Apparently it was laugh at first sight, as Weir recalled, 'I first saw her on an audition tape along with about 20 others, and before she'd opened her mouth I shouted, "I want to work with her. She's hilarious," and I was right. Miranda is a one-off.'

David Baddiel echoed this view in an article he dedicated to Hart: 'There's a phrase – funny boned – that is sometimes overused in comedy to describe those performers who can get laughs without saying anything: just by the way they are, the way they hold themselves, the way they move. It's commonly used to describe Eric Morecambe and Tommy Cooper. It should also be used to describe Miranda Hart.'

Charlie Higson admired how Hart has overcome the conventions of cool which can stifle TV comedy at times: 'When *Miranda* first appeared on our screens, some TV critics were sniffy – "This can't be right, it looks like an old-fashioned situation comedy! It's filmed on dodgy borrowed sets. It isn't modern and trendy and filled with jokes about anal sex." But they'd missed the point. The point being, of course, that *Miranda* is just gloriously funny. That's all you need to say.'

Even more startling, perhaps, were the reactions from fanatical viewers. There are a number of fan blogs that post quotes, pictures and clips from the show; fan videos uploaded of clip montages, and scenes of Miranda and Gary set to love ballads; there are Twitter accounts dedicated to tweeting Miranda's latest news. And then, there is Miranda's NBLF (Nutty But Lovely Fivesome). These are five young ladies that admire and idolise Miranda Hart. Simply put – they are her biggest fans. They are Rosie, Roma, Amber, Genevieve and Jess, the last of whom seems to be the leader of the gang. She's certainly the most committed – she posted a video to Twitter that began, 'Today, I have been making my room into a Miranda Hart shrine.'

It should be made clear that this isn't one of those creepy shrines with candles and voodoo – it's simply a wall papered with Miranda paraphernalia. There are stills from the series, promotional shots, a picture of her together with Hart, her programme from the recording, her 'production guest' ticket, the 'reserved' sign from her seat at the recording, her favourite quotes (ordered by series one, series two, interviews and *Hyperdrive*) and a printout of tweets she has received from the lady herself.

Another fan called Kirsty also posted a picture on Twitter, which showed her bedroom wall saturated with photos of Miranda.

Hart's family seems to like her sitcom, although she acknowledges that their approval may have a lot to do with the fact her style is mainstream. 'If I was doing really edgy or dark or rude stuff, I think my mum would be a bit like, "Oh yes. No, that's not my daughter"... wouldn't mention me down the WI, you know. So she got lucky with me from that point of view, but, yeah, I think they're really proud.'

With such fantastic ratings and a positive response, it seemed inevitable a second series would follow, and so it did. BBC Comedy commissioner Cheryl Taylor said at the end of 2009, 'It's rare that a debut series provokes such an ecstatic response and we are delighted that Miranda's special brand of warm and distinctive comedy will be back to delight audiences again next year.'

Ultimately, the main reason for the sitcom's success is Miranda Hart herself, both the writer and the character, as developed through her stand-up persona. Sally Kinnes of the *Sunday Times* wrote, 'Stand-up success and great sitcom-writing rarely go together, but Miranda Hart's semi-autobiographical material – posh girl from boarding school struggles to cope with body image, misanthropy and trouser presses – makes the perfect transition. It's like French and Saunders in the early days.'

But where does *Miranda* end and Miranda begin?

13

REALITY BLURS

'I'm not quite as mad as the sitcom Miranda!'
– Miranda

As Miranda Hart plays Miranda, a predictable question she is often asked is how much of her is in the character. She explained to BBC Writersroom how the character was born: 'Well, I developed this stand-up persona, and that's where it all started from. I realised I was getting laughs being a version of me.'

As many artists are advised when they start out, Miranda writes about what she knows, by starting from herself and exaggerating her persona in order to create the perfect sitcom character. 'I'm pleased to say I did have to exaggerate for comedic effect,' she said. 'It wasn't entirely autobiographical... But I do bring myself to all my performances. I've just taken that sort of feeling to its extreme.' She writes about her loves and her hates, and has even lifted some anecdotal material from her real life, but when it comes to the Miranda who owns a joke shop she stressed, 'I do feel like I'm playing a character. It's not really me.'

There are things she shares with her screen self. They both went to boarding school and shared a dorm with girls who had ridiculous nicknames, but Miranda insisted the real-life ones weren't quite as bad. 'My school didn't have lots of moneyed, King's Road Tilly types, so I got lucky, as boarding schools go.'

Shortly after Hart suffered a minor injury to her knee (while bending over to tie a shoelace), Stuart Husband visited Miranda's flat for a *Telegraph* interview and said it told him a lot about her. 'She values her family (multiple photos of whom are on display), friends... and enjoys defiantly low-brow evenings in (evidenced by her DVD boxed-sets, not of *The Sopranos* or *The Wire*, but of *Mistresses* and *Pineapple Dance Studios*).'

This seems to chime with her alter ego, but the big difference between the real and imaginary Miranda lies in their relationships with their families. In *Miranda*, Penny is nothing but a burden to her daughter, always pushing her to do better and saying how disappointed she is in her. It has led some to wonder how much Penny is like Hart's real mum, D. Miranda reassured, 'They're not dissimilar in looks, actually, but yeah, they're not alike character-wise.'

D has never pushed Miranda about getting married or having children. In fact, Miranda says that the only similarity between her real mum and Penny is their constant use of the phrase 'such fun'. Hart recalled, 'I definitely had my ear to the ground when my mother had her friends round: "Oh, we must have a quiche! Such fun!" I love that language.'

Even in the single episode he appears in, Miranda's sitcom dad, Charles, steals a line from Captain David Hart Dyke. 'There's a line my dad always says,' Miranda revealed. "I'm not excited yet but I'm sure it'll hit me any minute..."'

Miranda has bonded well with Patricia Hodge, and even refers to her as 'Mum Two'. When Hart appeared on a special version of *The Generation Game* in David Walliams' charity panel-show marathon *24 Hour Panel People* in March 2011, she revealed that her on-screen mum even signs her text messages with it.

For one red-button extra, Miranda interviewed both Hodge and her real mother. D revealed that people always think that Penny's character is based on her. 'It doesn't upset me, but it is very hard to get across to some people that it isn't based on me, and they can't actually believe it – [Miranda] must have got the idea from somewhere and therefore it must be me.' Nevertheless, D admitted that there are aspects of Penny that she would quite like to have: 'I think she's got a great sense of fun and does rather surprising things unexpectedly.'

In an attempt to use her as some sort of reliable witness, Miranda asked D if she felt she had used a lot of her own real-life character for the fictional Miranda. D responded, 'Not really, no. Although you were quite accident prone, you did trip over things.'

Miranda was delighted – a note from her mum! 'I'm so glad you said it,' she grinned. 'I spend a lot of time defending myself and going "sitcom me is not the real me" so I'm delighted that you've said it's not.'

Miranda's sitcom family members cause her nothing but strife and this is established from the very beginning of the show in the introductory monologue to camera: 'Previously in my life, my mother tried to marry me off…' Even the show's title sequence stresses her pressurised background, as co-writer James Cary has pointed out: '*Miranda* has a lovely, cheerful theme… but Miranda has pictures of her growing up and we begin the theme of family embarrassment and we're already beginning to invest in her emotionally.'

Another reason so many people love the character of sitcom Miranda – and something, to an extent, she has in common with the lady who created her – is her fabulous pratfalling. Miranda does her best to convince people that this trait is exclusive to the sitcom character but – sorry, Miranda – your mum's already told us you were very much like that.

Recent evidence came when Hart appeared on *Alan Carr's Chatty Man* on 7 February 2011, and viewers were treated to a real-life stumble. As she entered the studio to applause, she lost her footing and fell down the stairs. Carr exclaimed, 'You are so clumsy, what's the matter with you, woman?'

Highly embarrassed, Hart replied, 'I spend my life saying I'm nothing like the sitcom character… I just fell down the stairs!'

Once the interview was under way, Carr didn't let her forget what happened. She was explaining why she wrote herself a part which is the brunt of such cruel comments. 'I really do feel that I'm playing a character, so I don't feel I'm writing it about me, weirdly. Which is, obviously, slightly odd because we look very alike,'

Totally deadpan, Carr reminded her: 'Yes… and you've just fallen down the stairs as you came on.'

Busted. Then again, sitcom Miranda displays exaggerated clumsiness. Real-life Miranda does not tumble over any cardboard box in her path, nor does she fall over when a man enters the room; nor does she knock over a hat stand every time she leaves a room. Occasionally, though, just occasionally, she falls down studio stairs when on television.

What drags the sitcom's slapstick into the present day are the embarrassing social situations – something we all have to cope with. While some of the incidents in the show were completely fictional, many were drawn from Hart's real-life experience, and sometimes ridiculous things happened to her she thought too unbelievable for the sitcom. The most memorable example from the show is near the beginning of the very first episode – when a delivery man calls her 'Sir'. This has happened to Miranda but, as she has reassured, 'Luckily, in real life, they look at me and say "Sorry, Madam", but obviously in the sitcom he looked at me and carried on calling me sir, but that didn't happen in real life.' Some writers have criticised the show for its seemingly implausible storylines, but, as Miranda emphasised on Twitter, some of them really happened to her: 'Just got called sir in a shop. Yes, happens. Journos said was ridiculous to have that happen in a sitcom. My life too sitcom for a sitcom.' (It's worth noting that this tweet was sent on 20 August 2010, nearly a year after series one was broadcast, so the accusation had clearly been made before.)

Other situations drawn from Hart's real life appeared in series one's finale, 'Dog'. She told the regular panel on TV's *Loose Women* of actually 'getting locked in a park when it went dark and then not being able to fit through. In the real-life version there was a hedge and a gatepost and I tried to fit through and I couldn't. So I had to remove my jumper and sort of scrape through. In the sitcom version, obviously I got stuck just in a bra.'

So these things do happen to Hart, but they make up such a small percentage of the show. She builds on them, exaggerates them and creates more disastrous situations for this heightened version of herself. Yet she is still honest enough with interviewers to offer them a nugget of awkwardness such as this: 'I did go to the loo just now and walk into the men's by mistake. So I am still a bit of an idiot. But then I'm hoping, aren't we all?'

And this is perhaps the key to Miranda's appeal. In *Seinfeld, Subjectivity, and Sartre*, author Jennifer McMahon writes, 'Our favourite fictional characters and events are generally the ones who impress us with their realness. Successful fictions resonate with us. They tell us something about reality. Through the characters and situations they present, works of fiction offer us insight about human nature, ourselves, or our times.'

This may go some way to explain why shows featuring comedians playing exaggerated versions of themselves are so popular. Tony Hancock started the trend in Britain with *Hancock's Half Hour*, written by Ray Galton and Alan Simpson, in which Anthony Aloysius St John Hancock lived in a rundown part of East Cheam. It started on the radio in 1954, co-starring Sid James, Hattie Jacques, Bill Kerr and Kenneth Williams before transferring to television in 1956. Hattie Jacques also co-starred with Eric Sykes in *Sykes*, about an immature clumsy man who lived with his unmarried twin sister. Its run on the BBC from 1960 to 1979 was only brought to an end with Jacques' untimely death in 1980 of a heart attack.

The format of a star playing a version of themselves is especially big in America, perhaps because of the huge celebrity status many of its comedians hold. One of the earliest stars was Lucille Ball, who was the star of a number of eponymous sitcoms – *I Love Lucy*, *The Lucy Show*, *The Lucy-Desi Comedy Hour*, *Here's Lucy* and *Life With Lucy*. She worked for most of her life, first acting in the 1930s and still making films right into the 1970s. Other female American performers with their own show include Roseanne Barr, Ellen DeGeneres and Cybill Shepherd. Roseanne's character, like Miranda's, started out as a stand-up comedy routine. But the series ran for nine years and became the most watched television show in the US from 1989 to 1990, according to the Nielsen ratings. *Ellen* is a particularly interesting example of the formula, because the comedian's life informed what happened in the show. In 1997, DeGeneres came out as a lesbian on *The Oprah Winfrey Show*. Shortly afterwards in her sitcom, DeGeneres' character Ellen Morgan told her therapist (played by Winfrey in a special cameo appearance) that she was gay.

It's Garry Shandling's Show was notable for breaking down the fourth wall, allowing characters to address the audience. It starred the comedian Garry Shandling as himself – a neurotic stand-up, but one who knows he is a sitcom character. Even the supporting characters know they are in a show and many of the storylines involved the studio audience. Shandling's run of success continued with *The Larry Sanders Show*, where he played a talk-show host and celebrities played versions of themselves – much like in Ricky Gervais's subsequent series *Extras*. Having formerly hosted *The Tonight Show*, Shandling had experience to inform his performance. *The Larry Sanders Show* ran from 1992 to 1998 on HBO and was ranked in numerous lists as one of the best TV shows of all time.

One of the best-known and most popular eponymous sitcoms, perhaps ever, is *Seinfeld*. In the show, its star – comedian Jerry Seinfeld – even pitches it to commissioners as 'a show about nothing'. It was created by Seinfeld and Larry David and was set in Manhattan, following the chaotic lives of Jerry and his friends George Costanza, Elaine Benes and Cosmo Kramer. Larry David went on to make his own show, *Curb Your Enthusiasm*. He lives with his wife Cheryl and burdens his manager Jeff with the problems of his life – often having to apologise for offending or annoying people in social situations.

Skipping forward to more recent US sitcoms, there is *Two and a Half Men*, where the lead character Charlie Harper is largely based on Charlie Sheen's reputation as a womaniser and hedonist. He lives in his beachfront house in Malibu with his uptight brother Alan, and Alan's idle son Jake. Meanwhile, the provocative comedian Sarah Silverman played a fictionalised version of herself in *The Sarah Silverman Program*. Her character is an unemployed woman who spends her time managing to insult everyone around her. Many, though, preferred Silverman's stand-up work, and the show was cancelled after three seasons.

Still running, however, is *Louie*, a comedy series on FX starring the American stand-up Louis CK. The Emmy-award winning comic writes, directs, edits and stars in the show – it features his stand-up sets and sketches inspired by things that have happened in his life. But arguably the biggest star vehicle in US comedy at the moment is *30 Rock*. It stars Tina Fey as Liz Lemon and is based on her experience working on *Saturday Night Live*.

The glut of American shows of this nature inspired British comedians to do the same. In 1992, *Sean's Show*, starring Sean Hughes and shown by Channel 4, was similar in style to *It's Garry Shandling's Show*. It was set in his home and used devices to break down the fourth wall such as addressing the audience and walking through the set to get to other locations. It was nominated for Best Sitcom at the 1992 British Comedy Awards and he later had a series of programmes called *Sean's Shorts* before becoming a team captain on *Never Mind The Buzzcocks*. Other comedians followed suit with their own shows – *I, Lovett* starring Norman Lovett (best known as Holly from *Red Dwarf*); *Baddiel's Syndrome* where David Baddiel plays an architect who regularly sees his therapist (played by Stephen Fry); and *So What Now?*, a slapstick-fuelled comedy starring Lee Evans as himself.

A recent success of the genre is *Lead Balloon*, where Jack Dee plays a disgruntled, cynical comedian called Rick Spleen. Comparisons have been made with *Curb Your Enthusiasm*, largely because of the way most of the episodes see the comedian plagued with petty arguments and social embarrassments. As already noted, Miranda Hart played one such annoying character in Spleen's life, when she refused to negotiate on the price of a christening gift.

When comedians play versions of themselves, they can alter the public's perception of them. They have the creative control to rewrite themselves to how they want to be seen. In most cases, though, comedians don't take advantage of this as it's funnier to be ruder, louder, sillier or, in Miranda's case, more awkward versions of themselves.

Miranda's character is so real that it makes her appealing, as we can see a little of ourselves in her. We can laugh with her at the things we identify in ourselves or those around us, or we can laugh *at* her in the more ridiculous, surreal moments. Even Miranda can laugh at the character, as she has enough distance that it doesn't upset her, but it is based on how she was in the past: 'Now I'm socially competent, but in my twenties I was as scared as that sitcom character. In a comedy way I can be big, I can embrace my height, I can be posh, I can fall over, make a tit of myself socially, and it's all fine.'

Clare Balding, a fellow Downe House alumnus, recognises this trait: 'I think there is a part of all of us that is insecure, goofy and socially inept, and so we feel affection for and attachment to Miranda, the hapless heroine.'

This was proved by Miranda's legion of fans when the BBC blog asked for their 'real-life cringeworthy moments' based on this one from Miranda: 'I was out shopping yesterday when a gorgeous shop assistant asked me if I needed any help. As I turned around I felt a sneeze coming on. When nothing came out I panicked and persisted to scrunch up my face every few seconds, as if having a facial twitch was less embarrassing than sneezing. And OBVIOUSLY, as I was mid one facial scrunch, my ex walked past.'

My own personal favourite response came from Jess, who said, 'Being hated by your P.E. teacher can be very embarrassing, as I found out last week, when I was told to come up to the front of the class, and demonstrate how to serve in badminton, I swung the racquet, and hit myself in the face, causing my glasses to fall off, everyone thought it was hilarious, even the teacher... no wonder I hate P.E.'

More replies to Miranda's request came through via Twitter. Here is a stonker from @JonnyRiverhorse: 'Cough outrage Tuesday when, in a vain attempt to get to the corridor, I overstrained and broke wind with frightful venom!'

These are just two examples of the many answers that show Miranda is not alone in flirting with social awkwardness. Recognising our own everyday behaviour through comedy can also come from stand-up comedy acts. Just as we shout 'You do that!' to our loved ones when Michael McIntyre describes some aspect of human behaviour through observational comedy, so we watch *Miranda* and think to ourselves (though perhaps few would admit it out loud), 'I do that too!'

Miranda is proud of how she has turned out and wouldn't change anything about her nature. 'I'm sometimes hideously embarrassed at social occasions for being so ill-informed, especially because a lot of comedians are clever people... But I'm pleased about it, too, in many ways; it means I've been able to hold on to a kind of innocence.'

She takes the punch so that we can laugh without having to admit we do it too. 'No one goes, "You won't believe what I did yesterday," but I think that happens to everyone. I see my role as being the friend you can laugh at and think, Well, at least I'm not as bad as her!'

Her looks to camera only endear her to the audience further – we're in on the joke, and she's confessing to us. Writing in *The Stage*, Mark Wright pointed out, 'Crucially, we like her in a way we don't like David Brent. We sympathise with her, we want her to succeed, and we laugh – both with and at her.'

When Kira Cochrane went to interview Hart for the *Guardian*, she discovered: 'Every woman I have told about this interview has almost swooned, before wondering aloud how much Hart resembles the character she plays. I wonder too, and in the early minutes of our interview it seems simple. Hart is warm, friendly, quietly funny – like a much lower-key, much more grown-up version of her screen persona.'

It's not surprising that the sitcom character attracts men. Hart wrote on her BBC blog how, in episode three of the second series, she had to convince people that it is realistic that three different men would try it on with Miranda. 'I have to go, "I think Miranda has enough charm for him to be interested." And it all gets a little surreal and awkward!'

She went on to imagine that fiction might become fact. 'Hopefully, the three suitors might be prophetic in my real life – that would be nice. Well, I hear George Clooney is still single for one, and I've always had a penchant for Tennis champ Goran Ivanisevic, if anyone knows him…'

Three might be asking for two too many, but there is a certain someone in the show who seems to have taken a shine to Miranda: her knight in shining RAF cadet uniform – Gary Preston.

14

THE BOY NEXT DOOR

'It's nice to be involved in something like this – I don't think I've ever had this much attention from people in the streets as I do since I did Miranda!'

– Tom Ellis

Oh, Gary. Poor Miranda has had a crush on him for years, one which has only intensified. But it never quite seems to work out for the two of them. When he becomes the chef at Conky's Grill, the bistro next door to Miranda's joke shop, she can't get away from him and becomes obsessed.

Being so tall, Hart found it tricky to find the right actor. Tom Ellis is 6ft 3in, two inches taller than Miranda. But this was not the only reason he got the part, Miranda says it is 'because he's marvellous, obviously'.

Sorry, ladies, but let's just get one thing out of the way: Tom Ellis is not available. He is married to Tamzin Outhwaite and they make a great couple. When they won the Christmas edition of the ITV celebrity game show *All-Star Mr & Mrs*, on 20 December 2008, they showed they knew each other better than the other couples on that edition: Ronan Keating and his wife Yvonne, and Terry Venables and wife Yvette.

Ellis can boast of a varied acting CV. He has performed in other TV comedies – on *The Catherine Tate Show*, he twice played Detective Sergeant Sam Speed in a *Life on Mars* parody, as well as portraying Sam in *Pulling* and taking the lead male role in ITV's *Monday Monday*, in which Miranda had a regular supporting part. At the other end of the spectrum, he has featured in hard-hitting dramas such as *Accused*, created and co-written by Jimmy McGovern. Ellis has described *Accused* as 'very hard to watch. One of those dramas that doesn't come along very often; doesn't patronise the audience.' He added, 'It was probably my proudest moment actually, being in that.' As Neil, he played opposite Andy Serkis in the *Accused* episode 'Liam's Story', and told interviewer Lorraine Kelly, 'It was a privilege to work opposite him and observe someone working like that.'

This sort of challenging piece is the polar opposite to *Miranda*, but Ellis thrives on variety in his work, and is grateful for the chances he's been given: 'I'm lucky that I've been able to do that, have that kind of range going on. It's why I got into acting in the first place. I like varied parts, being given the opportunity to do different things. You know, I enjoy doing comedy, but I also enjoy doing straight acting and heavy, intense drama as well, if it comes along.'

Tom Ellis has taken part in some of Britain's most iconic programmes. In 29 episodes of *EastEnders*, he played the dishy Dr Oliver Cousins, who succeeded Drs Legg, Samuels, Singh, Fonseca, Trueman and Leroy as Walford's resident GP. He made his first appearance in January 2006 when Dot knocked him over and he got locked out of his house, while naked. Sounds more like something that would happen to

Miranda. Despite this rather farcical introduction to Albert Square, Dr Cousins played an important role in some major, serious storylines. He advised Honey about her unborn child, and found Ben Mitchell when he had run away. He also helped Little Mo with Freddie. He took pity on Mo and began to develop romantic feelings for her, taking her on a date. Eventually, he proposed and the two of them prepared to go to Leeds, but, when Stacey told her that she had seen Dawn kissing him, Mo pushed him to the ground. Shocked by her response, as it had only been a friendly kiss, Oliver ended their relationship. But, when Mo was about to leave the Square, the doctor had a change of heart and told her that he still loved her, asking her to change her mind and go with him to Leeds. She decided not to go, though, and left Walford with Freddie, leaving Oliver to go north alone.

You may also recognise Tom Ellis from another timeless TV favourite, *Doctor Who*. He is proud to say, 'I've ticked that box.' In a 2007 story, 'Last of the Time Lords', he played Thomas Milligan, a former NHS doctor who becomes a fugitive when the Master brings the Toclafane to Earth. 'I had a storyline with Martha. It was at the end of the third series when David Tennant was the Doctor. And, yeah, I helped Martha save the world – before I got killed by a sonic screwdriver! It happens.'

For an actor, a *Doctor Who* death is almost an honour, and, when the Master (played by John Simm) discovers them, he uses his laser screwdriver (superior to the Doctor's sonic one!) to kill Thomas. But when time was reversed so it never happened, he survived and later got engaged to Martha. It was later revealed in David Tennant's last episode, 'The End of

Time', that Martha had instead married Rose's old boyfriend Mickey Smith.

More recently, Ellis has travelled back in telly time by guesting in *Merlin* as King Cenred, a moody baddy with long dark hair. Ellis loved playing the part: 'It was great and I haven't had a lot of opportunities to play baddies. It is a bit of an acting cliché that actors love to play baddies, but I understand why now, because you just get to exorcise all the things you don't in real life.'

Being in *Merlin* was a lot of fun for Ellis, as not only did he get to play the bad guy like a cross between a pantomime baddie and a villain straight out of James Bond, but he also had a fantastic outfit. When *What's On TV* magazine asked him if he liked the costume, he exclaimed, 'I loved it! It was the best costume I've ever worn for anything! It was tailor-made for me, the most ridiculous leather suit which I could barely move in and an OTT wig. I looked a bit like Russell Brand really, so I've been told. An evil Russell Brand... I got to do everything I ever wanted to do when you're a kid.'

When he's not working, Ellis enjoys golf: 'It's my yoga, really. Time away just to think about nothing else.' He also likes to spend time with his two children – his toddler Florence, whom he had with Tamzin Outhwaite, and Nora, who is two years older and from a previous relationship. He likes to watch television with Florence, especially *Miranda*. 'I was in the scene and, when I left the scene on the telly, she went, "Uh! Where's Daddy?" and I went, "I'm sat right next to you," and she said, "Nooo! Daddy on the telly Daddy!"'

Fans of *Miranda* can't wait to see Miranda and Gary get together. In sitcom's history of 'will they, won't they?' they're fast becoming successors to Ross and Rachel from *Friends*. The website tvtropes.org, which calls itself 'a catalogue of the tricks of the trade for writing fiction' describes the 'Will They or Won't They' trope like this: 'Two characters, often combative but with obvious Unresolved Sexual Tension (or UST), resist going into a full blown relationship for a rather long time. Usually the two characters will be presented so that "they will" is the conclusion to root for; only rarely is the question of whether the writer think they should in any real doubt.'

It is true that Miranda and Gary are portrayed as such a good match that most fans are rooting for them to hook up with each other. But some can see that the comedy lies in their failure. Razzberry, a user of the forum on thestudentroom.co.uk, commented, 'I just prefer her as a single independent lady with an attempt to get guys, but failing! It was hilarious last week in the parachute place where she said she hadn't slept with a guy for 3 years! I do think Gary is awesome though, not going to lie. I think I just prefer Miranda and Gary as friends though.'

This stylistic device has been used throughout sitcom history, back to Rigsby and Miss Jones (*Rising Damp*) and Arkwright and Nurse Gladys Emmanuel (*Open All Hours*) right through to Carrie and Mr Big (*Sex and the City*) and Tim and Dawn (*The Office*).

After the first series had finished, news and gossip website Digital Spy asked Tom Ellis if his character could ever end up romantically involved with Miranda, and he replied, 'I don't know because, if they do, that will be the show over in many ways. They'll tease it out for a bit – it's the new Ross and Rachel, apparently!'

In a statement to the press, meanwhile, Miranda teased,

'There might be a little bit of a dalliance, yes. Whether it's with Gary or not, I can't possibly divulge.'

Series one of *Miranda* had ended on what Miranda describes as 'our attempt at a *Crossroads*-type cliffhanger', with Gary leaving for Hong Kong and Miranda having blown every chance to change his mind by telling him how she feels. Hart and Ellis both used social-networking sites to build the suspense and keep fans guessing. In September 2010, Tom (@tomellis17 on Twitter) wrote: 'Gary is in hong kong [sic] doing a new job so will not be around for series 2...', then followed up with: 'Or will he be back? ...hmm'.

In the weeks leading up to series two's premiere in November 2010, Ellis responded to fans' tweets with the following: 'For all who have seen the trailer and asked if I'm not coming back... I told you. Gary left! Still watch though coz Miranda is brilliant! Txx.' When the first episode of the second series had finished, revealing that Gary has returned, he admitted his prank. 'Well... didn't want to spoil the surprise!!! Thankyou [sic] tweeps for all your lovely messages... hope you enjoy the new series, havin [sic] fun filming!'

Now Gary was back in Miranda's world, hopes were high for the pair to get together. So much of the writing points to their being made for one another. In series one episode four, before Miranda goes on holiday to her hotel around the corner, a customer called Amanda sees them playing together with children's toys and assumes they are a couple with children. When Gary says to Miranda, 'Hello? Caterpillar duck race!' it demonstrates he has the same childlike love for life as Miranda. They are also assumed to be a couple when

Chris and Alison (Gary's annoying kissy friends) ask them to be godparents to their unborn child. Until, that is, Miranda ruins her chances by punching a vicar in the face.

Because Miranda speaks directly to the audience in her monologues, she makes it clear that she has feelings for Gary. She is usually very honest and reveals even the most embarrassing of truths, but she occasionally lies for comic effect.

Gary can be incredibly, heroically loyal towards Miranda. He spares her blushes in the park by covering up her semi-nudity when Tilly and Fanny walk past. He is willing to make a fool of himself in order to stop her from doing so. In series two episode four, when the bistro's new waitress Tamara (Stacy Liu) invites them to an art class, Stevie tries to embarrass Miranda by accusing her of not knowing who Botticelli is. Miranda flounders, but Gary comes to her rescue and mouths the answers behind their backs.

One of the key things that show Miranda and Gary would make a good couple is – like the character of Mr Darcy in *Bridget Jones's Diary* – he likes her just the way she is. In 'The New Me', series two's opening episode, in which Miranda is desperately trying to improve herself, Gary muses, 'I think I preferred the old Miranda anyway.' Which is just as well. Things were just starting to go well for her while he was in Hong Kong, and she had been developing a sense of composure. Yet, the moment Gary returns, she's back to her old self – falling off her stool and getting covered in cake.

It is so obvious to their friends that they have feelings for each other and would make a good couple that, in the third episode of series two ('Let's Do It'), Stevie and Clive force them to go on a date.

They are reluctant at first, insisting that they are just friends, but Gary is keener once he discovers the vouchers are for Wilson's (a restaurant whose food he is eager to sample) and talks Miranda into going. At Wilson's, they are out of their comfort zone and both extremely nervous. Gary suggests that the only solution is to sleep together.

Miranda says she thinks it is an excellent theory, but then confides to camera, 'He could have given me any theory to be honest!'

Back at Miranda's flat, they do their best to create a romantic atmosphere. She puts some music on, but the shuffle facility on her music player is a little too random – 'My Humps' by The Black Eyed Peas is hardly appropriate. She attempts low lighting, but ends up dimming the lights so low that Gary is sat in the dark. Eventually, they are about to kiss, their faces leaning towards one another, but, just as their lips touch, Gary belches in her face! After giving him some Gaviscon to relieve him, he is worried about his 'aniseedy breath', a claim Miranda dismisses. But, as they're about to kiss once more, Miranda panics and pulls away. They both agree that it has become awkward and over-planned so they agree to try again the next day when they are more relaxed.

When Gary shows up the next day, Miranda is too het up, and says to him that things aren't working out and that the pressure on them is too great.

Gary apologises but makes a surprise visit later that evening, wearing only his dressing gown. Just about to kiss – again! – they are interrupted, this time by Penny, Tilly and Stevie, returning to the flat with pizza.

Things go better for them as a couple once they decide to

remove the pressure of having sex. Gary specially arranges a romantic trip to a spa hotel. Miranda feels an overwhelming sense of relief, but, just as they're about to leave for their mini break, Clive gets annoyed with Tamara for gossiping and fires her, letting slip that he'd only given Tamara the job in the first place beacuse the were married.

Miranda is appalled and angry by this, while Gary tries to explain that it is only a technicality – that he did it as a favour to Tamara, so that she could get a visa to study in the UK. He is not doing well in seeking forgiveness and only makes it worse when he accidentally says, 'Come on, it's not like I'm still sleeping with her.'

A furious Miranda berates him for keeping such an enormous secret from her when they had been planning a romantic getaway together.

The next morning, Miranda goes to see Gary once more. When he asks if she thinks they can move on from this awkward situation, Miranda feels they can. Relieved, Gary starts telling her how Tamara has gone to give them space but she stops him and explains that she wants to move on in a different way; she wants to break up with him.

Even though it was Miranda who decided to break it off, it is clear she still loves him. In a subsequent episode ('Just Act Normal'), when Miranda is sitting in the psychiatrist's office, Gary can't help but burst in and announce to her that he is in love with her. When he gets down on one knee, the audience screams with excitement! But it's all a dream – Miranda imagined it. Gary never came in and she sits back down, telling the psychiatrist, 'Don't think about him. Don't miss him.'

Justifying the decision to have such a dramatic plot revelation as Gary being married, Miranda told Grace Dent in an interview, 'There's got to be a very, very good reason why Miranda and Gary don't get together. I can't bear will-they/won't-theys, they drive me insane.' One of her writers thought that the suggestion was too much and that the audience wouldn't believe it. The other, however, agreed that it had to be that big because, in Miranda's words, 'people would think "Oh just forgive him and get together, for goodness sake".' Such an unforgivable slip-up means that the couple are unlikely to end up together any time soon.

But, for the sitcom to continue, Miranda and Gary must repair their relationship to some extent. They decide to do this letting Miranda enact a small revenge on him. When he brings them a meal and asks if everything is OK, she says, 'Yes, fine. Yes,' and then she shouts, 'Apart from the fact you married somebody for a green card so have potato for hair!', before smearing mash into his hair. Nevertheless, ending the series with the pair spending Christmas together as friends again cements their status as a 'will they, won't they' couple. Sharing a bed, they are so relaxed with one another, yet an underlying awkwardness and nervousness suggests an abundance of unresolved sexual tension that could keep the suspense going ad infinitum.

Some journalists have suggested that Gary's character is perhaps not as profoundly drawn as it might be. 'If there is a subversive element,' wrote Dominic Maxwell in *The Times*, 'it's in the way she's written in a would-be boyfriend character (Tom Ellis) who is just there as eye-candy for Hart to humiliate herself in front of.'

Another journalist, meanwhile, remarked that Gary, 'in an interesting reversal of traditional sitcom gender objectifying, is underwritten to the point of non-existence'.

In *The Times* interview with Dominic Maxwell, Miranda reassured him that Gary's character does develop throughout the series but did confess, 'As I wrote it, I did think that this was quite satisfying, that I've done to a man what men have done to women for 40 years of sitcom!'

Tom Ellis didn't feel embarrassed about having to play this role though. 'It's just one of those things. I'd just approach it like any other part. I like to think that one of the things people like about Gary is that he's not too aware of it.' Ellis told Digital Spy that he had become good friends with Hart during the run of the first series, and certainly viewers could see their fantastic rapport for themselves when she interviewed him as a red-button extra. Ellis also admitted to having done 30 press-ups backstage before appearing in front of the cameras in just his boxer shorts, leading Hart to ask him what it was like to play her love interest. When she said to him, 'The romance is fun to play, but it's not always fun in real life, is it?' he laughed and, by way of teasing her, replied, 'Well... depends if your co-star has got horrendous trapped wind or not!'

Well then. There's the off-screen chemistry theory ruined.

15

YOU HAVE BEEN WATCHING

'I knew, before the first series went out, that the phrase "old-fashioned" would be levelled at me. But I regard that as a positive rather than a negative.'

– Miranda

'Comedy is the new rock'n'roll,' Janet Street-Porter proclaimed some 20 years ago. The idea of the touring comedian taking groupies back to the hotel was a myth that was soon exposed as nonsense (with a few rare exceptions). What remains, though, is the idea that, like music, it's cool to like some comedy, while other things are at best considered guilty pleasures. When it comes to television shows, this comedy 'cred' is usually inverse to ratings. Take *Last of the Summer Wine*, for example. The world's longest-running sitcom had consistently high ratings – peaking with 18.8 million viewers in 1985 – but many viewers and critics branded it 'boring, outdated, slow and unfunny'. In the last decade, the traditional sitcom has been deemed distinctly unfashionable, with comedy aficionados and judging panels favouring the awkward realism of *The Thick of It* and *The Office*. The word 'mainstream' has become something of an insult in comedy circles.

The British comedy-watching nation is now in need of a change, a move away from single-camera mockumentaries and dark humour. In stand-up comedy, this has come in the floppy-haired form of Michael McIntyre. Again, despite success on the comedy circuit and moving his way up to arenas via television, people complain that he's mainstream. Such an attitude makes Miranda angry: 'What's the argument? I'm often termed mainstream and it does feel like a derogatory term, but, without the mainstream, you can't have the other so why would you complain about it? Why would you look down on all of those people who bought his DVD and say, "You're a bit thick"? I get very cross.'

But it seems to be what the nation wants. There is the argument that, when Britain is going through tough times (cough, economic crisis, cough), then the public want to escape with silliness and laughs. It's what has happened throughout history – from the King's jester to satire on *10 O'Clock Live* – and it's what comedians are there for.

As well as mainstream, Miranda has been labelled old-fashioned, both by supporters and detractors. But what is meant by old-fashioned? Let's take a little journey through the history of the British sitcom.

During the 1960s and 1970s, some of the most popular British sitcoms were *Dad's Army*, *It Ain't Half Hot Mum* and *Are You Being Served?*, all studio audience series, and all produced and co-written by the venerable David Croft. Then, in 2004, the BBC conducted a poll to discover what was considered to be Britain's Best Sitcom. *Only Fools and Horses*, which was shot in front of a studio audience, took top spot, and you had to scroll right down to number 19 to find *The Royle Family*, the first mention of a show without a studio audience.

Even as recently as the 1990s, the studio audience sitcom was in rude health thanks to *Absolutely Fabulous*, *One Foot in the Grave*, *Red Dwarf* and *Men Behaving Badly*. But Mark Freeland, head of comedy productions at the BBC, believes that something changed in 1997: 'The turning point was *I'm Alan Partridge*, when they came up with the hybrid format of filming with an audience, but putting four walls up. They shot single-camera in a cube, but with the audience watching on monitors. It teetered between the two formats, and it put a question mark under traditional sitcom.'

The next major development seemed to come in 2001 with the arrival of BBC Two's *The Office*, with a brand of awkward realism which followed in the footsteps of the John Morton mock-documentary series *People Like Us*. *The Office* became a critical hit, attracted large audiences for the channel and left an indelible mark on British comedy. For years afterwards, most new shows were only shot using single cameras and were inspired by the mockumentary style. Lee Mack (*Not Going Out*) has commented, 'Since *The Office*, everyone has this idea that comedy is only good if it reflects the way people really speak. But that's nonsense – and it's a problem that's unique to comedy. If you went to a Picasso exhibition and said, "I love this painting of a horse," and someone chirped up, "It doesn't look anything like a horse – it's not real," they'd be seen as a real heathen.'

In recent years, admittedly, the most talked-about sitcoms have all been free of a studio audience: *Peep Show*, *The Inbetweeners*, *Gavin & Stacey*, *The Thick of It* and

Outnumbered. Even when *Miranda* premiered, commissions for new shows shot without an audience continued to dominate. There was *Grandma's House*, a Simon Amstell vehicle where his neurotic family try to cope with his career following his departure from *Never Mind The Buzzcocks*. There was *The Trip*, in which Rob Brydon and Steve Coogan play versions of themselves on a restaurant tour of the north of England. *Getting On*, with Jo Brand, Joanna Scanlan and Vicki Pepperdine, focused on the tensions and struggles of an NHS hospital ward for the elderly. Elsewhere, Tom Hollander played an inner-city vicar in *Rev*, and Alan Davies portrayed a celebrity chef in *Whites*.

But, while *The Trip* was a favourite with many critics and comedy fans, it was *Miranda* that achieved larger audiences. As the second series of *Miranda* began in November 2010, it was announced that its viewing figures each Monday not only bettered those of *Panorama* (aired on BBC One at the same time), but also were more than double the numbers for *The Trip* (another BBC Two Monday comedy).

It seemed that escapist comedy was what the British public was in need of. *Miranda* brought a fresh face and a modern angle to the traditional sitcom, and seemed to have inspired other commissions such as BBC One's post-watershed *Mrs Brown's Boys*. Even before the first episode was shown, it had gained a notoriety for its sweary nature, not least Brendan O'Carroll's foul-mouthed Nan. There were 36 'feck's in the first episode alone. Yet, aside from the filth, *Mrs Brown's Boys* has all the makings of a traditional British sitcom: studio audience, small set, recurring characters and catchphrases.

Some viewers were left cold by the new show. Akava77

commented on the BBC website, 'A dreadfully bad sitcom with cartoon opening credits, filmed in front of a studio audience where you can see the audience and camera/sound crew, over the top characters, silly make up and wigs, characters talking directly to the camera, daft voices, catchphrases and canned laughter at every single line said by every character.'

But enough people liked it, and a second series was commissioned. Even comedy critic Bruce Dessau, despite cautious reservation, could see some of its appeal: 'Part of me wonders what the BBC was thinking when it chose to air *Mrs Brown's Boys*, but another part of me thinks that it has come at precisely the right time. There has been much talk of a return to post-*Office* mainstream studio-based humour since the success of *Miranda* – and sitcoms don't come much more mainstream than this.'

So, not only was *Miranda* a success, it has ushered in a new age of TV comedy, but, as one door has opened, another has to inevitably close. On 25 March 2011, Danny Cohen, controller of BBC One, announced the end of *My Family*, which had run for 11 series starring Robert Lindsay and Zoe Wanamaker. As well as being a long-standing fixture on the channel's schedule, it holds an important place in sitcom history, as it was a conscious attempt by the BBC to use an American production process to create a show. In charge was Fred Barron, an executive who had worked on *Seinfeld* and *The Larry Sanders Show* in the US, and who appointed a team of writers, a set-up wildly different to that of Miranda's solo project. 'Up to 10 or 12 people were writing around a table and storylining,' Hart explained. 'I think two of them went away and actually wrote that episode but it would always be storylined by a group of people.'

Many are sad to see the demise of *My Family*, but critic Bruce Dessau summed up a lot of opinions when he suggested, 'After more than 100 episodes, the decision comes not before time. Unless the writing is up to *Simpsons*-standard, there is only so long a television family can realistically exist without viewers getting tired of joining them in their living room.' And, for many, losing the show's best-loved character Nick, the eldest son who was played by Kris Marshall, signalled the beginning of the end. Dessau continued, 'Younger characters have been introduced but the show has never recaptured its golden era of father–son hijinks between Lindsay and Kris Marshall, who left the series so long ago there must be people who think the only work he has ever done is irritate BT subscribers.'

Miranda, on learning of *My Family*'s cancellation, said that, after 11 years, 'It's not a slight to be taken off air, it's an amazing achievement.' She went on to say that it will be remembered for Lindsay and Wanamaker: 'They put a lot of work in and they did fantastic performances that really endeared the nation to them. They were great, great comedy actors.' So we bid goodbye to the Harpers and welcome in Miranda and her family.

Perhaps the thing that links *Miranda* and *My Family*, apart from the presence of appreciative studio audiences, is that it was loved by the viewers, even while critics were less enthusiastic. So what is it about *Miranda* that has such wide appeal? Surely we can't all empathise with a tall and clumsy, middle-class lady who spends her inheritance on a joke shop?

Or can we? The problems she faces are universal – how to get the guy and, ultimately, how not to look like an idiot. And, of course, being a sitcom character, she spectacularly fails at both.

Plenty love *Miranda* – the ratings alone have proved that – but many consider it a guilty pleasure. When Hart appeared on *Loose Women*, she believed that shows filmed in front of a live studio audience 'by their very nature, seem uncool. You've got the audience laughing, they're just less real.' She considered that it's also that they haven't been around for a long time.

Panellist Sherrie Hewson (previously a cast member of *Coronation Street*) suggested to her that the rocketing ratings were a sure sign that audiences wanted more of this type of comedy. At this point, the studio audience cheered a 'Yehhhh!' of approval, and Sherrie concluded, 'There you go, it's the right time.'

Miranda's past led her to love this light-entertainment style of comedy. While the alternative comedy scene was growing in comedy clubs in London and across the country, Miranda was at boarding school in Berkshire watching videos of Morecambe and Wise. Her favourite sitcoms were *Are You Being Served?* and *Fawlty Towers*. After she left boarding school, the 1990s brought *Absolutely Fabulous* and *Gimme Gimme Gimme* to feed her love of slapstick. 'So I remained in this buffoony, clowny era, and just thought nothing had changed. Alternative comedy passed me by. I was like: "Who is Alexei Sayle?"'

Ever since Miranda, at the age of seven, had seen Eric Morecambe turn to look at the camera as part of the act, she thought, I want to do that one day. It became one of the things that made her want to get into comedy and she has made that kind of comedy her own. During a series of promotions for its 'precision-engineered' comedy (which also used material from *Rev* and *Stewart Lee's Comedy Vehicle*), BBC Two chose the *Miranda* clip showing her look to camera in the very first episode, reacting to when the delivery man called her 'Sir'.

One critic has described how Hart's intricate performance delivered so much: 'It's not just a look to camera. It's about four reactions, each one timed to perfection, each angle of the head expressing a tiny modulation in how she feels about it. Miranda can make a look to camera mean so many things: hope, joy, frustration, anger and despair, while still letting it do what it always needs to do in comedy – which is to punctuate the joke.'

In one look, Miranda will let the audience in on her secret naughtiness, whether it's that she's confessing ('I do do that'), or that she's desperate to get out of a situation ('What am I doing?!'). This endears her to us, as we all have these faults and her honesty about it is extremely amusing. As Larry David, star of *Curb Your Enthusiasm*, told Ricky Gervais, 'No one ever expresses the bad thoughts but the bad thoughts are funny.'

One of the other 'old-fashioned' devices used in *Miranda* is the 1970s-style ending. As each episode finishes, the words 'You Have Been Watching' appear on-screen as the individual members of the cast wave to the camera, much in the manner of David Croft's sitcoms like *Hi-de-Hi!* and *Dad's Army*. Hart explained why she chose to do this. 'They're so out of vogue, those shows, or there's this slightly snobby attitude to them, so I thought, Well, I'm just going to embrace the genre for what it is. So I thought I'm going to blooming well do the 70s ending.'

Hart told one red-carpet interviewer that she still puts on Eric Morecambe videos now. 'The light-entertainment 1970s campness is my thing.' She also said that Not Going Out was an easy job to say yes to, partly to be able to work with Lee Mack and Tim Vine, but also because it gave her 'the opportunity to do a studio audience sitcom which is a genre I love and, although making a bit of a comeback now, was hardly in existence a few years ago when I started to work'. But, as many commentators have noted, Miranda played a big role in that comeback.

On a red-button interview as an extra for its first series, Frank Skinner said, 'There does seem to be a swingback but I do think – certainly as far as sitcoms are concerned – I think you've pioneered that.' In 2004, Skinner had his own ITV sitcom, Shane, shot in front of a studio audience, but it was badly received and Skinner himself later admitted, 'It was quite poor… In fact, the second series is still in a vault at ITV. So bad a sitcom, ITV wouldn't put it out! I'm going to use that on the publicity for the DVD.'

Where Miranda succeeded, and Shane didn't, was in the writing. Hart was aware of the differences between stand-up and sitcom, and understood the dynamics of filming in front of a live audience. Skinner told Miranda that he wrote his sitcom the same way he wrote his stand-up, and believed that was why it had failed. 'I think plot, characterisation, all those things, some people see as essential. I just tended to like to get really big gags.' And this seemed to come through to the viewers; as one commented on IMDb: 'Basically, it's his stand-up act CRAMMED into a sitcom format.'

Miranda, on the other hand, spent weeks with the help of experienced sitcom writers, honing the characters and painstakingly weaving together the different storylines.

As well as the writing, another key thing to consider with studio audience sitcoms is how it affects performance. There is a temptation for actors to play up to the audience, particularly for comedians who are used to bouncing off the crowd at gigs. Miranda spoke to her co-stars Sally Phillips (Tilly) and Adrian Scarborough (Dreamboat Charlie) about how they feel about acting in front of a live audience. Scarborough said that there wasn't much difference in his approach to the acting, but it is more like theatre and compared it to his previous experience performing farce on stage. The main difference for him in sitcom performance was that it was more nerve-racking: 'The bowel movements are different. More active on the live.'

Sally Phillips believed that the audience becomes part of the experience. 'You have to wait for their laugh, quite apart from anything else... With single camera I am generally trying to make the person I'm acting with laugh. On this, I'm not trying to make them laugh, that would be bad.' She also says that, because of the writing and the retro style of the show, harking back to the 'grand old days of studio audience sitcoms', the performances are bigger. 'I think other studio audience sitcoms done in this country are not necessarily as big as this, performance-wise.'

Miranda finds it a tense experience too: 'Studio shows are really terrifying because you have two-and-a-half days to get a half-hour show together. You do it in front of a live audience, you have two takes, max, and then that's that, and then it goes on telly.' If she considers this too much, it makes her nervous at the pressure of the situation, but usually Miranda just enjoys performing in front of her audience, not thinking too hard about the idea it will be broadcast. Essentially, it all comes down to the classic, almost clichéd, insecurity shared by many comic performers. 'The idea of it being out there is nerve-racking, because if people don't like it they basically don't like me.'

Although Hart avoids reviews, people have (particularly on Twitter) alerted her to negative ones. Her biggest pet hate is being accused of adding a laughter track or 'canned laughter' to the show. From the moment the first series aired, she tweeted, 'Those saying get rid of "laughter track" on the show. It ISN'T a laughter track. Was filmed in front of a LIVE audience. Sorry, they laughed!' and then, 'Whilst on the subject. "Canned" laughter hasn't been around since 60s. All sitcoms with laughter are filmed in front of live audience. FACT.'

David Baddiel felt so strongly about the matter that he wrote a rather ranty piece for *The Times* about it: 'Maybe *Rowan and Martin's Laugh-In* used canned laughter, and, you know what, so probably did *The Hair Bear Bunch*, but it hasn't been used in any mainstream sitcom since. And yet every single review/preview of Miranda Hart's new show, *Miranda* on BBC Two, that I've read, including the many positive ones, refers to the sound of the studio audience heard during the show either as canned, or as a "laugh track".'

Baddiel blamed it on a general misunderstanding of

sitcoms that, just because *Miranda* is filmed with multiple cameras in a studio, it should be considered old-fashioned. He pointed out that the single-camera, non-audience format is so much the norm nowadays that *Miranda* is actually 'a radical departure'.

One interesting example where critics' snobbishness towards audience laughter was misplaced came in 2002 when BBC Two broadcast the second series of *I'm Alan Partridge*. With some five years between series, some complained about the 'addition' of a laughter track, yet in fact the first series had also taken place with an audience. Defending himself on Nicky Campbell's Radio Five Live show at the time of the original series two broadcasts, the show's producer and co-writer Armando Iannucci pointed out, 'It's not canned laughter. We recorded it in front of a studio audience. If anything, I tried to tone it down. If Steve blows his nose there is a round of applause. I can't say, "Can you not laugh at this?" or "Can you laugh a little bit less than that?" The first series also had the laughter as well.'

Iannucci also explained that the type of comedy suited the audience format, compared with more recent 'downbeat' comedies: 'If we wanted to make *The Office*, we would have made another series of *The Office* but it's a different world. *The Office* is very real, whereas Alan is very grotesque – Steve calls him uber-real... Maybe following on from *The Office* people were expecting more of the same. But there is a laughter track on *Blackadder*, and *Morecambe and Wise* wasn't spoiled by the intrusive inclusion of a laughter track.'

In *The Times* in 2009, David Baddiel also noted that 'when critics equate multicam audience sitcom with a perceived lack of sophistication, they seem to forget that *Seinfeld*, *Frasier* and *Friends* were all produced in this way'.

Chuck Lorre, creator of two of America's top-rated sitcoms, *Two and a Half Men* and *The Big Bang Theory*, explained his love of the traditional audience sitcom to *The New Yorker*: 'It's a very intimate genre. There's no music. There's no camera magic. There are no editing tricks. It's not a visual medium. It's about people and words.'

As an interesting aside, when Larry David and Jerry Seinfeld first pitched what became *Seinfeld* to NBC, they wanted it to be done in a mockumentary style. Canadian critic Jaime Weinman explained in the *Independent* the restriction they faced: 'The network said, '"No, you're doing it on three cameras, in front of an audience." So they accepted that, but they did it their own way. They broke the rules and changed people's idea of what you could do with that format. All that has to happen now is for some network to force some writer to produce a sitcom for a studio audience. He won't know the old tricks that people are tired of, so he'll come up with new ones.'

It's exactly the sort of philosophy that led Hart to come up with *Miranda* for a UK audience.

Despite all these disclaimers, Hart still found she had to explain the laughter of the studio audience after two series of her own show. Speaking to Fern Britton in late March 2011, she said, 'The fear of not hearing a laugh in the first five minutes of your script is terrifying.' When Fern asked, 'Do you ever sneak in a laugh on the edit?', Miranda held firm: 'No, no. People still think it's canned laughter. Even TV journalists have said to me, "I love your show, it's a shame you had to put the laughter on". It's filmed in front of a studio audience! Look at me getting het up – I find it really annoying! No, it is real. A real audience and real laughter and, no, we wouldn't put additional laughter on.'

With *Miranda*, there's no need for a laughter track, because genuine laughter is being heard. Apart from the show being a success with audiences sat at home watching television, there is the fact that things are always funnier live. Hart explained to BBC Writersroom: 'You've had the warm-up, you've had me tripping over a cable on the way to do some warm-up... Even in between scenes when you're doing costume changes, there's the warm-up and there's this great atmosphere and people want to laugh or they like you or someone in the show so there's a general feeling of goodwill. There's no one really going, "Come on then. I've come all this way. I bet you're rubbish."'

Journalist Stephen Armstrong, in a piece for *The Sunday Times*, attended a recording of the show, and reported that the audience was a cross-section of the British public, 'hipsters, housewives and handymen'. The one thing they had in common was a love for Miss Hart. 'When Miranda stepped onto the studio floor and asked how many people had been at the previous week's show, more than half of them put their hands up and cheered. Studio audiences may respond like that for *Have I Got News For You*, but not for an as yet unscreened BBC Two scripted sitcom with no big names. As the show unfolded, though, it was clear why they had returned.'

Somehow, Hart had recaptured the feeling of a huge, knockabout 1970s British classic comedy such as *Are You*

Being Served?, but with a goofy modern edge. One of Miranda's biggest fans, a 16-year-old called Jess who is part of Miranda's NBLF (Nutty But Lovely Fivesome), has stated on her YouTube account that Miranda is her hero and 'the most amazing time of [her] life was meeting Miranda Hart after sitcom recording (14.11.10)'.

It seems, though, that critics and bloggers will still carp about Miranda's style as either negatively old-fashioned or a guilty pleasure. One *Daily Mail* critic, Paul Connolly, wrote, '*Miranda* really shouldn't work. If it were any more mired in Seventies sitcom clichés it would feature Terry Scott and June Whitfield in a shop called Grace Brothers. It's also terribly blighted by awful canned laughter and comedy signposts probably visible from Mars. Yet, despite all this, Miranda is occasionally very funny indeed.'

Quite apart from yet another misunderstanding of studio audience laughter, the writer is mostly right about the secret to *Miranda*'s success. But why does it have to be funny *despite* these things, rather than *because* of them? One of the writers on the show, James Cary, says, 'A show is no better or worse for harking back to the old days or having a feel of a bygone era about it. *Miranda* has attracted praise for being old-fashioned. But that is precisely the reason that some people hate it – or more specifically say daft things like "I shouldn't like it but…".'

So what is the future of British sitcom? Has *Miranda* heralded a move forward in looking backwards? It certainly seems so. Both *Miranda* and *Mrs Brown's Boys* have been recommissioned, and, for its third series, Miranda Hart and co. will be heading to BBC One primetime. Both shows play with the format, using new ways to break down the fourth wall and interact with the audience directly. But, as critic Bruce Dessau put it, 'This is not Brechtian *Verfremdunseffekt*, it is more about having a giggle.' And there's not much wrong with that, eh?

It's this spirit of fun that has made *Miranda* such a hit. And there are hints that to enjoy the show may soon become a socially acceptable stance. Hart has said that people have started telling her on the street that it is their guilty pleasure. 'It now feels like people are allowed to openly like an uncool show... I just thought, That's the kind of comedy I love, so why not embrace the genre wholly and go, guys, this is what I'm doing, and you really will have to like it or lump it.'

16

CLASS DISMISSED

'Forget class, it's the laughs that count in comedy.'
– Ray Galton and Alan Simpson,
creators of *Steptoe and Son*

Her privileged upbringing informs much of Miranda Hart's writing, both in the characters she has created, and the situations they are put in. While she has tried to step away from that background, for example in downplaying her accent when she was temping, she has defended others from similar origins: 'I have had a few conversations with people going, "Oh, I can't bear Jodie Kidd or Tara Palmer-Tomkinson, they're just spoiled," and then I find myself defending public-school people and going, "They can have suffered." It doesn't matter if you were brought up in a castle, you can still have tough times. I wasn't brought up in a castle, though!'

In late 2010, something happened that seemed to lock the comedy industry in a passionate debate. The *Daily Mail* reported that Danny Cohen, controller of BBC One, said that there were too many middle-class sitcoms, drowning out the 'blue-collar' sitcoms of the past, such as *Porridge*, *Only Fools and Horses* and *Steptoe and Son*.

At first, there was doubt as to the reliability of the statement. As writer James Cary noted, 'It isn't clear exactly when, where and how Danny Cohen said this, although he's made no secret of this desire over the last few weeks.'

Many of the papers quoted BBC insiders, who gave more insight into what the BBC One controller wanted. The *Telegraph* had this from someone who worked at the Beeb: '[Cohen] feels the BBC has lost its variety and become focused on formats about comfortable, well-off, middle-class families whose lives are perhaps more reflective of BBC staff than viewers in other parts of the UK.'

But it was the separation of class that upset some people, the idea that shows were being target at disparate groups. Another insider quoted in the *Daily Mail* said, 'If you look at *My Family* and *Outnumbered* they are a bit more middle class. It may be that, rather than having a comedy based in a nice house in Wandsworth, you could have it in a factory or something like that. The key point is to make everyone feel like they are engaged with BBC One.'

There was something of a knee-jerk reaction to this from some journalists. One *Daily Mail* reporter wrote, 'The suggestion that the BBC is "too middle class" has echoes of former director general Greg Dyke's claim in 2001 that the corporation was "hideously white".'

To avoid further speculation, Danny Cohen issued a press statement refuting any agenda based on class: 'We will work hard to capture the lives and experiences of a broad range of British people, but it's not right to suggest any one group will be given priority over others. BBC One is focused on working with Britain's most talented comedy writers and performers to get the best programming for our viewers.'

Despite Cohen's efforts, this did not calm the storm and the debate continued to rage. Ray Galton and Alan Simpson, the writers of *Steptoe and Son* and *Hancock's Half Hour*, who have been honoured with OBEs for their contribution to British television, felt impassioned to write a reactive piece for the *Daily Mail* about Cohen's reported remarks. 'You might think we'd be right behind this,' they wrote. 'After all, you can't get much more working-class than the two of us – the son of a milkman and the child of a bus conductor. And the characters of *Steptoe and Son*, the sitcom we created nearly 50 years ago, were working class, too.' But they went on to explain that, in their view, humour was more important than class: 'Cohen is missing the point, because good comedy is classless. It's not working-class characters in working-class situations that are inherently funny. It's people, families, relationships – wherever you find them – that make audiences laugh.'

The success of *Miranda* bears this out, and the audience figures suggest that people don't exclusively enjoy watching comedies which reflect their own lifestyles. James Cary has pointed out, 'Let us not forget that, at its peak, *Bread* pulled in about 22 million viewers. Let us also not forget that *To the Manor Born* pulled in 24 million viewers. Was it the same 20-odd million watching both programmes? Probably. I used to watch both of them. I didn't care. They were both brilliant.'

Writing for the *Telegraph*, Andrew Pettie echoed this sentiment: 'The idea that you should commission TV programmes along class lines is patronising and absurd; it implies that viewers only respond to a fictional world that mirrors their own. And what an idiotic notion that is: 10 million viewers were glued to the climax of *Downton Abbey*, yet I can't imagine many live in stately homes or ring a tiny, silver bell when they feel like changing the channel.'

From its first episode, screened five decades ago, Galton and Simpson's *Steptoe and Son* attracted a huge audience of all classes. It was an enormous success, running from 1962 to 1974. 'Though our protagonists were working-class men, our audiences came from all walks of life,' Steptoe's creators claimed, and added, 'The show attracted 28 million viewers at its peak... We were so popular that the Prime Minister, Harold Wilson, asked the BBC to delay transmission of our show on the night of the 1966 General Election until after the polls closed, so people could go out to vote rather than plonk themselves down in front of *Steptoe*.'

A key appeal of television is to reflect the lives of others and to explain different worlds, whether that be on the news, in documentaries or through soaps, dramas and sitcoms. Comedy writer Jeremy Lloyd (*Are You Being Served?*, *'Allo 'Allo!*) also entered the debate, insisting that the current state of Britain should not affect programming: 'Nor is the woeful state of our economy a reason to focus on blue-collar Britain. At times of difficulty we want to be taken out of ourselves, to laugh, to enjoy flights of fantasy. We do not always want to see our lives reflected back at us. That is what soap operas are for.'

Sam Leith at the *Guardian* extended the discussion to look at other class biases across television, but disagreed with a point made by Jeremy Lloyd: 'So we can concede Cohen's point; while suggesting, too, that he turns his eye to a far greater imbalance in the programming of another TV genre. What everyone with an earldom and a grouse moor will wonder is: where are the non-working-class soap operas?'

The truth is it doesn't matter – famous fans of *EastEnders* include Camilla, the Duchess of Cornwall. People will watch what they like, irrespective of their background or that of the characters in the show. Some comedy fans thought the whole debate laughable and made sarcastic comments on discussion boards. On the forum of the British Comedy Guide, one user called Dan, or 'swertyd', said, 'I watched that *The Smoking Room* and thought it was really good. But I've never smoked and generally get pissed off by those who do. Also, I like *Red Dwarf* a lot but have never been a spaceman nor have I been in the future. What should I watch? If somebody could inform me, that would be very pleasant.'

Comedy transcends class and unites what at other times may be disparate groups of people. The novelist Zadie Smith wrote about this in her essay *Dead Man Laughing*. She explained how going to Cambridge University and entering a middle-class world meant she had little in common with her father – apart from their appreciation of comedy: 'When meditating on the sitcom, you extrapolate from the details, which in Britain are almost always signifier of social class: Hancock's battered homburg, Fawlty's cravat, Partridge's driving gloves, Brent's fake Italian suits. It's a relief to be able to laugh at these things. In British comedy, the painful class dividers of real life are neutralised and exposed. In my family, at least, it was a way of talking about things we didn't want to talk about.'

To suggest that *Miranda*, which affectionately mocks middle-class and upper-class life, is only for those it depicts is ridiculous – it is for others to laugh at, and those who recognise themselves to laugh with. Jeremy Lloyd also wondered whether sitcoms endorse or send up the lifestyles of the people they depict. 'Take *The Good Life*, another enormous success in its day. Did it promote the woolly idealism of the middle classes, or make them look absurd? Or was it just plain funny?'

Boyd Hilton, *Heat* magazine's TV and reviews editor, says that the executives seem to be the only people not to realise that comedy appeals to all walks of life. 'I bet most viewers of all social backgrounds would be chuffed to see *Miranda*, for example, on BBC1, even though that show is also "painfully" middle-class (not painful for me, you understand, but painful perhaps for people who worry about these things – ie middle-class TV bigwigs).'

Other BBC shows whose impeccably middle-class credentials must have worried some of the Corporation's executives include the now-cancelled *My Family* and *Outnumbered*. *My Family* is set in a leafy part of West London, where dentist Ben Harper and his wife Susan live in an impressive family home. Together they have three children and Susan, who works in an art gallery, has an MBE for her charity work. *Outnumbered*, starring Claire Skinner and Hugh Dennis, is set in a similarly imposing house set in the fictional borough of Limebridge. Parents Pete and Sue are a teacher and part-time PA who deal with their rowdy and disobedient children while trying to save face with friends and neighbours. So far, so middle class. So what?

A puzzled Vicky Frost wrote in the *Guardian*, 'It's the kind of idea that leaves me scratching my head... Miranda, joke and trinket shop owner with pushy mother and "jolly hockey sticks" school friends, would presumably count as solidly middle-class. And yet I've always thought of her comedy – being rubbish with boys, rubbish at not being clumsy, rubbish at managing her mother – as being universal.'

Let's look back to James Cary's recipe for sitcom success: 'character + conflict + confinement +catastrophe +catchphrase +casting = comedy'. All those Cs – but no mention of class.

Conflict and confinement, agree Galton and Simpson, are far more important aspects: 'For all it mattered, Albert and Harold could have been vets or carpenters. What was most important was that they aspired to be somewhere else, but were stuck in their lives and with each other. Old man Albert Steptoe, played by Wilfrid Brambell, knew that if he loosened his grasp on his 38-year-old son Harold (Harry H. Corbett) he'd never return. But snobbish Harold saw glimpses of life outside Oil Drum Lane and knew he was missing out.'

Fellow veteran comedy writer Jeremy Lloyd feels much the same, arguing that 'situation' is the less important component of the sitcom: 'It is a mistake... to assume that a setting, be it a housing estate or a mansion, is what defines the humour on offer.'

More important than class or profession is that the characters are trapped and have aspirations they can never realise. Miranda is doubly trapped – both by her mother and the societal expectations imposed on her. Galton and Simpson wrote of her, 'Though her character is from a well-to-do family, she is still a loser with ambitions that will never be fulfilled and a love life that will never succeed.'

It could also be argued that, despite Danny Cohen's reported call for more 'blue-collar' sitcoms, times have changed. The *Guardian*'s Sam Leith wrote, 'The simple thing to say is that, since a working class doesn't exist in the form it did 40 years ago, sitcoms depicting it as if it did aren't to be expected. The notable successes in recent years – *The Royle Family* and *Shameless* – both portrayed a working class unrecognisable to the Galton and Simpson generation.'

Leith went on to suggest that Cohen's statement may have been a warning against a growing belief that everyone is now middle class, 'not because it's unrepresentative, but because it's less funny. The best British sitcoms have tended to probe the deepest British anxiety: that is, class itself.'

It is true that British comedy focuses on class, not just in sitcom, but in stand-up comedy and sketches. Armstrong and Miller's sketches involving the World War Two RAF pilots who talk like 21st-century 'youths' is a case in point. Catherine Tate's schoolgirl character Lauren 'Am I Bovvered?' and *Little Britain*'s Vicky 'No but yeah but' Pollard are examples of popular working-class characters, while Harry Enfield's Tim Nice But Dim and *The Fast Show*'s Ralph, played by Charlie Higson, are affectionate caricatures of upper-class society. In stand-up comedy, Steve Coogan's Paul and Pauline Calf characters are much-loved portrayals of Manchester's working class. More recently, Russell Kane's award-winning Edinburgh show, *Smokescreens and Castles*, focused on the differences between his archetypal working-class father and him, an arts graduate with a love for yoga and Penguin Classics. It was the first show in history to win both the Edinburgh Comedy

Award and the Barry Award for the best show at the Melbourne International Comedy Awards.

The debate about BBC One sitcoms and class inspired members of the public to speak up about contemporary comedy about Britain's working-class population. They may not be the bygone, almost romantic, portrayal of the working classes in Galton and Simpson's era, but readers of the *Guardian* website offered some modern illustrations: 'How is *The Office* not a working-class comedy?' asks stlemur, while LondonPhil suggests, 'aren't *Gavin & Stacey* working-class?' The same could be said for *dinnerladies*, *Peter Kay's Phoenix Nights*, *Still Game*, *Gimme Gimme Gimme*, *Rab C Nesbitt*, *Early Doors*, *Time Gentlemen Please* and BBC One's latest BAFTA-nominated hit *Mrs Brown's Boys*.

Miranda's transfer to BBC One for its third series seems to fly in the face of the recent concerns about sitcoms being too middle class, and suggests that such a commissioning agenda wasn't so clear cut. It doesn't get much more middle class than *Miranda* – the product of a public-school education who spends her inheritance on a joke shop, but spends most of her time as a lady of leisure, panicking about various social occasions. There are no worries about where the next rent cheque is coming from; it is more about reacting to her mother's middle-class expectations and eccentricities. One of the most vivid examples of this is when Penny comes to the shop to give Miranda 'social training' ahead of attending the Henley Regatta.

Some of the idiosyncrasies are based on recognisable aspects of middle- and upper-class society, while the writers give it an additional surreal quality. The idea that there is a 'laugh of the season', usually a pop song for ladies to base their laughs on

– in the first series it is 'Barbie Girl' by Aqua and in the second series 'Poker Face' by Lady Gaga.

But, however hard Penny tries to coach her, Miranda usually ends up making a fool of herself in social situations, whether it's by accidentally getting naked at a formal garden party – 'The shirt's run off with the jumper like a whore!' – or not knowing how to respond to questions about the Chinese human rights record: 'I think... if my thighs are sweaty and I stand up, it sounds like I've done a fart.' The fact that she moves in these circles magnifies the social embarrassment as the situations have such strict codes of conduct and rules of interaction. Miranda removing her top by accident wouldn't have quite the same comic impact if the joke had appeared in *The Royle Family*.

As well as examining social etiquette, the show's class is cemented in the language it uses. In addition to using some ridiculously posh names, the sitcom has developed a lingo of its own, invented by Tilly, Sally Phillips' character. It is the sort of language which Miranda is desperate to avoid using whenever possible. While on a date with Dreamboat Charlie, she panics and says to Gary and Clive that if she went with him she would end up with a black Labrador called Jaspar, pronounced 'jar-spar'.

Miranda reveals herself to be a total outcast, neither fitting in with Penny and Tilly's sort, nor being comfortable with those outside their class bubble. She gently mocks but tries to blend in with both, mimicking the voices of the girls who come into the shop as well as the shop assistants at the bed store – 'I've caught her accent!'

What was revealed by this discussion was that class is

irrelevant, as long as the show is funny. Galton and Simpson have pointed out what would be lost if only working-class sitcoms were commissioned: 'If BBC1's campaign to move away from "middle-class" comedies is successful, we'd tragically be denied the recent delight of *Miranda*, starring Miranda Hart, who has just collected three gongs at the British Comedy Awards.'

The idea of comedy meeting quotas or ticking the boxes of various demographics annoyed some, including writer Jeremy Lloyd: 'I was lucky enough to write when there were few such restrictions. I was not expected to reflect the working, middle or upper classes. I was simply expected to write something that was funny. It's comedy, not politics, after all.'

In the light of Miranda winning a hat-trick of British Comedy Awards (notably one award voted for by the public), Vicky Frost for the *Guardian* added her thoughts: 'As *Miranda*'s hard-won people's choice award on Saturday night showed, there's a lot of people who find someone going on a bonkers escapade, falling down and then mugging frantically to camera hilarious. Whether Miranda is shop owner or shop assistant has very little to do with it.'

Perhaps surprisingly, one of the most insightful arguments against this class-selection plan came from former Conservative politician Ann Widdecombe. She compared the argument about class in sitcoms to how she felt as a woman in parliament – that it doesn't matter what gender an MP is as long as they are a good one: 'Excellence should never play second fiddle to political correctness. Why does that seem so obvious to me and so unthinkable to some media bosses and the PM's office alike?'

Galton and Simpson concluded their opinion piece in the *Daily Mail* with a simple statement: 'The best comedies are funny regardless of whether their characters operate at the depths of society or in middle-class comfort.'

And instead of avoiding middle-class sitcoms such as *Miranda*, Danny Cohen has in fact moved the programme from BBC Two to BBC One. So the profile of the show is only likely to rise still further.

17

THE ART OF
THE PRATFALL

*'Miranda Hart deserves a medal, or better still a BAFTA,
for reminding us that slapstick can be funny.'*
— Brian Viner, *the Independent*

When *Miranda* arrived on BBC Two in November 2009, journalists and bloggers alike commented that it hailed the return of slapstick. It is often cited as one of the key reasons for the sitcom's success, though that same aspect has led some to avoid it. *Miranda* is ridding slapstick of its labels of 'simplistic' or 'old-fashioned' by bringing it to a new audience and reinventing it for the 21st century. Its central character is a female Frank Spencer coping with modern problems such as negotiating gym contracts, getting trapped in sushi bars and trying not to end up naked in public parks.

Miranda loves slapstick and appreciates how her physical stature has enhanced her performance. 'I like stumbling, but I prefer falling. Actually, now my height is a huge advantage. It makes slapstick comedy seem far more natural. Think of John Cleese towering over Manuel. If anything, the producers have to stop me doing pratfalls every few seconds.'

As a child, Miranda was upset at being different and so clumsy, 'because [she] didn't realise how wide [her] wingspan was'. Now, she has made a career out of flailing her limbs in front of millions of devoted viewers. She has even jokingly cited Naomi Campbell as a fellow tall lady of slapstick: 'Yes, I'm like Naomi in so many ways. I've watched her falling off her Westwood platforms thousands of times for inspiration. I guess I didn't realise how awkward I felt about being tall until I started playing on it. And then I found that pratfalling comes very naturally to me.'

While *Miranda* is the first slapstick-heavy sitcom on primetime BBC for a while, slapstick is still popular, it's just usually found in different places. Think of the YouTube videos that get passed around – even cats are becoming the new Chaplins. You don't even need to look beyond your television set. Saturday-night listings are filled with it, but this time the public is the star. Reality television and game shows have brought a surge of slapstick to our weekend viewing. If you like *Hole in the Wall*, *Total Wipeout* or the long-running *You've Been Framed*, then you like slapstick.

But where did this fascination with slapstick start? It has been around since long before the inception of television itself, and can be found in the work of Monty Python, Vic and Bob, Mr Bean, and even the alternative comedy of the 1980s. The birth of modern slapstick came with the first-ever publicly screened film by the Lumiere brothers, who were French pioneers of moving pictures. The film, which has been imitated numerous times, was shown in a Parisian café in 1895 showing a gardener having a little trouble with his hose. A prankster steps on the hose and the water stops flowing.

The gardener, perturbed, looks down the hose to see what might be the problem and – yes, of course you guessed it – the water flow resumes and the gardener is met with a forceful spurt in the face. Much fist-shaking and chasing ensues.

But we need to go back even further for the first recorded mention of slapstick – to the 16th-century Comedia Dell'Arte, when an Italian improvisational theatre group merged physical theatre with that inexplicably hilarious possibility of pain. Slapstick spread as an art form, gracing theatres and music halls across Europe – until the Lumiere brothers shifted it into a new era with the screening of their film. Moving pictures were the hot new thing and, without sound, performances needed to be visual. The perfect medium for slapstick.

Even in our own lifetimes, many of us were brought up with slapstick – watching Punch beat his wife Judy, the crocodile and the policeman to a pulp, usually over nothing but a much-coveted string of sausages. Clowns at birthday parties and at circuses throughout our childhood combine slapstick and juggling to create an act using heightened moments of violence as absurd situations escalate. And, put simply, what's funnier than pushing your sibling over? Apart from Stephen Fry spectacularly walloping Hugh Laurie, I can't think of anything.

But why do we find others' pain so comical? Freud has discussed it in his 'Wit and Its Relation to the Unconscious', but perhaps the easiest way to sum it up here is that we all have an instinctive desire to witness cruelty at some level. Slapstick gives us the chance to experience this vicariously without guilt – we can watch people suffering without it being real. The Germans perhaps put it best with their term *schadenfreude*, which is derived from *Schaden* (harm) and *Freude* (joy). Although it does not translate into English, *schadenfreude* translates to slapstick because it means we can laugh at the pain because it isn't happening to us. As Mel Brooks, director of comedies such as *Blazing Saddles* and *The Producers*, says, 'Tragedy is when I cut my finger. Comedy is when you fall into an open sewer and die.'

If you think this is something we develop as we get older and become more cynical, I urge you to look up the hit internet video 'Charlie bit my finger – again!', in which a baby laughs hysterically at his brother cries of pain after biting his finger. More than 300 million people can't be wrong – it's just funny.

Slapstick is a primitive, instinctive form of humour. Many think it childish or simple, some see it as a guilty pleasure, but, as audience ratings consistently prove, it is universal. As comedian Ben Miller says, it 'gets you somewhere right in your gut'. The dictionary defines slapstick as 'comedy based on deliberately clumsy actions and humorously embarrassing events' and also 'a device consisting of two flexible pieces of wood joined together at one end, used by clowns and in pantomime to produce a loud slapping noise'. So... it's literally a slap stick.

The first stars of screen slapstick predate television and even talkies and, as the American film industry grew, hundreds of silent comedies were released between 1910 and 1929. This golden age of slapstick saw household names born, stars that are still renowned today – Laurel and Hardy, Harold Lloyd, Charlie Chaplin and Buster Keaton. Paul Merton brought these performers back into the public consciousness with his BBC

Four series and subsequent tour *Silent Clowns*. The comedian shared his passion for the subject with theatre audiences across the country, showing films by these four acts interspersed with entertaining and informative chat.

There was one Buster Keaton piece in particular shown on the tour that struck audiences. Keaton is well known for performing his own stunts and a set piece in *Steamboat Bill, Jr.* (1928) has become one of the most iconic cinematic images ever, certainly in silent comedy. Buster is standing in the middle of a street when the front of a house falls on him. He narrowly escapes death, a window slotting perfectly over him. Merton has commented, 'In 2007, I showed this film to 1,500 people at The Colston Hall in Bristol. The spontaneous round of applause that rang around the hall as Buster stepped safely away from the wreckage will long remain in my memory.'

Veteran comedian Barry Cryer has said of the sequence: 'You can watch it again and again and still marvel at it, the perfection of the calculation involved and the skill of his relaxed persona.'

The danger involved in the stunt is another reason for its legacy. The front of the house was substantially weighted and, had it hit him, he almost certainly would have died. Many imitations followed on television, from *Some Mothers Do 'Ave 'Em* to *The Goodies*, but none made quite the impression of the first wave of film slapstick stars.

While the American Keaton was astounding us with his stunts, far and away the biggest star of the era was from London. Charlie Chaplin had all the elements of great slapstick – athleticism and timing – but he also brought poignancy and satire to the genre with his feature *The Great*

Dictator. Chaplin was a perfectionist. While his performances seemed spontaneous, he rehearsed sequences up to 30 or 40 times before he was happy with the take. Sadly, the arrival of sound signalled the beginning of the end for Chaplin. People didn't like his voice and that was the end of his career. Fortunately, though, Chaplin inspired many future comedy stars in Britain, the closest to a silent clown being Rowan Atkinson as Mr Bean. The fact that he doesn't speak words gives him an alien quality and helps to create a purely visual comedy. It also means that it transcends language and has become one of British comedy's most successful characters, selling to more than 200 countries worldwide. They say that imitation is the most sincere form of flattery, but Alexei Sayle's parody of Mr Bean, Monsieur Aubergine, played with the infuriating side of the character. 'Monsieur Aubergine was in the real world, so it was sort of playing with that. If someone was really behaving like that in the real world, just how obnoxious would they be?'

The smoothest transition from silent films to talkies was experienced by Laurel and Hardy. Stan and Ollie's voices seemed to suit their characters and they broadly stuck to visual comedy. Stan Laurel, who wrote the scripts, was talented in creating situations conducive to physical comedy.

By the 1950s, slapstick was sweeping across British entertainment on television, and stars like Norman Wisdom and Charlie Drake became hugely popular. Television was nearly always live, there wasn't the option to strive for perfectionism (a luxury Chaplin had enjoyed in cinema), and so things inevitably did go wrong. In one sequence, Drake was dragged through a bookcase during a live broadcast.

The furniture itself was designed to break away, but the shelves were loaded with books and were very heavy. The actor passed out mid-scene from the blow but, rather than give him medical assistance, his co-star picked him up and threw him out of the set window. The show must go on, as they say.

One much-loved British performer was Max Wall, who kept one act going his entire working life. Having started off in music halls, he would basically gurn and do funny walks right into his seventies. But it worked. His most famous character was Professor Wallofski who, according to some, performed the moonwalk years before Michael Jackson.

The biggest star of the 1950s was Mr Pastry, a slapstick character played by Richard Hearne. Though largely forgotten now, he was such a success that, in the 1970s, Hearne was asked to take over from Jon Pertwee as the Doctor in *Doctor Who*. However, when Hearne insisted that he should play the Doctor in the style of Mr Pastry, the producer of the show decided to go with Tom Baker instead, who has become many fans' favourite Doctor.

The Goons were the first to bring slapstick to the radio, with their uniquely surreal brand of humour. They proved, according to Neil Innes of The Bonzo Dog Doo-Dah Band, that 'the pen is mightier than the budget'. How to make a visual joke in an audio medium? A problem Miranda Hart would face during the making of *Joke Shop* on BBC Radio 2.

The Goon Show, which ran on BBC Radio throughout the 1950s, was a hugely influential show, especially to an exciting new breed of Oxbridge-educated future comedians who would later call themselves Monty Python. Since their ground-breaking TV series, *Monty Python's Flying Circus* (1969–74), they have been routinely regarded as comedy heroes by comedians, but the Pythons themselves were inspired by the Goons. *The Goon Show* added surrealism to slapstick, and the Pythons added to that intellectualism and a level of sophistication. Where they used slapstick, they would confound expectation and play with established rules of the form. Their unique take on slapstick was successful worldwide and they sold out the Hollywood Bowl with their 1980 live show.

The rise of Python coincided with that of *The Goodies* (Tim Brooke-Taylor, Bill Oddie and Graeme Garden), with a brand of slapstick which appealed to all ages. The whole family from kids to parents and even grandparents enjoyed this silly show. Some critics suggested it was a kids' show, but – as with *Miranda* – high ratings proved that this is what the audience wanted. *Miranda*'s Sally Phillips (aka Tilly) has remarked that slapstick is ageless. '[It's] something adults and children can share – chases and smacking each other over the head.' The childlike nature of *The Goodies* made for great escapism and the way the trio played with tradition showed their familiarity with the old greats.

But undoubtedly the biggest family favourite of the 1970s, and a huge inspiration to Miranda Hart, was *The Morecambe and Wise Show*. They used slapstick throughout the show, from Eric smacking Ernie round the head to carefully choreographed set pieces. Their impeccably timed breakfast routine has become one of their best known, and many present-day stars acknowledge the influence of Eric Morecambe. Mathew Horne, star of *Gavin and Stacey*, is one:

'The way he moved his body was funny and he knew that. He knew how to use it as a flourish on the end of jokes.'

The 1970s was the golden age of television slapstick in Britain but the biggest and most memorable character in sitcom was the hapless, clumsy Frank Spencer, played in *Some Mothers Do 'Ave 'Em* by Michael Crawford. Crawford, a huge star on stage and screen, performed his own perilous stunts. He has become an iconic slapstick star and some journalists have made comparisons with Miranda, referring to her as 'Francesca Spencer'.

By the time the 1980s came around, audiences were ready for change. It came in the form of 'alternative comedy' from the likes of Rik Mayall, Ade Edmondson, Ben Elton and Alexei Sayle. *The Young Ones* continued the slapstick tradition but took it to new heights of violence. The nation was politically divided and the anarchic students expressed the anger of many through their aggression and hostility. The stars of the show were Rik and Ade whose act 'The Dangerous Brothers' had become much talked about on the cabaret circuit. With no stunt doubles, the cast regularly got cuts and bruises. In the 1990s, the pair went on to create their sitcom *Bottom* which pushed the limits of slapstick. The extreme violence of their work adhered to Freud's theory of our desire to see suffering, and making the characters so pathetic – but likeably so – made them perfect victims.

Even though *Bottom* finished on television in 1995, live shows continued until 2003, and in *Let's Dance for Comic Relief 2011*, the pair reunited in a frying-pan-to-the-face version of *Swan Lake*. Their *Young Ones* co-star Alexei Sayle has said that, during the show's original run in the 1980s, he thought 'they'd be doing that stuff until they were 90'. And he may be right. Fans are excited about a rumoured forthcoming sitcom set in a nursing home that Edmondson describes as 'like *Bottom*, but we will be hitting each other with colostomy bags'. Even a life-threatening quad-bike accident in 1998 didn't seem to stop Rik Mayall for too long. In his autobiography *Bigger Than Hitler, Bigger Than Christ*, he joked that he 'rose from the dead'.

The 1990s brought the joyous antics of Vic Reeves and Bob Mortimer, with cartoon-like slapstick which was so absurd and likeable that they went from student cult hit to running series after series of *Shooting Stars*. And they're still at it today. Their comedy comprises elements of Jacques Tati, Laurel and Hardy, and even Max Wall's absurd body movements. Vic Reeves has described the act as unjustified violence: 'There's no reason for it. It's almost like we enjoy doing it. When we hit each other, we do actually hit each other – we've got the scars to prove it.'

More recently, Lee Evans brought slapstick physicality to his stand-up comedy and acting work; Jennifer Saunders and Joanna Lumley's characters did inimitable, drunken pratfalls in *Ab Fab*; and *The League of Gentlemen* examined the darker side of the genre. In recent times, sketch act We Are Klang have been described as the new Goodies, bringing silly violence to a traditional sitcom set.

These days, stunt doubles for comedians are more necessary due to health and safety requirements. In a reunion show for the three members of The Goodies, the producer insisted that they didn't ride the famous three-seater bicycle because they couldn't insure them.

Miranda has confessed to occasionally using a stuntman, but does perform many of the stunts herself. On director David Baddiel's video diary for his film *The Infidel*, he spoke to Hart about slapstick. She had cuts and bruises all over her arm and he apologised, asking if she normally has a stunt double. She admitted she sometimes does, but the last time she did she had to have a man to match her height. 'It was actually embarrassing for us both. He had to wear a wedding dress, put his hair up, and the worst thing was someone came up to me thinking that I was the guy.'

Although a double is used, the majority of slapstick moments – falling off stools, over boxes, into a hat stand – were performed by Miranda herself. This took its toll on her body, as she revealed on Twitter: 'Day 2 of rehearsals and a packet of peas has come out to stop bruising. I am basically an athlete. One look at me and that is obvious.'

As more rules and regulations hit TV, the public went elsewhere for their hit of slapstick. Internet video sites such as YouTube became the go-to place for computer users and *You've Been Framed*, *Hole in the Wall* and *Total Wipeout* have been feeding the technophobes' appetites. With things getting more and more violent and uncensored slapstick testing out limits, it was about time for a gentler form of slapstick to fill the gap. Cue *Miranda*.

As slapstick has reinvented itself many times over the years, comedians have had to find new ways of performing the same old gags. Miranda has become its poster girl with her impeccably timed pratfalls that add to her social awkwardness. It shows the joke-shop owner doing her very best to fit in and be liked, but ultimately failing, and often embarrassing herself through her physicality. One of the most memorable moments from the second series is when she is walking with her mother Penny talking about how embarrassed she was at a funeral. She didn't know who had died and was forced to make a speech about the deceased. Pacing through the graveyard to escape the awkward situation, she says that it was 'mortifying! I wish the ground could have swallowed me up', and instantly falls headfirst into an open grave. Despite being quite clearly telegraphed, the gag is so perfectly timed that most viewers quite understandably emitted a raucous belly laugh.

On set, immediately after the scene was filmed, Miranda said, 'It was actually quite frightening because normally, if I fall over, the crash mat is just there, and this was like a massive hole. You know, so I was falling quite fast. I was a little bit nervous.' But the comedian was so sure about the gag that she committed to the laugh and, quite literally, threw herself into it. On Alan Carr's talk show *Chatty Man*, she said that, despite being scared, she loved doing it because she knew it would work: 'It's not that often I'm confident that something will get a laugh but I kind of thought, If this doesn't get a laugh, I'm in trouble. So I really enjoyed it.' On her blog, she revealed that it is her favourite ever pratfall and she is very proud of it.

Another favourite slapstick moment is the yoga-ball stunt in the series one episode 'Job'. The crew members were concerned about Hart performing it, but she reassured them by saying, 'I am going to put two yoga balls slightly apart, run up to them, my torso will be on the front one and my legs on the second and I will travel across the gym.' Her insistence she had done it before calmed their insurance worries, but she actually did it before with two large rolls of bubble wrap while working in an office. She spectacularly re-enacted the yoga-ball moment live on *The Graham Norton Show*, much to the delight of her fellow guests and the studio audience.

A recurring theme in Miranda's slapstick is her trying to look cool or attempting to impress someone and ending up falling off, on to or over something. She is constantly trying to 'sweep' out of Gary's restaurant, only to tumble against the coat rack. In the very first episode, she falls over some boxes and tries to regain her composure, saying, 'It's all about the recovery, isn't it?' before collapsing into a second pile of stock. With all this falling over, you might expect Miranda to be covered in cuts and bruises and you'd probably be right. But, thankfully, there's nothing more serious than that. When Stuart Husband interviewed her for the *Telegraph*, he discovered the star 'receiving visitors in a horizontal manner'. No, not in that way (how rude!), but because of her damaged knee. Rather than from an elaborate stunt, it was nothing more than bending over to tie up her shoelaces while filming the second series.

Miranda isn't the only cast member to regularly fall over. Stevie, the dedicated joke-shop manager played by Sarah Hadland, is forever pushed off her stool for landing her friend in trouble or embarrassment, or for simply being competition for a man. Hadland has said of the series' use of slapstick and cartoon violence, 'It's not cruel, it's not being horrible – we're all completely flawed characters, all of us are a bit inept. So I think that helps. It's not cruel in any way. Except the pushing that goes on, which is fairly cruel.' But this sort of behaviour only endears us even more to the characters, resulting in even bigger laughs. Sarah jokes, 'I mean I'm in hospital when we're not filming. I'm basically undergoing reconstructive surgery.'

The relentless tripping, stumbling, galumphing and falling is one of the show's biggest appeals, but some were unsure about sitcom slapstick returning to our screens. 'Physical humour has become as unfashionable as Jim Davidson in the world of television comedy and much of Miranda's work comes across as camp and a bit daft,' remarked one *Metro* reviewer.

Others were converted, including one writer for website Unreality Primetime: 'It's funny; it's very funny, and I really wasn't expecting it to be, primarily because before I watched it myself, I'd heard the word "slapstick" in relation to it, and I'm always wary of that.'

But Miranda proved her worth in the ways of stacking it, and fellow comedian David Baddiel extolled her talent: 'The idea that a tall woman falling over is just a tall woman falling over is nonsense. Slapstick is the most complex weapon to employ in any comic armoury: it requires enormous technical skill and choreography not to look naff.'

So, despite cynics, *Miranda* has proved that we have an appetite for slapstick and filled the hole created by mockumentaries and health and safety constraints. Miranda retains her childishness and avoids the boringness of adulthood by slipping on social banana skins. She looks at adult problems with an immaturity we can enjoy vicariously. I'm sure not many of us would have the guts to attempt to get out of gym membership by threatening to wee in a ball pool or fill the swimming pool with dogs. Miranda does that for us. 'Anything for a gag. I'm committed,' she has said.

Slapstick will always be around, it may go in and out of fashion, but we have a basic urge to laugh at people falling over. For comedy historians, it's fascinating to see how silent comedy stars from decades ago still inform what comedians do today. And it's universal – it doesn't matter what gender you are, how old you are, or where you're from. As Vic Reeves says, 'The first things as a kid that you laugh at are poo and falling over. I've brought up kids and I've studied them to see what makes them laugh and that's it. And it should carry on through the rest of your life.'

18

THE DIFFICULT
SECOND ALBUM

*'More Miranda? That news puts an enormous smile on my face.
From its life on radio and all the way through to BBC One –
that's a great story.'*
– Mark Freeland, Head of Comedy at the BBC

It was a combination of all these previously discussed aspects, then – the old-fashioned style, the slapstick, the characters, the casting and the brilliant writing – that helped make the first series of *Miranda* such a success in late 2009. It was, however, something of a surprise hit, audiences growing as word spread. It became one of those shows talked about at work the next day, and it seemed inevitable that a second series would be commissioned.

News that the BBC would make another series came as something of a relief for the show's star and creator: 'I was far more nervous than I thought I would be about the series going out,' Miranda said in December 2010. 'I am not only relieved but totally overwhelmed by the response and thrilled that people have enjoyed the series. I am very grateful for all the support and to the BBC for giving me the chance to do another series next year. A daunting, but delightful Christmas present!'

Janice Hadlow, controller of BBC Two, announced by way of a press release: 'Miranda is a fantastic talent and it's no surprise that her first television series has been an instant hit.'

The show's executive producer Jo Sargent, who originally cast Miranda when she was producer of *Absolutely Fabulous*, commented, 'We are delighted to be working with Miranda on a second series. She is a unique and extraordinary comic talent who has the ability to talk to a broad audience who can identify with her and all her quirks and foibles.'

Would series two see Miranda struggle with 'second-album syndrome'? Anticipation was high among journalists and fans alike. Jack Seale, writer for the *Radio Times*, wrote, 'For us fans, Miranda and chums are a fun gang that we feel a part of – and, while it's funny when she gets stuck in a chair or trips over a hat stand, the scripts are much sharper and more heartfelt than they initially appear.'

Filming for series two began on 19 September 2010. Hart announced on Twitter on that date: 'First scene of series two in the bag. Oooooh.' But the shoot hit its first obstacle when an unexpected injury for one crew member meant further filming had to be delayed. People who had audience tickets for the filming expressed their disappointment on Twitter, so Miranda replied to each of them with an apology: 'SO sorry. There was a serious injury we hoped would be overcome for show but will take longer. Did all we could. We're equally gutted. [sic]'

The disappointed fans were given tickets to alternative recordings, where possible, and on Monday, 15 November at 8.30, less than two months after filming had begun, 'The New Me' became the first episode of series two to be broadcast. As usual, Hart wrote a trailer blog on the BBC website: 'The first question people are asking me is: did Gary go to Hong Kong/will he come back? Well, the answer to that is so top secret that not even I know the answer – and I wrote the episode. I will reveal this though: this series there are some serious boy problems and excitements along the way. Oooh, web exclusive alert.'

The series opens with Miranda in a state – she's not coping well with Gary having left for Hong Kong. She spends all day in her pyjamas and a dirty fleece, eating biscuits and generally sulking. Stevie shows her a postcard that arrived from Gary – it's a very brief generic message and Miranda is hugely disappointed, so she decides it's time to move on and be a better person. She dreams up a brilliantly observed monologue that sums up just the sort of woman Miranda despises – most likely because she knows she can never be like them. But things don't exactly start off well. At a sushi lunch with Tilly and their old head girl Stinky (Belinda Stewart-Wilson), Miranda gets her necklace caught and ends up having to mount the conveyor belt. They go to Conky's Grill instead, where they meet Gary's replacement, Danny (played by Michael Landes). They all swoon at his good looks and American accent. Miranda makes her usual glittering first impression – as she later recounts to Stevie, 'I farted in front of him, blamed it on an imaginary dog and sang in his face.'

She goes shopping for a new bed to replace the one she broke by jumping up and down on while listening to S Club 7, and trying to catch the sweets that Stevie was throwing at her. A customer assumes that she is working as the shop's new assistant Sandy and, despite Miranda's protests, she ends up working a four-hour shift. She does find new strength, though, when she talks to the girls in the staff room. They talk about how rubbish men are, and encourage Miranda to move on. The only trouble is, of course, that they are talking to her as if she's their new colleague, Sandy. Having decided to renounce men, Miranda quickly changes her mind when Danny comes into the shop to ask her out. The date goes miraculously well and he ends up at her flat. Despite the fact that Penny is present the entire time, trying to hide but topping up his whiskey glass when he turns his head, Miranda manages to make a good impression.

The next day, she goes to the restaurant and Tilly, Stinky and Clive are all astonished when Danny kisses her. Everything seems to be going according to her 'new me' plan, but then... Gary walks in! She immediately falls off her stool, a cake falls and splats all over her. Gary gets his old job back and Danny decides to take a job in Birmingham that he saw advertised. Everything is back to normal again.

And critics and fans were delighted with it. Miranda's Twitter account was flooded with adoration from fans. Phil Hogan wrote for *The Observer*, 'The second series of *Miranda* started as her fans hope it means to go on, with a taxi whipping off her party dress and roaring away with it caught in the door. Magnificent... what a show! Listen to that live studio audience – a pit of hyenas feeding on their own laughter. More! More!'

Miranda obliged the following week in an episode called 'Before I Die': 'So, here we are: episode two. Bit of a strange episode this – I usually choose a theme for each episode and try and make the stories as interesting as possible with as many twists and turns around that theme, but this episode I remember throwing more threads than normal at it. So hopefully it will gel and not be too manic!'

The first storyline begins – bam! – as Miranda struggles to work her fancy new phone and accidentally deletes a message she missed the beginning of. This means that she ends up at a funeral without knowing who has died. The situation gets worse when she is asked to give a eulogy for the deceased and has to play something of a parlour game, responding to the congregation's reaction to make her next guess. She manages to scrape through the situation but is mortified with embarrassment nonetheless. Charging back through the graveyard, Miranda tells her mother that she wishes the ground could have swallowed her up when... she falls into an open grave. She is naturally shaken and starts to consider her own mortality and what people might say at her funeral. She decides she needs to make more of a difference so puts her name down to do voluntary work at the local hospice but, in typical Miranda style, she ends up getting thrown out for scaring them into a screaming state. Even singing wartime classic 'The White Cliffs of Dover' doesn't manage to calm them down. She decides to try something else and signs up for a parachute jump.

Chris and Alison (who previously appeared in the tango-lesson sequence of the series one episode 'Teacher') make another appearance in this episode. Hart informed her blog readers that they aren't based on anyone in particular, but they represent the sort of couple 'who are nauseatingly "couple-y"...' She went on: 'Couples that speak at the same time, think it is fun to wear matching jumpers, show far too many public displays of affection and give far too much information about their personal life when we really really really don't want to hear it. Particularly when it comes to breast feeding or how somebody's labour was – shush, shut up, we don't want to know.'

Miranda's character is similarly appalled when they ask her and Gary to be godparents to their unborn child, impressed by all the good that she is doing. Not because she doesn't want to be a godmother, but because it means Miranda would also be Alison's birthing partner. She tries to get out of it, but, when Alison is sickeningly supportive of her doubts, she realises there is only one thing she can do: 'I will have to do something intrinsically evil.'

So she goes to the library to borrow *Mein Kampf*. However, she falls asleep in the children's area with a kids' book on her lap and the librarian assumes she is there to read a story. Miranda goes along with the charade, but regrets it when a delighted Chris and Alison spot her. 'She's going to be our own Mary Poppins!' they exclaim.

Now at her wits' end, Miranda decides the only way to get out of the situation is quite simple. Having punched a vicar ('I just punched a vicar!'), she then begins to get recognised – firstly by someone who knew she was volunteering at the hospital, and then by a lady who also signed up for the parachute jump. Penny is astonished to see this and proudly introduces her to other guests.

The third episode, 'Let's Do It', is what Miranda has called the 'sexi-pode'. Hart heralded its broadcast with a blog announcement: 'Oh yes, my alter-ego gets some male attention this week. So prepare for my attempt at romance. Hopefully,

I will have pulled it off – as it very much were. (Steady on, family show.)'

It begins with Tilly's husband Rupert back home on leave, so Penny is even more desperate than usual to find Miranda a man. They are planning for Tilly's wedding and Penny is dreading Miranda turning up without a date. But Stevie and Clive know who Miranda should go with, and so stage an intervention, forcing Gary and Miranda to go on a date. Gary agrees but Miranda is a little more wary and answers his question: 'Humiliation, embarrassment, fire, explosions, collisions, tears, nudity and death. But that was just bad luck including a rogue crème brûlée torch – it's very unlikely to happen twice. So let's go for it.'

On the date, Gary suggests that, to get rid of the awkwardness between them, they should sleep together. But this doesn't quite go to plan, as we've already seen. Things become more complicated when Miranda meets Tilly for a wedmin lunch ('wedding admin, keep up'). Dreamboat Charlie is there, the awful man she went on a blind date with in the first series. He is trying to get Miranda's knickers off, as usual, and Rupert ('Call me The Bear!'), Tilly's fiancé, gets rather too close for comfort.

Miranda and Gary sneak off to the park and he suggests that they do it *al fresco* (which Miranda confuses with the phrase 'al dente'). Penny and Tilly, looking at flowers for wedding inspiration, interrupt the pair, and they give the pathetic excuse that they were looking for animals, 'because apparently animals have escaped from the local circus'.

With Miranda having told Gary she finds rushing for any spare moment is far too pressurised, Tilly and Rupert come by the flat. Stevie tells Miranda that she should set a honey trap so that Tilly can find out what Rupert is really like. But just as this seems to be going a little too well for Miranda's comfort, Dreamboat Charlie turns up at her window and climbs into the kitchen. She hides him in the bathroom while Rupert is waiting in the bedroom. Exhausted, she turns to camera with a knowing look and says, 'This is turning into a French farce!' Then Gary arrives in only a dressing gown and things are looking up, but in burst Penny, Tilly and Stevie, seeing Miranda with the half-naked Gary. Then Dreamboat Charlie throws the bathroom door open, revealing him wearing very little and shouting 'Mirandy!' Rupert exits the bedroom in just his underwear proclaiming, 'I must have you!', before spotting that his fiancée is in the room. Everyone stares in shocked silence apart from Penny, who is delighted: 'Go, Miranda!'

Miranda tells Gary she can explain the situation, but that she had better look after Tilly first.

Gary tells her not to worry and that it will happen if it's meant to. Miranda turns to camera and says, exasperated, 'It better!'

'This episode I call my soap opera episode,' Hart said on her blog of 'A New Low', the fourth episode, 'as there's a bit of a sad twist at the end. Ooh, exciting, how can you NOT tune in now?! Marvellouso, enjoy-ingtons.'

Miranda and Stevie compete over which of them is better friends with Conky's Grill's new waitress Tamara, while Clive is getting increasingly annoyed as she does very little work. Stevie and Miranda go to an art class with Tamara and, when it finishes, reluctantly agree to go clubbing, determined not to show their age. Returning home from the club, they're exhausted but Tamara is still hyper and wants to stay up to see the sun rise. When she calls them middle-aged, assuming them to be in their mid-forties, they try their hardest to prove they're still young and can have fun. In order to stay awake they drink (and eat) coffee, smash cymbals to wake each other up and even resort to licking batteries (do not try this at home!).

At 9am, Tamara is still tirelessly enthusiastic and suggests they go swimming and shopping. In the changing rooms, Miranda struggles with getting into her swimsuit without showing any flesh. Meanwhile, Gary has told Miranda that he's booked a spa break, but – what with the male nude at the art class, embarrassment from changing at the pool and then being made to imagine her mother naked – she is all cringed out. In an attempt to learn to love her body, she decides to volunteer as a life model for the art class.

Afterwards, Miranda is feeling confident, but this soon dissipates when she discovers that Gary is married to Tamara. Miranda and Gary have a massive argument and she ends up breaking it off with him. Tamara has left to give them space, but, as a way of saying sorry, she leaves her nude painting of Miranda as a gift. The whole cast stand around and stare at it as the 'You Have Been Watching' credits roll.

Viewing figures dipped a little that night, but it wasn't that *Miranda*'s popularity was waning; the show was competing with a special live episode of *Coronation Street* (which was celebrating its 50th anniversary) on ITV. Tom Ellis's reaction on Twitter reminded viewers of the sitcom's Tuesday night repeat: 'Ok so we lost a few viewers to corrie last night but don't worry coz Miranda is repeated tonight at 10pm bbc2...miss it miss out! X.'

The fifth episode, 'Just Act Normal', was something of a departure from the show's usual format, as Hart explained on her blog: 'It's set in one room and all played in real time. I have always wanted to write one of those sitcom episodes, having been inspired by David Renwick's *One Foot In the Grave* episodes, when he would just have Victor at home for half an hour or two people stuck in a car. And of course I was initially inspired by *Hancock's Half Hour* where it would just be Tony Hancock for, well, half an hour. (I know, aren't I clever?).'

Hart explained that she found it a struggle to write because of the restrictions of the one set. 'It all becomes jokes which I don't really do. It also gave me massive respect for the writers of *Roger and Val*... which I think is a wonderful show.'

Roger and Val Have Just Got In, written by sisters Beth and Emma Kilfoyle, featured just its two central characters, played by Dawn French and Alfred Molina, in a situation conducted in real time.

'A New Low', then, finds Miranda and Penny spending the whole 30 minutes of the episode in the office of psychiatrist Dr Hopkins, who is played by the comic actor Mark Heap. They're there because, to stop Miranda being arrested, Penny told the police that she was 'one pashmina short of a wardrobe'. Miranda got into a bit of a pickle pretending she was a boy's teacher in order to excuse shouting at him (because he made her drop her ice cream). She ended up having to buy the whole class ice creams and then forgot to pay, so she had to run away. Well, actually she galloped. And so, Miranda and her mother agreed to visit a psychiatrist and get an assessment in order for Miranda to avoid being arrested.

Throughout the time they spend in Dr Hopkins' office, Penny is constantly reminding her daughter to act normal, but this only distresses her and she ends up acting even more strangely. The appointment starts badly – Dr Hopkins walks in to see Miranda drinking water from his briefcase – and only goes downhill from there. When they see him making notes, they are determined to see what he has written. Penny distracts him with a song and a dance while Miranda has a look but, alas, his notes are in shorthand.

At the end of the session, they manage to get hold of his notebook and are furious that he has been working on his Christmas shopping list. They ask what the bit written in shorthand is and he says, 'Just some thoughts as the top of the session.' They demand he tell them what he has written, so he obliges: 'Mother and daughter. Mother's protective instinct has become dominating fuelled by fear of how she's perceived by outer world. Daughter seeks mother's guidance and approval as she has yet to find her own voice.'

They pause. Then reply in unison, 'Absolute rubbish!'

'Haaaaappppyyyy Chhrriiissstmassss!' Miranda greeted her blog readers ahead of series two's festive finale. 'I LOVE Christmas. Can't get enough of mulled wine, a roaring fire, fairy lights, mince pies, even ice skating. I'm quite good – I can even go backwards. Oh yes, you heard it here first.'

With 'The Perfect Christmas', Miranda had her own very special Yuletide edition of her sitcom, a prospect she found most exciting. 'I was thrilled to be able to write a Christmas episode. It was like we had our own Christmas when we filmed it.' The scenes shot on location were filmed much earlier than the studio session (in September) and Miranda made a little confession about how warm she was dressed in knitwear: 'If you so desire, you can look closely at the scene of me in the post office and there is definitely a very sweaty upper lip area. I know – sexy. Hello boys!'

'The Perfect Christmas' begins with a special festive version of the titles, complete with jingle bells, and a Santa hat atop Miranda's bonce. In her introductory monologue, she tells the viewers that she and Gary have made up (by her putting mashed potato in his hair). Tom Conti has joined the cast to play her character's father, and makes a spectacular entrance, tripping over a suitcase on the floor. As well as the Christmas presents she has ordered online that are yet to be delivered, Miranda has things on her mind. She has a rash on her breast, so goes to see Dr Gail, who turns out to be a male doctor, and a rather attractive one at that. Miranda tries to flirt with him by assuring him that her other breast is completely normal. It doesn't work, but she leaves knowing that, thankfully, there is nothing to worry about.

While she was out, Miranda has missed the delivery of her Christmas presents and Stevie has been too busy with a rush of customers, so she calls the depot to rearrange delivery for Christmas Eve. While at the restaurant, Miranda is subjected to the sight of her mother trotting in dressed as a reindeer and singing 'Jingle Bells'. She tries to get out of going to the family pre-Christmas jumper party, but of course fails, thanks to Penny's 'Such fun!' philosophy. At the party, she is surprised to be introduced to the now-familiar Dr Gail, but she suggests to him that they should pretend not to know each other. 'We could have an affair,' she adds optimistically.

The next day, Miranda takes charge of the joke shop in

order to look out for the delivery man, but while she is hiding from carol singers – and forcing her customers to do so as well – a depot card drops through the letterbox, and she has missed it. Never mind – when her friends' Christmas plans fall through, she suggests they could celebrate the perfect Christmas at her flat.

The night before Christmas finds her and her guests playing charades, excitedly expecting the big day. Overnight, Gary and Miranda have to share the sofa bed in the lounge (the others have vowed not to, owing to her wind). Gary tells her not to worry about getting him a present because having his friend back is the best present he could have.

Touched, Miranda asks, 'Really?' and Gary jokes, 'No! Where's my present, you bitch?'

Christmas Day starts well, but, when relations between her guests descend into bickering, Miranda decides to run away to her mother's for the day. As she tries to sneak away, one by one the other guests catch and join her, until she realises they're all with her and stops trying to escape. Former post office villain Ray turns out to be a good Samaritan when he turns up at the house and agrees to let Miranda have her delivery of presents. The episode ends with the entire cast gathered around a piano for a rendition of 'We Wish You a Merry Christmas'.

Though Miranda Hart does enjoy spending Christmas with her parents, she has confessed that 'by the fifth day I'm craving time on my own... I'll go into small-talk meltdown if I have to answer another "Isn't the weather cold?" "What are you doing for the New Year?" or "Is the family well?"'

A few days before the final episode aired on 20 December

2010, Hart gave her Twitter followers an idea of how she preferred to spend the Christmas season: 'Off to see @louiespence in panto with Sarah Hadland. Evenings don't get much better than that.'

Miranda's Christmas special saw a record number of viewers for the show, attracting an impressive 4.4 million. Comedy website Chortle reported that this was 50 per cent more than the last series' finale 'and 73 per cent higher than BBC Two normally gets in the 8.30pm Monday slot. Overall, the series averaged 3.2 million viewers per episode, up more than 25 per cent on the 2.5 million of the first series.'

Critics were just as positive about *Miranda*'s second coming: 'It is solid, heartening fare and I nearly laughed my leg off,' wrote Lucy Mangan in the *Guardian*.

But it had been hard work. Before it was announced that another series would be made, Hart told *Stylist* magazine, 'I don't think I'm ready to write again yet. I'd like to do a third series, but there's nothing official yet and I definitely need a break to really think about where I want to go to get the joy back.'

The announcement came amid *Miranda*'s awards mania and she seemed a bit overwhelmed by how fast things were moving. She told Channel 4's Alan Carr, 'We only finished recording the second [series] on December 6th, so really recently. So I'm kind of taking a bit of a break to see what I want to do with the next series and when...'

Confirmation came with an announcement to fans on Hart's official website, at www.mirandahart.com: 'Thank you for all your enquiries about being in the audience of the sitcom recordings of Series 3. It won't be filming until sometime in

2012, dates yet to be arranged, but there might be news at the end of this year about it. So keep popping back.'

But bigger news was on the horizon. Not only would *Miranda* return for a third series, it would also be moving to a new home at the higher-profile BBC One. George Entwistle, Acting Director of BBC Vision, said in a press release, 'Miranda's been a tremendous hit with audiences on BBC Two and I'm very glad she's let us persuade her to move to BBC One, where we believe we can build an even bigger following for her multi-award-winning show.'

Hart herself came across as excited, but a little nervous about the decision to switch channels. 'I am very grateful to BBC Two for supporting and nurturing me, and trusting my vision for the show. Two will always feel like home. Now I feel like I am renting a swish apartment that I hope I don't look out of place in or break all the furniture!'

This has created even more pressure on Hart for writing the third series. She considers it harder writing for BBC One. 'You have to have proper jokes, and jokes are really hard to write. It's much easier being characterful and oblique on a niche channel where you don't need laughs.'

But judging from what has been before, it's sure to be a series worth waiting for.

19

THE RISE OF THE OFFICE TEMP

*'Initially I treated the job at Comic Relief as just another of
my many temp jobs whilst trying to get in to acting. However, within
a few weeks I realised what a special place it was.'*
– Miranda

Until 2005, when she was offered the part of Teal in
Hyperdrive, Miranda was still temping as a PA. From
2001 to 2003, this was with Comic Relief and she formed an
unbreakable bond with the charity: 'I would take minutes of the
meetings that decided where the grants would go. So I learned
a huge amount and that changed my outlook completely. It's an
extraordinary place, the passion and commitment there.'

In 2007, four years after working at Comic Relief, Hart
appeared in one of its fundraising shows. *Hyperdrive* series
one had already aired and she was beginning to gain
recognition, so was asked to take part in that year's *Comic
Relief Does Fame Academy*. The show was a celebrity spin-
off from the BBC's singing talent competition that
introduced David Sneddon, Alex Parks and – most
enduringly – Lemar (Obika). Three Comic Relief spin-offs
had been organised in 2003, 2005 and now 2007. Hart's

profile on the *Fame Academy* website sounded promising: 'Her musical abilities include singing mezzo soprano, playing piano to grade 6, performing basic tap, jazz and period dance.' In the harsh reality of the studio lights, however, she didn't quite achieve her potential. On the opening night, Miranda and her fellow students sang one song each. The celebs performing alongside Miranda were Rowland Rivron, Linda Robson, Tim Vine, Zoë Salmon, Mel Giedroyc, Fred MacAulay, Angellica Bell, Ray Stubbs, Colin Murray, Shaun Williamson, Tricia Penrose and the eventual winner Tara Palmer-Tomkinson.

Hosts Patrick Kielty and Claudia Winkleman introduced the songs, while the judging panel, Craig Revel Horwood, Lesley Garrett and Richard Park, told the celebrities what they thought. The phone vote put Miranda, Angellica Bell and Rowland Rivron in the bottom three, meaning they had to perform again, this time for the judges to save them. Lesley saved Miranda but both Craig and Richard chose to keep Angellica, so she was saved. It was down to the eleven other celebrities to decide who should stay. Here Miranda showed her popularity, receiving ten votes, while Rowland only got one for his performance of 'Stand By Your Man'. Rivron's solo vote was from Colin Murray who wanted to keep the number of men in the competition up, otherwise 'everyone would be talking about *Sex and the City* all the time'. But Rowland was eliminated and Miranda got the chance to perform again. Dawn French, who was supporting Miranda's progress in the contest, joked, 'Miranda? Not particularly funny, but a fabulous singer.'

In the second heat of the competition, Miranda performed

her version of 'Physical' by Olivia Newton-John, dressed in workout clothes, and rolling around seductively on stage. Future *Strictly Come Dancing* judge Craig Revel Horwood described it as 'limp, lacklustre and not funny' and even jovial host Kielty said it was 'slightly more mental than physical'. Yet again Hart was placed in the bottom three, but this time no one came to her rescue and she became the second contestant to be 'expelled' from the Academy.

The 'Physical' sequence has occasionally come back to haunt her ever since. In 2008, when she was a contestant on *Have I Got News For You*, they showed the clip and she tried to hide under the table in embarrassment. It was shown again on ITV's *Daybreak* in February 2011, and Adrian Chiles said, 'That's excruciating! Were you trying to sing that badly?'

She explained that she was so nervous that she couldn't control her throat or voice.

Comic Relief rested the *Fame Academy* contest after 2007, replacing it for the next event in 2009 with *Let's Dance for Comic Relief*. With her penchant for physical comedy and fundraising, it seems a perfect vehicle for her antics and it wouldn't be surprising to see her taking part in the future. However, for the 2009 edition of the biennial fundraiser, Hart got another opportunity to become involved, and her chance came via French and Saunders, who were fast becoming mentors of hers. She appeared in *Gimme Gimme Gimmick*, a spoof version of Phyllida Lloyd's film version of the Abba musical, *Mamma Mia!* Miranda took the part of the film's director, joined by an all-star cast including Sienna Miller, Alan Carr, Joanna Lumley, Matt Lucas, Sue Perkins and Mel Giedroyc. The extended trailer and 'making-of' showed a tongue-in-cheek version of the film, which the voiceover described as 'the genius of Abba, with words in between'. Although an affectionate parody, Saunders' feelings about the film were made clear in an interview with the *Daily Mail*. 'Did I hate it? Um, well, it served its purpose, let's put it that way.'

Hart felt privileged to play the role and let her fans know about her Red Nose Day appearance via Twitter. 'Happy RND. Watch beginning to end, don't blink because you'll miss my vital role in F&S sketch. And that's what tonight is really about. Me.'

Her inept director character was chosen to 'direct' the film because as her equally incompetent producer (Sue Perkins) put it, 'She'd done working with actors before and she was the right person to put it in the camera.'

Hart gives a fantastic performance as the nervously fumbling director, desperately trying to muster up enough confidence to actually direct the actors: 'Can everybody stay where they can see the camera, please? That's the first rule of filming apparently. And stay in the middle of the photograph and bend down if you're tall.'

In 2002, Comic Relief and BBC Sport joined forces to create a new fundraising event, Sport Relief. It is staged every other year, alternating with Red Nose Day, so there is now a Comic Relief drive every year. In its time, it has seen some pretty amazing achievements from the public and celebrities alike. Memorable moments have included Bob Mortimer beating Les Dennis in the ring as part of the first-ever Celebrity Boxing, David Walliams swimming the English Channel in 2006 and the Gibraltar Strait in 2008, and Eddie Izzard's astonishing 43 marathons over 51 days. Until only a week before he set off, Izzard had never run a marathon, but he managed to complete one six days a week for a solid seven weeks, covering 1,166 miles. This phenomenal feat raised over £1,152,510 for Sport Relief.

In 2010, former Channel swimmer David Walliams led a team of celebrities, including Miranda, on an epic bike ride from John O'Groats to Land's End in what was called The Million Pound Bike Ride. He said that he thought this would be more fun than his solo swim because of the camaraderie and group support. Comedian Jimmy Carr said his biggest concern was 'falling off the bike and it not being captured on camera'. Also in the team were such luminaries as Davina McCall, Patrick Kielty and the television presenter Fearne Cotton, who in 2009 accompanied another group of celebrities who climbed Mount Kilimanjaro in aid of Comic Relief. Cotton expressed great passion for the work the charity has done over the years: 'Going out to Africa or visiting charities and organisations in the UK is so fulfilling. There's no better feeling than seeing how that money's directly helping people.' With the cycling marathon, though, came some minor worries about her own welfare: 'I've got concerns that I'll never have children after doing this, due to what's going to happen to my lady parts.'

Also joining the team was the fresh-faced stand-up comedian Russell Howard. He said the reason he agreed to do it was that everything would be organised for him. Howard is pretty fit so wasn't concerned too much about the cycling, but rather scared of potential monsters: 'I'm a bit of a wuss... You know you read these stories about wild cats that roam? It'll be just my luck if like this massive panther just took a bite out of me. And I die – dressed in Lycra.'

But what of Miranda Hart's concerns for the event? She felt nervous, certainly. 'Since Monday night when we did our night cycle training, I have felt nauseous and I'm told that is being out of shape and I've got to push through it, so that makes me nervous.' It didn't help her that, while the rest of the team had been training, Miranda had been taking a holiday in Thailand and became ill on her return. She said, 'Our trainer made the mistake of saying, "Don't stop eating anything, eat loads of carbs." It was fine for the others who'd been in training, but I was taking his diet advice without doing the training, so I piled on the pounds and got steadily more unfit.'

By the time the cycling marathon came around, she had only done a full two hours of training on one occasion, which she would have to complete twice a day throughout the challenge. While on holiday, she had posted a picture to Twitter of her sunning herself, with the comment: 'Whilst @ThisisDavina et al are on bikes training, I am doing this in Thailand. And they're all fit already. Help!'

On her blog, Fearne described how gruelling the training was: 'At the weekend myself and David Walliams, team captain of said challenge, headed out to Marlow where our wonderful trainer Greg lives. He took us on a 90 minute cycle of doom around the local hills. I unintentionally dismounted (fell off) twice, and David got four punctures in 90 minutes which I believe is a world record.'

When Hart returned, she tweeted: 'Back in blighty and not entirely happy about it. Was meant to come back thinner and fitter. Pun coming – fat chance.' After her first training session she said that she hurt in places she didn't know existed, and that her throat was still preventing her from exercising properly. On 13 February, she told her Twitter followers, 'Two weeks tomorrow we go to Scotland for cycle challenge. I only managed 20 mins on bike today. This is proper scary. bring back healthy me. [sic]'

She battled on with the training, determined to succeed. The night ride cycle training was particularly demanding and she ended up crying three times, as 'every pedal vaguely upward was painful'.

Davina McCall was just as committed, as gruelling as the training was: 'Even if I'm dying, I will give it everything I've got.'

So, on 1 March 2010, the team assembled at John O'Groats to set off. Their trainer, Olympian Greg White, explained what they had ahead of them: 'This is a really tough challenge. We've got a group of unfit celebrities who've never ridden a racing bike before who are going to embark on a 1,000 mile trip across the roughest terrain in the UK in the middle of March where we could be down to minus five or ten degrees centigrade. With wind chill, that could be down to minus 15, in the snow.'

The seven riders (minus Jimmy Carr who was on tour) set off and cycled the first 12 miles as a group. Miranda took a tumble immediately. 'I fell off at the start, when I was standing. It was slightly embarrassing. And because it was embarrassing and there was a lovely crowd, I felt like I couldn't go, "actually, that really hurts".'

After the first stretch, they had a continuous relay; if they were to achieve Walliams' ambitious target of reaching Land's End in just four days, they would have to go at a sprinting pace. David continued alone, while the others stopped for breakfast and to find their tour bus. It was somewhat smaller than they had anticipated, as Davina observed, 'Miranda doesn't fit anywhere on this bus.'

Four miles into his solo ride, David was forced to endure a snowstorm but remained optimistic about the situation: 'It's lovely and cooling though, on your face.'

Because of the ambitious time limit, the team were using racing bikes, which aren't suitable for icy conditions – so there were a lot of 'unintentional dismounts'. Meanwhile, on the bus, Miranda applied an ice pack to her bloody knee.

Davina took the second shift, talking to the camera as she cycled. 'After everything I've seen on all my amazing trips with Sport Relief and Comic Relief, that if I get asked to do something and I possibly can to raise a bit of wonga, I'll bloody do it. And that's that.'

Miranda was getting more and more anxious about her night cycle. Before the ride, all of the team members had been given comprehensive fitness tests. Miranda's GP did not approve of the ride, giving strict orders that she was only to cycle an hour at a time. So, while Russell Howard took the helm, Miranda shared her anxiety with her Twitter followers: 'Waiting for my cycle stint. an hour to go. very dark, very cold, very nervous! onwards. [sic]'

Under the pitch-black night sky, Hart so wanted to support her teammates that she defied her doctor and opted to do an extra hour of cycling. But it was a massive struggle – 'I want to cry, I feel so weak' – and 15 minutes before her handover she was forced to dismount and walk. David Walliams took over and, back on the bus, Miranda explained how faint she had become. It was totally understandable; she had been riding in icy winds, in the dark, for an hour and 45 minutes. She told Fearne how she was embarrassed about snubbing the crowds: 'I got in the car, there was a whole mass of lovely people with bagpipes and I just stormed off...' Her usual candid self, she posted details of her ordeal on Twitter: 'Couldnt climb the wall i hit on my stint, had to walk up hill in -6. Had first weep of trip! Dont want to let anyone down but this is HARD. [sic]'

The celebrities were finding it hard to sleep on the bus, what with the noise and cramped conditions. One thing they had, though, was warmth. Riders had to face temperatures as cold as minus 15 Celsius, and, having suffered this for hours on end, the pacemaker had to stop at risk of hypothermia. A real trooper, Davina continued alone, keeping herself company by talking to the camera. The whole team was finding it so hard. Even on the first night, Patrick Kielty said he had got to bed at 6am, but 'cried until quarter to eight'.

Spirits were raised when they learned that, on the first day alone, they had raised over a quarter of a million pounds. Still, everyone's mind remained on the job in hand and Miranda was starting to worry about slowing the team down. She shared her view of the experience with a documentary cameraman who was filming their efforts: 'The joke is on me because, when I got asked to do the ride, I thought it would be fun! There are small pockets of fun in a 24-hour period but it's predominantly hell on this very earth. But you have to keep going because people sponsor you and the cause is so worth every pedal.'

Having now crossed the border from Scotland into England, the third day found the group tackling the toughest terrain yet – the Lake District. Luckily, it was the day when Jimmy Carr could finally join them to help out. He had been away on a stand-up tour and could only commit to the one day. He hadn't joined them in any of the training sessions as he said, 'training is basically cheating'. He found the ride quite a shock: 'This is hard,' he told the crew while cycling. 'I've done eight miles so far, which is officially the furthest I've ever cycled in my life.' He ended up getting the slowest time of all. But he brought a fresh perspective to the group and was surprised how well they were coping: 'Everyone seems in pretty good spirits. I mean David seems pretty tired but Davina seems massively upbeat.'

Miranda was given the morning off. She explained on Twitter: '...can't walk up step let alone pedal. Got to get over this wall for my 2 hours this pm.' She got a lot of support from her fans on Twitter as well as from her fellow cyclists. 'Very painful ride as back went ten mins in but just had a shower and looking forward to sleep. @ThisisDavina and @fearnecotton keep me sane. [sic]'

Peter Jones, the extremely tall entrepreneur from *Dragons' Den*, came to meet the team and towered over them all, even David Walliams. He had been helping by encouraging businesses across the country to donate to the cause and had the pleasure of telling them how much money they had raised. And by 1pm on the third day they had raised £627,000. This was fantastic news, but the pressure was on to reach the million-pound target by the time they reached Land's End. Walliams joked, 'You're like a lovely uncle giving us lots of money to spend on sweets.'

On the fourth and final day, spirits were high and the end was in sight. David teased Miranda, 'Do you feel guilty taking some of the glory? Do you feel a little bit ashamed, in a way, that you've sort of conned the public?'

She took the joke in good humour, but answered seriously, 'Well, I would have but I've done so much more than I thought I would. And actually I made up time for the team yesterday because I went so fast.'

Throughout the journey, it was Patrick Kielty who was the cyclist with the highest average speed, at one point reaching 45mph on a downhill stretch. Psychologically, though, he was losing his strength: 'What happens on the trip is our energy levels just go and go and go, so, when you want to cry, you want to cry like there's a dead dog in your house.'

As the team had started together, so they finished together. They completed the last eight miles as a group; symbolic of the journey they had taken together. As they crossed the line, crowds of supporters cheered and applauded their fantastic achievement. Among those there to greet them were Dawn French and Peter Jones who gave Walliams the final total. He announced to those gathered that, during their 82-hour cycle, they had raised £1,006,509. With the addition of donations after the event, the final amount raised totalled £1,337,099. All their hard work, determination and commitment meant that hundreds around the world could have a better life.

It had been quite a slog. After the event, Miranda told a BBC entertainment reporter that it wasn't just the cycling that had been a trial: 'The bus stank, I get travel sick and I couldn't stand upright in it. Me and David Walliams couldn't stand up.' They asked what the bus had smelled of and she replied: 'Mainly David Walliams. He's very manly. The only way that he was manly was by odour.'

David Walliams also told the press: 'It has been an amazing challenge, so much harder and more gruelling than any of us thought it would be. To have raised a million pounds in four days is a fantastic thing – thanks so much for everyone who sponsored us, it kept us going.'

Not everyone had the same attitude, though. Miranda shared a nasty tweet she received, which suggested she only did the ride for self-promotion: 'Before the cycle ride you were that unknown fat woman of the TV. It has now raised your profile so mission accomplishe. [sic]'

She replied with impressive restraint but with just a little sarcasm: 'Yeah, sweating up a mountain with no make-up and a cycle helmet, crying is the kind of publicity we court. Twas genuine. Chill. [sic]'

Of course, the majority were totally behind the group, including the then Prime Minister Gordon Brown. He invited Miranda, Fearne and Jimmy to Downing Street along with Christine Bleakley, who had crossed the Channel on water skis, *Blue Peter* presenter Helen Skelton, who had kayaked 2,000 miles along the Amazon, and Lawrence Dallaglio, who had cycled to every Six Nations stadium during the tournament. The PM said, 'I am always moved and inspired when I hear about people who have gone to incredible lengths to raise money for important causes. But these celebrities haven't just inspired me – they have also inspired people across the country to get involved in Sport Relief by raising money and getting active at the same time.'

Miranda reported on Twitter that she had left a signed photo of herself on the PM's staircase. 'On a less boring note i dreamt i met Gordon Brown, curtsied then farted a i rose to a stand again. I dream sitcom. [sic]'

Good old Miranda. Yet only one year on from Sport Relief

2010, and her celebrity status would have stratospherically risen. She would play a much more prominent role in Comic Relief 2011.

20

DOING SOMETHING FUNNY FOR MONEY

'It's safe to say, on the basis of her towering presence in this year's show, that Miranda Hart is properly, Comic Relief famous.'
– Stephen Armstrong, *The Sunday Times.*

By 2011, Miranda Hart had come a long way since working as the Comic Relief office temp. Now she was one of the big stars of its special fundraising events. Only the very best and most respected comedy favourites are asked to contribute their very own sketch or insert to Red Nose Day. Even during the 2010 Sport Relief event, Hart had felt strange about returning to the offices of her former day job: 'Walking down that corridor that I used to work in every day but being on the other side was really weird but very exciting.' But this Red Nose Day, she was even bigger news, having won numerous awards for her eponymously titled sitcom and becoming one of Britain's most recognised comedy actresses.

A number of interviews Miranda did promoted the cause. She appeared on ITV's *Daybreak* wearing one of the campaign's T-shirts, designed by Vivienne Westwood. 'I'm wearing the Miranda T-shirt obviously, another Queen!' she says, though this was of a different Miranda: Miranda Richardson as Queenie from *Blackadder II*. In a big fundraising year for the charity, the government joined in, promising to match Comic Relief's own commitment to spend £10 million on health and education in Africa. Andrew Mitchell, the International Development Secretary, said, 'Even in these tough economic times, the British public has given an incredible response to Comic Relief's appeal, showing yet again their compassion and generosity. The government will come in behind the public's effort, to support and amplify the choices that British people have made.'

Large corporations became involved, too. Walkers Crisps joined in the fun again in 2011, creating four new flavours named after British comedians: Jimmy con Carrne (Jimmy Carr), Steak and Al Pie (Al Murray), as well as Frank Skinner's Roast Dinner and Stephen Fry Up. British Airways, too, played their part, setting a new Guinness World Record for the 'highest stand-up comedy gig in the world'. The night's acts, Dara O'Briain, Jack Whitehall and Jon Richardson, who performed at 35,000ft on board an A321 aircraft, helped BA raise £800,747 for the charity. BT sponsored the Red Nose Desert Trek, where a group of celebrities including Dermot O'Leary, Ronni Ancona, Scott Mills and Craig David braved the Kaisut Desert for a 100-kilometre walk, in temperatures which reached 38 degrees Celsius.

Blue Peter presenter Helen Skelton, who had kayaked the River Amazon in the previous year, walked a tightrope between the two towers of Battersea Power Station. At 200 feet, it became another record for the show, as it was the highest a British woman had ever walked a tightrope.

Meanwhile, *Famous, Rich and in the Slums* was a documentary made for the show in which Comic Relief stalwart Lenny Henry and a group of celebrities lived, worked and experienced the plight of someone living in the slums of Kiber in Kenya.

Comic Relief decided to look into what embarrasses Britons in The Big Red Face Report. The survey showed: 'The top five most common British embarrassments were farting in public (32 per cent), walking around with flies undone (26 per cent), moaning about a colleague and being overheard (16 per cent), falling asleep, snoring and dribbling on public transport (12 per cent) and calling your partner by the wrong name (12 per cent).'

But the famous had their own juicy confessions of embarrassment to share, like Miranda Hart: 'I went to a toilet on a train and I thought I had locked the door. I was just taking my trousers down, and as I did that the train did one of those "lurch" stops. I fell through the door of the toilet which hadn't been locked, and was trouserless and pantless in front of a buffet queue in the train carriage.'

Other events included one in which BBC Radio DJs and presenters (one from each national network) swapped their mixing desks for a single mic on a stage as they took part in *Stand Up for Comic Relief*. Dev (Radio 1), Tony Blackburn (Radio 2), Tom Service (Radio 3), Jenni Murray (Radio 4), Tony Livesey (5 Live) and Shaun Keaveny (6 Music) all went in front of a live audience at the Comedy Store in London to perform a three-minute stand-up set. Listeners voted Jenni Murray – whose spot including jokes about how to target younger listeners on Radio 4 – as their favourite. Mark Steel, the comedian who mentored her, said, 'Jenni's been a delight... whenever you've been listening to her on *Woman's Hour*, you must be aware that, no matter how serious the subject, underneath there's a huge cauldron of bubbling stand-up mirth.'

One of the biggest marathon events ahead of Red Nose Day itself was yet another challenge for David Walliams – *24 Hour Panel People*. Across one whole 24-hour period, he either hosted or took part in some of the most iconic game shows of British television including *Just A Minute*, *Blankety Blank*, *Never Mind The Buzzcocks*, *Call My Bluff*, *Mock The Week*, *Mastermind*, *Room 101* and *QI*. On the highlights show, a voiceover announced that 'People all over the world were watching online to find out if David could be funny for 24 hours straight. It was the most talked-about thing on Twitter, trending globally from Peru to Australia, with over 24,000 tweets in 24 hours.'

And Miranda was one of them, tweeting, 'There is a strong chance my life won't improve after what is lined up for *24 Hour Panel People* this afternoon.'

Hart took part in a special revival of *The Generation Game* with Patricia Hodge as her teammate. They were up against Walliams and his mum, while Vernon Kay played host. There was a high level of competitive spirit between the two teams, and Miranda started early with the fighting talk. Five hours into Walliams' 24-hour stint, Vernon suggested that Walliams was already flagging as he didn't have a witty riposte ready, to which Walliams replied, 'At least this is my real mum not a pretend, made-up one from a TV show. My mum's not ashamed of me; she'll come on television!'

The teams were tasked with the classic *Generation Game* pot-moulding challenge, or 'throwing a pot', as it's officially called. The professional demonstrates, first how to shape the pot and then add the handle. Smoothing the clay for the handle involves a rather suggestive hand movement. The potter explained, 'It's a bit like milking a cow, some people say,' while the audience shrieked with hysterical laughter. To this, Miranda feigned ignorance: 'Why are you laughing?!'

The mums went first. Patricia Hodge was very good at it, as she had tried it before. David's mum was no expert, but made a reasonable attempt. Then it was the comedians' turn. Miranda's pot collapsed, so she improvised and made it into a basket. David's too fell over, but he tried to excuse the disaster by saying, 'It's abstract, that was the idea!' David and his mum were awarded six out of ten, while Miranda and Patricia won with eight. Walliams' reaction was sulky: 'I think it's an insult to pottery.'

Nevertheless, Walliams managed to stay awake throughout his 24-hour panel-show marathon, which proved to be a fantastic success. Afterwards, he said, 'It was as tough as I thought it would be, particularly at the end just having to keep the show together, being so exhausted and not being able to think straight any more.' Tired eyes proved the biggest risk to it all falling apart: 'I just couldn't read the autocue any more because my eyes couldn't focus, which is quite a scary thing, especially as there was an audience here.'

As well as exciting firsts like *24 Hour Panel People*, 2011's fundraiser also saw the return of *Let's Dance for Comic Relief*, the show that had previously seen Robert Webb perform *that* 'What A Feeling!' routine from *Flashdance* and

Rufus Hound present a moustachioed homage to Cheryl Cole. Cross-dressing returned as a popular theme in the third series of the show, much to the delight of many viewers, but not some critics. Michael Hogan wrote on the *Guardian*'s TV and Radio blog: 'So many *Let's Dance* stars are flogging the cross-dressing clotheshorse that it's almost ruining this fun show.'

Whether a fan or not, there was no denying men dressed as women and vice versa was in abundance. Of the six acts left in the final, four were cross-dressed – Russell Kane in what many thought a scarily accurate rendition of Beyoncé's 'Crazy in Love', Noel Fielding flailing about in a scarlet dress to 'Wuthering Heights' by Kate Bush, Katie Price donning a 'tache for her best Freddie Mercury in Queen's 'I Want To Break Free', and Ade Edmondson in full ballet garb for a slapstick rendition of 'The Dying Swan'. The other two acts in the final were the 80s Super Group with 'Greased Lightning', and Charlie Baker and James Thornton tap-dancing their way through 'Puttin' on the Ritz'.

Miranda also appeared in the *Let's Dance* final, but rather than dancing (that would come later) she was a celebrity judge alongside Louie Spence and the series two winner Rufus Hound. When Katie Price performed her hoover-pushing routine of 'I Want To Break Free', Miranda said of her tiny leather mini, 'First off, can I have me skirt back? She's ruined it by putting an extra panel in.'

Ahead of the final result, the *Guardian*'s Hogan wrote, 'Tip to win? Well, excuse the told-you-so smugsies but I predicted the winner would come from the Kane/Fielding/Edmondson ladyboy stable. If I had to stick my neck out, I'd plump for Kane. Mainly because despite looking like an horrifically burnt Gillian McKeith on a hen night, he makes me both aroused and bilious at the same time – a rare skill.'

Kane was a popular choice, even the bookies' favourite with odds of 11/8 to win. But expectations were confounded when comedian Charlie Baker and *Emmerdale* actor James Thornton beat him to the winners' podium. They were visibly surprised by their victory, gushing with gratitude. 'I want to say thanks to everyone who voted at home,' said Thornton. 'We've raised so much money for a brilliant cause and that's what it's all about. We've had a real laugh while we've been doing it, cheers guys!'

Louie Spence in particular had been rooting for them and sang their praises highly: 'You had great fluidity through the moves as well. It was beautiful and your rhythms were great, so well done. I would be more than happy to be your Ginger Rogers!'

What turned out to be one of the year's more controversial fundraising efforts was Twitrelief. This was the brainchild of scriptwriter and Comic Relief fundraiser Emma Freud and the actress Emma Kennedy. Freud was trying to think of ways to raise money through Twitter when, over Christmas dinner, Kennedy told her about Twitchange, an enterprise set up by Eva Longoria in 2010 which auctioned off a follow from a celebrity tweeter. (For the uninitiated – where have you been? – for someone to see your tweets on their homepage, they need to follow you. So, if a celebrity follows you, they will be able to read your posts and you will be able to send each other private messages.)

The Twitchange idea had raised a lot of money and Freud was keen to see how it could work for Comic Relief. 'Twitrelief was Kennedy's idea,' Freud explained. 'She said she was sure people would pay for celebrities to follow them on Twitter. I said, "Yeah, about 50p." She said, "Seriously – in America, I was auctioned for 1500 dollars." Emma Kennedy? Emma Kennedy the ENGLISH comedy actress and author? Went for over a grand in the States?'

Freud was now convinced by the idea's potential, so they went about their mission. In a matter of days they had more than 100 celebrities signed up for Operation Twitrelief. Originally, the idea was for the celebrity to follow you for 90 days, but soon they started adding extras. Miranda put up a signed script of her sitcom, while others' offerings were a little more extravagant and eccentric. Organiser Emma Freud added the opportunity of a walk-on part in her partner Richard Curtis's next film. Robert Webb said he would perform live a favourite sketch or moment from *Peep Show* for the winning bidder via a Skype video call. Chris Addison's follow came with the bonus of a swear-packed phone call from *The Thick of It*'s Malcolm Tucker (played by Peter Capaldi). Rufus Hound even agreed to get a tattoo of the bidder's choice on his leg – you could even choose which leg it would adorn. But it was the comedian David Schneider who offered one of the most original extras: 'As well as following the person on Twitter, I will literally follow them in real life. I will walk behind them for one hour, at a designated distance which they can choose.'

But when it was launched, on 10 March, Twitrelief met with some criticism from other users. CreativeReview said, 'We don't want to shoot down important fundraising work, but how horribly ill-conceived and ego-stroking is #twitrelief?'

Others were rather more aggressive or rude with their disapproval, causing upset to many of those involved. The main arguments against it were that, by offering follows at a price, it suggested that celebrities were superior; that it was not what Twitter is 'for'; and that celebrities should donate themselves rather than getting the public to do it for them.

Graham Linehan wrote a blog post quoting complaints that came through and answering them with his side of the story. He reasoned that celebrities did not think themselves superior, that 'it's a dangerous road to start telling people how to use their account' and that the follow would not replace donations. Responding to one user who suggested they could afford to donate one month's wages, Linehan offered: 'James Corden, to take one example, has been filming for Comic Relief for three weeks, so in effect he has already given up a month's wages.'

Miranda summed up many people's opinion in one tweet: 'For those moaning about #twitrelief I'll say this – it will raise enough money to change people's lives. Poverty exists. Ooh, serious tweet.'

Many positive comments about the event circulated, but, as Linehan wrote on his blog, 'The damage had already been done, at least where Miranda Hart was concerned. By the end of the afternoon, she had had enough.'

Miranda announced that she was leaving Twitter 'for SO many reasons', and that she would pay her bidder back as her donation. Although she had previously received some negative comments via Twitter, the reactions to Twitrelief were what had prompted her to leave: 'Oh, hate of twitter nothing to do with people saying the odd nasty to me – don't give two hoots about that. 140 character to short to explain [sic]'.

Despite this hiccup, Twitrelief ended up an enormous success. On 21 March, three days after Red Nose Day itself, it was announced: 'So, after all the bids were in last night, the grand #twitrelief total was... *drumroll*... A MASSIVE £286,074.23!!! Can't thank you enough!'

Less controversy came with the sillier, lighter event, *The Masters of the Kazooniverse*. Staged at the Royal Albert Hall on 14 March, Miranda was among 3,910 people (including over 80 celebrities) who managed to beat the world record for the largest kazoo ensemble, previously set by 3,861 people in Sydney. Led by the professional group Masters of the Kazooniverse, the London venue was buzzing to mass kazoo renditions of 'The Ride of the Valkyries' and the 'Dambusters Theme'. The concert was compered by Katie Derham and Basil Brush and was broadcast on Radio 3 on Red Nose Day. 'We loved the idea of marrying what we do in comedy with what they do with classical music,' said Emma Freud. 'The original plan was to have just a few kazooers on stage but I mentioned it to [Emma] Kennedy and suddenly there were 87.'

Before the Royal Albert Hall show, Miranda said, 'It's fantastic how many people are taking part in this brilliant fundraising event. It's going to be a real spectacle. I just need to work out what a kazoo actually is, and then work out how to play it. It's fun even saying "kazoo" so I can't wait.'

When the result had been made official, Craig Glenday, Editor-in-Chief of Guinness World Records, said, '[We] would like to congratulate everyone that hummed their way into the record books during Radio 3's Red Nose Show to set a new record for the largest ever kazoo ensemble.'

All this build-up meant expectations were high for Red Nose Day itself – where Miranda would shine. She said, 'It has some huge television moments, like Dawn French kissing Hugh Grant. There's always some terribly exciting thing that I'm sure will happen again on the 18th of March.'

Part of the excitement of RND comes from the fact that it is broadcast live, so the unexpected can, and often does, happen.

Guardian writer Michael Hogan also reviewed the evening's highlights for the *Telegraph*: 'Live TV took its toll too, with technical glitches and awkward gaps, but that's part of the seat-of-the-pants appeal of such events.' As usual, silly skits and sketches were interspersed with appeals for donations, through emotive films. Hogan continued, 'The Africa films were remarkably powerful, especially those fronted by David Tennant, Lenny Henry and Jack Dee. Proceedings started at 7pm and many viewers would have been in tears by 7.08pm. It's hard to see how anyone could not donate under those circumstances.'

As important as these inserts are for Comic Relief, viewers also want to be entertained by the one-off specials from Britain's top presenters, actors and comedians. The proceedings began brilliantly with a special episode of *Outnumbered*, in which the family accosted tennis ace Andy Murray, a *Doctor Who* mini-episode that found the Tardis within the Tardis, and Harry Hill looking for wildlife in his off-the-wall version of *Autumnwatch*.

Then we were treated to Miranda's first appearance of the evening, in Comic Relief's take on *Masterchef*. Along with fellow unlikely cooks Claudia Winkleman and Ruby Wax, she had the challenge of preparing and serving a meal to Prime

Minister David Cameron and his guests: 'Cooking doesn't get tougher than this!'

It wasn't the first time a PM had appeared in Comic Relief, as Tony Blair appeared opposite Catherine Tate's character Lauren 'Am I bovvered?' Cooper in 2007.

Ruby began the meal by serving up a crab salad starter, which she managed to leave riddled with shell, putting Cameron at risk of breaking a tooth. Claudia was in charge of the main dish and somewhat over-spiced her chilli con carne. Surprising everyone – Winkleman especially – the Prime Minister enjoyed it, but quickly added that it wasn't as good as his wife Samantha's. Miranda made her own meringues and dished up a dessert of trifle with, in true childish *Miranda* style, gummy bears instead of jelly. The team was amused but impressed and crowned her the winner, adding yet another trophy to her ever-growing cabinet.

Next up was Jennifer Saunders' return to Comic Relief, but this time with the notable absence of her former comedy partner Dawn French. *Uptown Downstairs Abbey* was an affectionate spoof of two TV dramas: Julian Fellowes' *Downton Abbey* and the recent revival of the 1970s hit *Upstairs Downstairs*. Apart from being a brilliantly observed parody, the skit was notable for its impressive cast. Joining Jennifer Saunders were comedy stars Harry Enfield, Joanna Lumley, Victoria Wood and Tim Vine, as well as *Sex and the City* star Kim Cattrall, who is a fan of *Downton Abbey*.

It wasn't long before Miranda Hart's starring moment – her very own Comic Relief special. She teased about what might be to come on Twitter at the end of February: 'Sworn to secrecy but there's a strong chance my Comic Relief sketch could finish me physically and comedically. Ooh I'm a tease. 18th march. [sic]'

Her special saw her and her sitcom family take over Pineapple Dance Studios, famous after Sky One's show that made a star out of Louie Spence. Hart appeared on Graham Norton's chat show ahead of Red Nose Day and he asked her if she was a dancer, because he had heard she had a health scare on a dance floor. She laughed at the suggestion, saying, 'Well I dance like we all dance, with a couple of sherries in us!' and explained further: 'Towards the end of a night, about 5am, 10 or 12 of us were left on the dance floor and I suddenly collapsed in agonising pain to the floor and turned sheet-white, writhing round. So everyone said, "Right. Call an ambulance, it's clearly appendicitis," and then apparently I did the biggest fart you have ever heard! And then leapt up and went, "I'm fine now," as the ambulance was pulling up.'

The first part of Miranda's special was in the style of a *Pineapple Dance Studios* episode, complete with a commentary from the series' resident narrator, Michael Buerk. Miranda and 'her tiny elf of a friend' Stevie are manning the dance studios' reception, gazing at hunks like its dance teacher Andrew Stone. Meanwhile, Penny – who according to the voiceover 'trained at the Bath School of Dance where she spent several summers under Lionel Blair' – is teaching a class.

Gary enters dressed in a vest and pork-pie hat, while Buerk explains: 'Gary has been told that, because his name is one letter away from gay, he's a likely dancer.'

Heather Small arrives to practise in one of the rehearsal rooms, but Miranda panics when they run out of cups, instead offering her water to lap up like a cat. Stevie tries to teach Small to sing 'Proud'.

Then Louis Spence turns up with JLS, while Buerk tells us some backstory: 'Miranda and Louie have always been rivals. The first time Louie took Miranda up the West End it was a turning point – in that he turned gay.'

She was supposed to have arranged a dancer for JLS and hasn't, but Penny doesn't seem concerned. The boys aren't worried either, as they say they've seen some dancers and think they can make it work. Part one of the *Miranda* special, then, ends on a cliffhanger: 'But how?'

The second half of the special, which appeared later in the evening, begins with Lenny Henry and Fearne Cotton introducing JLS to the live studio to perform their single 'Eyes Wide Shut'. But at the point where rapper Tinie Tempah would usually join in, Miranda storms the stage, supported by her back-up dancers Penny, Stevie and Gary. It was a performance that drove the studio audience wild; Miranda's rap could hardly be heard for the screams of delight. One critic simply said, 'Miranda strutting her stuff around Pineapple Dance Studio was amazeballs.'

Red Nose Day 2011 was a colossal success, raising a total of £75 million – the highest amount raised on the night in the 23 years the show's been running. And it was a fantastic moment for Miranda, too. She stood out in a show of excellence that, at its peak, was watched by more than 12.4 million people.

In 2012, Red Nose Day stepped aside as Sports Relief took charge and Miranda, once again, took to the challenge. Her biggest feat this year was hosting. Only the top comedians are trusted to host this live television event. She co-hosted with David Walliams while others performing the duty were regulars Davina McCall, Dermot O'Leary, Claudia Winkleman, Fearne Cotton, Patrick Kielty, James Corden and first-time presenter John Bishop. Miranda was in the cool gang now and rose to the occasion for her BBC Two stint from 10pm.

Besides presenting, her run-in with JLS during last year's Comic Relief was enough of a hit to grant her a full sketch. In this sketch, Miranda, Stevie and Penny are at the Royal Albert Hall to watch the tennis. Following a wardrobe faux pas and many awkward VIP room exchanges, Miranda rushes to a dressing room and changes into the kit there. She is mistaken for tennis player Goran Ivanisevic and is forced to play Ivanisevic's competition, Tim Henman, on court. Things go surprisingly well and, returning to the dressing room, she gets a kiss from an enamoured Ivanisevic. In the behind the scenes feature for the sketch, Miranda points out how beneficial it can be writing for yourself!

The night was a success and the total raised on the night of the broadcast was more than £50 million.

21

WHAT'S NEXT?

'This has been my ambition since I was six – it is literally a dream come true.'

– Miranda

From comedy sketches at university, to stand-up and character comedy on the circuit, to Edinburgh Fringe stints and to the BBC in London, Miranda Hart's had quite a journey. But she was something of a late starter due to her politics degree, a difficult period of agoraphobia and rejection from casting agents. After a dalliance with radio, and supporting roles in other people's work, her considerable breakthrough in 2009 made a great impression on the BBC Two schedule. In June 2011, repeats of the series were shown on BBC One for the very first time, in preparation for the channel showing a third series, probably in 2012.

Miranda-fever had spread beyond Britain too. Eén, a television channel in Belgium (similar to our own BBC One), broadcasts the show, leading *Hyperdrive* writer Andy Riley to tweet in April 2011 that such was its popularity there that 'seriously, Miranda would have trouble walking down the street in Antwerp now'. The Australian Broadcasting Corporation (ABC) finished showing the first series in April 2011 and immediately ordered the second series, which is expected to air there in late 2011.

So, while other parts of the world get to know and love *Miranda*, we in Britain are eagerly awaiting the third series. On *The Graham Norton Show*, she revealed that she would start writing series three in May 2011 and her website stated that filming will not begin until sometime in 2012. Fans may be left panicking – making a cushion with Miranda's face on, obsessively watching the series one DVD until they know the outtakes off by heart, re-reading this book (thank you), or making fruit friends called Miranda, Penny, Stevie, Gary and Tilly. But stop – let's just regroup for a moment. Miranda isn't going anywhere. Since series two, she has been entertaining the nation in various situations that are not a joke shop in Surrey.

Following her stint as charity goddess for Comic Relief, she continued her good work with two live benefits in quick succession. On 21 March 2011, the Teenage Cancer Trust Comedy Night kicked off the annual series of concerts curated by the charity's patron: Roger Daltrey, frontman of The Who. John Bishop compered a line-up of top acts including Kevin Bridges, Greg Davies, Angelos Epithemiou, Seann Walsh and star of Comic Relief Smithy (aka James Corden). It was the third time Corden had appeared at the charity's Royal Albert Hall shows. He said, 'It's going to be an incredible night! The atmosphere at the Teenage Cancer Trust gigs is always electric and we've got a fantastic line-up, I'm really looking forward to it!'

But written underneath the line-up on the Trust's website was this teaser: 'There will be a surprise appearance by a very special comedy guest.'

After all of the acts had performed, 'television icon du jour Miranda Hart came galloping through the audience', wrote comedy critic Bruce Dessau. 'Corden returned and they reunited for a dirty dance to '(I've Had) The Time of My Life', though Corden drew the line at hoisting up Hart Patrick Swayze-style. Fair enough, this was already a high-flying show.'

The following week, Miranda co-hosted Mencap's April Fools benefit gig at London's Hammersmith Apollo. It was a truly impressive line-up, with Chris Addison tweeting it as 'the best bill I've ever been on'. Miranda and her fellow compere Jo Brand introduced to the stage the likes of Kevin Eldon and young stand-up star Jack Whitehall, as well as Catherine Tate and Lee Mack. The latter pair revived a sketch from their ten-year-old Edinburgh show which introduced Tate's foul-mouthed Nan character to the world. Also appearing were Harry Hill, who entered the stage on a tiny bicycle, Canadian gag merchant Stewart Francis, Lucy Porter (who should have been off work on maternity leave) and, closing the show, Sean Lock. The *Telegraph*'s comedy critic Dominic Cavendish described the event as 'like a time-compressed Comic Relief night'.

For those who prefer to stay in, though, there remains plenty of scope for Miranda-spotting. Hart will host a new panel show for TV called *Britain's Favourite*. At the time of writing, it is still in development after a pilot recording at BBC Television Centre on 21 February 2011. The format pits teams of comedians against each other in ranking famous people from a group, who have nothing in common but their first name. It was summed up as being 'like Top Trumps with celebrities'. The pilot attempted to find the best Steve, with the creators offering some suggestions: 'Is Stephen Hawking better than Steve Davis? Is *Six Million Dollar Man* Steve Austin superior to Steven Seagal? What about England captain Steven Gerrard? Is Shakin' Stevens even a Steve?"

The producers promise plenty of silliness in *Britain's Favourite*, including 'a battle to do the best impression of Steve McFadden, a challenge to find the best Steve in the audience, a list of people who didn't make the shortlist, such as Seve Ballesteros (out by just one letter) and a chance to see all the best bits from Steve Guttenberg's career (a 15-second montage)'.

Miranda has mixed feelings about panel shows. She has enjoyed appearing on formats such as *Would I Lie to You?*, but she has also commented, 'It is quite hard because male banter is quite different' and 'The kind of comedians that go on panel shows are often very clever and know a lot, which I don't – I'm coming at it from a characterful, clowny, comic persona.' So a show with such silly games as the producers described seems just like Miranda's sort of thing.

There has been some criticism that British panel shows are male-dominated and a hard gig for female comics. Miranda has said, 'My theory of why women find it hard on panel shows is that it can be as simple a thing as the quality of your voice. Because it's a different register, when you speak, everyone turns to look at you, so what you've got to say has to be even more pithy. It's hard to join in that rolling chatter. As it would be for a woman down the pub with ten male friends.'

Isy Suttie (who plays Dobby on *Peep Show*) told one interviewer that she tried out for panel shows but found it difficult to 'get a word in edgeways'. She said, 'I don't necessarily want to fight to get my voice heard. Maybe that is a male thing – who's got the biggest conker in the playground.'

Similarly, in Giles Coren's piece about the shortage of women in comedy, he quoted an anonymous female comedian who told him about her experience on *Have I Got News For You*: 'I ended up garbling my jokes because I had to talk so fast to stop Paul Merton interrupting. Pause and he steals your punchline. Then they edit it down and, by the time they get to the final cut, even my mum wouldn't have noticed I was on.'

But Miranda has proved herself as a good panel-show guest and even host. She first appeared on *Have I Got News For You* in 2008 and the show interviewed her for their website, asking what her hopes, fears and dreams were of being on. 'My hopes, fears and dreams are all based around some kind of love tryst between me, Ian, Paul and Jack [Dee],' she told them. She went on to talk about how making the panel show more like her radio series *Miranda Hart's Joke Shop* could improve it: 'Jack Dee opening the show with a fart could only be a great start to an episode of *Have I Got News For You*. Particularly if there wasn't a whoopee cushion on his chair.'

When the topical panel show reached its 38th series in October 2009, Miranda was invited to be a guest host. She was quite nervous at the prospect, as she candidly revealed on Twitter: 'Tomorrow night I will be hosting *Have I Got News For You*. Tomorrow day I will be shitting myself.' She told the

Telegraph how she wasn't quite prepared for the job: 'It's a bit tricky to go on *Have I Got News For You* when you haven't read a newspaper in 20 years. But I'm pleased about it, too, in many ways; it means I've been able to hold on to a kind of innocence.'

Although she was received well, there was some criticism of a joke she read from the autocue. They were talking about Prince Philip meeting the Indian president Pratibha Patil and him saying to Atul Patel, the businessman, 'There's a lot of your family here tonight.' Miranda said, 'There is no place for racism in the modern world and the sooner that Greek twit and his Kraut wife realise it, the better.' The *Daily Mail* reported that 50 of the show's five million viewers had complained, but comedy website Chortle pointed out that, on the BBC's Points of View website, only one comment was made.

As Miranda did not write the joke, focus fell to the broadcaster to explain its actions just weeks after it was lambasted for clearing an offensive joke Frankie Boyle made about the Queen on *Mock the Week*. A BBC spokesman said, '[*Have I Got News For You*] is a topical, satirical news quiz and as such tackles issues of the week in a comedic and challenging way. The joke Miranda delivered was about abusive racist language following on from the news story that Prince Philip had made what were considered offensive remarks at a meeting of Indian representatives.'

When they appeared together on Channel Five's daytime discussion show *The Wright Stuff* a few weeks later, Scott Mills asked Miranda about the incident and her view on censorship of offensive comedy. She joked that it wasn't relevant to her as 'a chocolate willy is about as racy as I get', but went on to say that she thought there was a place 'for comedy to be anarchic and anti-establishment' and that comedy shouldn't be confined by rules. 'But equally,' she added, 'I think people – weirdly – do knock *My Family* and those sorts of shows and say it's uncool. So both are getting attacked. It's weird.'

In the autumn of 2010, Hart returned to host *Have I Got News For You* for a second time, but now they knew what to expect. 'The producers know how badly read I am,' Miranda said, 'and are very good at not making me feel like an idiot.' They also managed to make the most of the popularity her sitcom persona had garnered: 'Series 40 saw a host – Miranda Hart – falling off the chair for the first time, albeit deliberately. The same episode also saw a radical new camera angle being used to allow for Miranda's trademark looks to camera.'

By now, Miranda had proved herself as a bankable hit, and on Friday 9 December 2011, she made her third appearance as host. Miranda's favourite panel show, though, was *Would I Lie To You?*, presented by Rob Brydon. After playing the game for the first time in August 2009, she said on Twitter: 'Would I lie to you has become the only panel show I have actually fully enjoyed doing. Its a fun game. [sic]' The object of the game is for contestants to relate stories and facts about themselves, and the other team must guess whether they are true or not. Miranda was on David Mitchell's team with the Welsh comedian Rhod Gilbert. It was her job to convince Lee Mack, Rufus Hound and Hugh Fearnley-Whittingstall of her statement: 'I always test the temperature of my bath with my ear.' Hugh asked why she didn't use the conventional elbow method and she said, 'Firstly, it amuses me to test it with my ear. Secondly, I'm a big fan of the bath and I like to get it right and I think it's more sensitive.' To further convince them, she explained that she uses her ear to test the temperature of hot food as well. But they didn't believe it.

Rufus said, 'The physics of this is all wrong,' so, to win them over, she demonstrated the bending action, with Rhod Gilbert playing the role of bath. Their demonstration was so convincing that the team changed their minds, now firm in their belief that the story was true. It was, in fact, a lie.

Until the arrival of *Miranda* series three in autumn 2012, fans can keep themselves amused with further Hart interviews and panel-show appearances. But what is still to come? Will *Miranda* join the likes of *Only Fools and Horses* and *My Family* as a long-running BBC sitcom? Or will Hart eventually decide she's had enough of the show and want to try something else? Backstage at the British Comedy Awards in January 2011, she said, 'To just do something completely different would be really nice.' Perhaps she'll take to treading the boards: 'What I'd love to do is make my West End debut. That would be lovely and then I could write in the day, though that is probably completely unrealistic.' With her teenage love of musical theatre, she said that she would love to play Miss Hannigan, the cruel lady who runs the orphanage in *Annie*. Then again, as she told Dominic Maxwell at *The Times*, 'I'd love to do farce, I'd bring back Ray Cooney.'

Having shown she can look the part when in costume for the *Tipping the Velvet* party in series one, Miranda has also said she would like to try some acting away from comedy: 'It'd be great to do something like *Downton Abbey*.' While she has not yet appeared alongside the Earl of Grantham, on 22 January 2012, she made her first appearance in *Call the Midwife*. The second episode, 'The Browne Incident', focused on her character – Camilla Fortescue-Cholmondeley-Browne (Chummy). She arrives at Nonnatus House and is a welcome pair of hands. At first it is hard for her to fit in, as Sister Evangelina (played by Pam Ferris) has little sympathy for her as her inability to ride a bicycle makes her late for appointments. The other midwives try their best to help her learn, but her first attempt ends in a dramatic collision with the local policeman, PC Noakes. She also finds that all of the dresses are too small and tells Jenny, 'I've always been a longshanks. Even as a child, in India, I was always taller than my brothers. Poor old mater, she used to be in tears.'

Sister Evangelina becomes something of an inverted snob when Chummy lets slip that she has met Princess Margaret and that her father was knighted for services to the Viceroy. The fact that Chummy would rather go to Africa rubs her up the wrong way, too. Chummy tells her she has been called to work there by God, 'When I close my eyes to pray, I see all these little black faces'. Unimpressed, Sister Evangelina snips, 'You don't have to up sticks to Africa to see them, you just need to go a bit nearer the docks. It's not that far – by bicycle.'

But Chummy proves herself when called out to her first job – the baby is in the breach position. She sends local boy Jack to call for extra support, but Dr Turner and Sister Evangelina arrive just in time to see her successfully delivering the baby, and she finally earns their respect.

The main storyline she has throughout the series is her relationship with Constable Noakes, the police officer she almost ran down on her bike. There is something of the sitcom Miranda in their first exchange. They flirt a little, but then she ruins the atmosphere, 'Uphold the law, good sir!' then reprimanding herself, 'Chummy! Why on earth did I say that?'

On a visit to Nonnatus House, Constable Noakes remarks that Chummy look well and she reciprocates the compliment. As Stevie and Clive did with Miranda and Gary, Sister Evangelina decides to stage an intervention, 'Enough, I cannot watch any more. Constable Noakes, would you like to take Nurse Browne to the pictures on Friday evening?' He says that he would and Sister continues, 'Nurse Browne, would you like to go?' Chummy says she'd love to. 'Excellent, how marvellous for you both, and now I can get on and enjoy my cake'.

Their courtship goes well until Chummy's mother comes from Madeira to inspect her daughter's man in uniform. After an awkward tea, in which Chummy's mother refuses the salmon sandwiches because they are tinned rather than smoked, she announces to her daughter, 'I'd sooner you were a missionary than lived like this and walked out with a man like that. Because at least our friends would comprehend it when we told them. You'd be a spinster but you'd be doing good works.'

A loyal daughter, she submits and breaks off the relationship, telling PC Noakes, 'I've hardly ever felt comfortable anywhere. And when I have it's been with you. It's been the most extraordinary thing. I felt small and in my proper place and not at risk of breaking anything precious. But now, all of a sudden, I don't feel that anymore. I think it's best for both of us if we put a stop to this. Goodbye Peter, it was all rather splendid.'

After some soul-searching – Jenny explaining that the man she loves is unattainable, while there's nothing standing in her and Peter's way and a new mother explaining how the father of her children made her 'feel small in his arms, like [she] was always meant to be there' – she goes to visit him at the station. 'I'm turning myself in,' she tells him. 'I'm guilty of criminal cowardice and robbing two people of something that would make them very happy.' They declare their love for one another and prepare to marry.

Later her mother rings to discuss the wedding dress and when Chummy pushes back she insists that it is white. No longer scared, Chummy tells her that she is 'no longer entitled' to wear white. Something of a scandal at the time.

A second series was commissioned immediately after the first episode, as it attracted almost 10-million viewers. Episode 4, 'Baby Snatcher', overtook Downton Abbey as the largest audience in Britain for the first series of an original drama. Not too shabby.

But where is the limit?

Her roles in *Magicians* and *The Infidel* gave her a taste for the big screen, and maybe her awards in television could act as a springboard into major film exposure. She said that people ask her if she thinks about trying America: 'I'm like, really? Let's just see how it goes. I like to take my time and don't like to take anything for granted... So, one step at a time.'

Whatever Miranda's career goals are, her fans have had ideas for her. On 7 April 2011, BBCMiranda on Twitter posted: 'Miranda has came #11 in @SFXMagazine's Recent poll "Who would make the best first female Doctor Who?" [sic]'

Meanwhile, a Facebook group has been created where fans plead for Miranda to star in the iconic time-travelling show, even suggesting character ideas and traits. The creator of the group said, 'I'd want her to play an alien but a nice one who helps them', while someone added, 'that wud be fun... you cud be a alien who likes Abba n like sherbert dip! [sic]'

Outside of her comedy career, there are dreams that she has not yet realised: 'It's a cliché but swimming with dolphins is on the list, along with being able to cook, going to see Polar Bears in the wild,' and Miranda's long-held ambition of 'winning the Ladies Singles Championship at Wimbledon'.

Emma John at the *Guardian* asked her about her tennis hopes. 'Don't let the dream die,' Miranda said to her. 'Laura Robson, she should watch out – I had some tennis lessons this summer and it went very well.' Perhaps something Hart could consider for a future Sport Relief challenge?

But her ultimate ambition – to star in her own sitcom at the BBC – has now been realised, and was successful beyond anything she could have hoped for. She has been showered with critical acclaim, awards, attention and affection from the British public and beyond. And to think that she was so close to giving up before she got offered the part in *Hyperdrive*. She has laughed off the idea that she is a role model to budding comedians and writers, but it has become clear that there are many people out there who idolise and revere her. So for those of you after Miranda's advice on how to approach getting into comedy, here are her wise words: 'Write what you think is funny, not what you think broadcasters want. Just write what you want to write.'

Her story is surely nowhere near ending; it has hardly yet

begun. Keep your eyes and ears open for where she'll be next because one thing's perfectly clear – Miranda Hart's story is one that is to be continued...